Death and the Migrant

Death and the Migrant

Bodies, Borders and Care

Yasmin Gunaratnam

Bloomsbury Academic
An imprint of Bloomsbury Publishing Plc

BLOOMSBURY
LONDON • NEW DELHI • NEW YORK • SYDNEY

Bloomsbury Academic

An imprint of Bloomsbury Publishing Plc

50 Bedford Square
London
WC1B 3DP
UK

1385 Broadway
New York
NY 10018
USA

www.bloomsbury.com

BLOOMSBURY and the Diana logo are trademarks of Bloomsbury Publishing Plc

First published 2013
Paperback edition first published 2015

© Yasmin Gunaratnam, 2013

British Library Cataloguing-in-Publication Data
A catalogue record for this book is available from the British Library.

ISBN: HB: 978-1-7809-3405-1
PB: 978-1-4742-3826-7
ePDF: 978-1-4725-1534-6
ePUB: 978-1-4725-1533-9

Library of Congress Cataloging-in-Publication Data
A catalog record for the book is available from the Library of Congress.

Typeset by Newgen Knowledge Works (P) Ltd., Chennai, India

For all those facing and caring at life's borders

Contents

Illustrations ix

Acknowledgements x

Preface xii

Elephant Pass(t) xvi

1 Death and the Migrant – An Introduction 1

Diasporic dying 8

Hospice-tality and the geo-social 12

Mortal chorographies 16

The book 20

2 Eros 23

The promise 27

David 30

The face 34

Dust and guts 37

3 Thanatos 41

4 A Catch 43

Dirt 44

Paranoia 47

Comin throu the rye 50

Patience 52

5 Never Mind 57

Silver lining 59

Les Fleurs du Mal 65

6 Dissimulation 67

Shock 68

Body heat 73

7   Moving On   77
     Faith   78

8   Music   81
     Noise   82
     Hospice-tality   87

9   The Prince and the Pee   91
     Tings   94

10   Failing, Falling   99
     Inklings   101
     The high wire   103
     Not-knowing   105
     In the skin of a lion   109

11   Home   115
     Body work   116
     Slowly, slowly   120
     Genograms   124
     A view   127
     A cough   129

12   Pain   133
     Total pain: 'All of me is wrong'   138
     Case stories   142
     Being affected to learn   143

13   The Foreigner Question – An Epilogue   147
     Sweet chariot   149
     Geese   152

14   Appendix: Research and Methods   155
     Stories, writing, care   158

Notes   163
Bibliography   183
Index   193

Illustrations

Thank you to the copyright holders for their permission to reproduce the images used in this book.

1.1	Grandmother	1
1.2	Hands	2
1.3	Olga and rosary	6
1.4	Opioids	15
2.1	St Christopher's Hospice	23
2.2	Cicely Saunders and David Tasma's window	31
2.3	David Tasma's grave	32
2.4	Cicely Saunders' diary	33
2.5	David Tasma	35
2.6	Balkanizing taxonomy, light boxes	36
2.7	Balkanizing taxonomy, jars	37
6.1	HIV, sub-Saharan Africa	68
8.1	Air diffuser in hospice ward	85
11.1	At home	116
11.2	Shakti	117
11.3	Washing bodies	119
11.4	Home furnishings	124
12.1	Cicely Saunders with patient	139

Acknowledgements

Many people have contributed to this book. Thank you to: Bob and Marjorie Bailey, Joanna Bornat, John Burnside, Denise Brady, Neera Deepak, Nigel Dodds, Helen Findlay and Majliss Care, Dagmar Lorenz-Meyer, Nela Milic, Colin Murray Parkes, Patricio Rojas Navarro, David Oliviere, Ann Phoenix, Nicola Rattray, Heather Richardson, Stephen Rumford, Suzanne Scafe, Vic Siedler, Gail Wilson, Michelle Winslow, the staff at St Christopher's Hospice and King's College (London) Archives, Caroline Wintersgill and Mark Richardson at Bloomsbury.

I am truly, madly, deeply indebted to the enthusiasm and generosity of Libby Sallnow and Nadia Bettega, both of whom gave me and the book considerable time. Nadia's images have transformed and lured my writing. Nigel Clark always believed in what I was trying to do, walking and talking with me through ideas and stuck places and allowing me to filch from his library. My thinking has been stretched and invigorated by students and colleagues in the Sociology Department at Goldsmiths. I was able to finish the book because of a term of study leave. Heartfelt thanks to Mariam Motamedi Fraser and Nirmal Puwar for their spirited dialogue and friendship.

My family, dispersed to all sides of the globe, are a continual reminder of the deep bonds, surprises and losses of migration. My head and my heart are so often all over the place. Sometimes I wish that the world really was getting smaller. Real love and virtual hugs to the Gunaratnams, Sourjahs and VanReyks; to David, Tracy, Carl and Darrell, and to my parents. Zac, thank you for the lessons in football, love and ethics. I will keep practicing.

This book would not have been possible without the people who gave me their time, trust, and stories. I will not forget. Thank you.

I am grateful to the publishers for their permission to reprint versions of 'Auditory Space, Ethics and Hospitality: "Noise", Alterity and Care at the End of Life' in *Body and Society*, 15 (4) (2009), 1–19; 'Learning to be Affected: Social Suffering and Total Pain at Life's Borders' in *The Sociological Review*, 60 (Issue Supplement. S1) (2012), 108–23. My poem *The Bed* in The Prince and the Pee was originally published in Caroline Malone, Liz Forbat, Martin Robb and Janet

Seden, eds. *Relating Experience: Stories from Health and Social Care*. London: Routledge and Open University, 120–1.

The author and publisher would like to thank the following for permission to use copyright material:

John Burnside for the poem 'Geese' from *Asylum Dance* Jonathan Cape, London, 2000.
Irit Rogoff, 'The Exergue – "All is Fair in Love and War"'. *Dictionary of War*, June 2006–February 2007, http://dictionaryofwar.org/node/415.
Michel Serres. *The Troubadour of Knowledge*, trans. Sheila Faria Glaser and William Paulson, University of Michigan Press, Ann Arbor, 1997.

Every effort has been made to trace all the copyright holders. If any acknowledgements have not been made, or if additional information can be given, the publisher will be pleased to make the necessary amendments at the first opportunity.

Preface

It is 1992. Winter is on its way. The Buddhist vihara in Croydon on Sundays is more frenetic than usual, with children rushing from one activity to another. My brother and I are at a Sinhala class trying to relearn a language that we have forgotten. Our teacher, a monk, is patient and kind, if a little puzzled that we are adults of Tamil and Euro-Sinhalese heritage, brought up as Catholics.

Our teacher does not seem to have a methodology. We learn a wild assortment of grammar and vocabulary that changes every week so that it is difficult to grasp underlying patterns. The monk knows that we are planning a visit to Sri Lanka. This week he asks if there are any phrases that we would like to learn for our trip 'What do you want to say?' Pen poised to capture phonetically the monk's translations in my exercise book I ask 'How do you say "I am bringing my mother's ashes to be buried?"'

In my mind's eye I was already imagining arriving at the Bandaranaike Airport in Negombo. The scene is sensuous, bursting with heat, noise, kinetic energy and smells. It is a memory as much as fantasy. I had been at the airport earlier that same year with my father's ashes. My mother had been there then to explain and to hand over the paperwork to the immigration officials. Now we would be on our own. Small certitudes shaken, losses strung like lanterns across time, oceans and language. How do you say in a language, that has at one time or another despised the heritage worn in each of your names, 'I'm lost. What now?'

This is a book of stories about an unfolding wave of transnational dying and end of life care in British cities. It is also a book about shared human predicaments – about how ordinary people do philosophy, how they live with estrangement, how they improvise their way across chasms.

I first got caught up in this world of border crossings in 1985 when, at the age of 55, my father was brain damaged following cardiac by-pass surgery. My mother, brother and I looked after him for seven and a half years and I forgot all about wanting to do any postgraduate research. My mother, a nurse, died at home under hospice care, six weeks after she had been diagnosed with cancer of the pancreas. Despite the relative advantages that their professions provided, my parents' lives in England and their work in the National Health Service (NHS) had not always been easy. Both had worked long and unsociable hours. Although none of us ever talked about our experiences of racism at work or at school, I now wonder about whether my parents felt what the sociologist Pierre Bourdieu has described as *positional suffering*[1] – the uncanny experience of being able to participate in a sphere of privilege 'just enough' to be able to feel your own marginality.

After their deaths I became more interested in migration, illness and care. At the time I had wanted to do two things. The first was to understand an emptiness. The second was to improve care. The void was a silence as much as my personal losses. It was an absence in the library, in the archive, in the cultural imagination. I was tearing through libraries, searching for anything about migrant death and bereavement. Surely there must be others who have gone through this? I may have been looking in the wrong places, but I found little. The absence of a contemporary dialogue about diasporic dying became a provocation that would shunt the trajectory of my life, leading to ethnographic doctoral research in a hospice and an eventual return to academic life.

Through my research and my ongoing work in palliative care education, I have witnessed the unfolding of patterns and novelty, especially with the ageing and dying of our post-war cohort of migrants. There have been concerns about inequalities in accessing palliative care and about whether care is culturally sensitive. But sometimes the differences that migrants signify and make real are not problems at all. They flow into the singularities and roominess that is good care. This is one of the forgotten legacies of migration. I am not only referring to the ways in which care systems in the global North spin on an axis of migrant labour and vast disparities of health and other resources, I have in mind the ways in which care is being continually endowed and reimagined because of difference, from within institutions, at bedsides and in front-rooms, building new hospitalities.

The professional chameleon Cicely Saunders (philosopher/nurse/social worker/doctor), who is regarded as consolidating the contemporary hospice movement, credits her ideas about hospice care to her relationship in 1948 with a dying Polish Jew and refugee, David Tasma. Saunders' idealized vision for the first modern hospice – St Christopher's in south London – is such an apt inscription for global multicultures 'A working community of the unalike'.[2]

When I hear patients talking about their craving for some meaningful contact with care practitioners – 'He didn't even spend two minutes with me on his ward round' – I imagine David Tasma, an accidental survivor and orphan of the Holocaust, on the threshold of anonymity and a short life. Despite feeling that he was uneducated and despite stumbling over the English language, David had the audacity to imagine that there must be better ways of caring for dying people. He had the nerve to ask the very proper and very English Cicely Saunders for something real, for 'what is in your mind and in your heart'.

At the time when Cicely and David met, the NHS was in its formative years, recruiting migrant care professionals and other care workers, to supplement post-war labour deficiencies. This 'perverse subsidy'[3] has continued, and to the detriment of the economies and households from which migrants come. At the same time governments continue to stoke public fears about welfare scroungers and treatment tourists. A nation's health is always a global matter, a twirling dance around the geo-political deathbed. I know something about this because my father was one of the more than 12,000 overseas-trained doctors licensed by the United Kingdom between 1966 and 1974, to fill the skills shortage in the NHS.[4] He died in the hospital where he had worked for much of his life in the United Kingdom. It is another side to Ed Sissman's poem 'A Death Place' that opens with the lines 'Very few people know where they will die, / But I do: in a brick-faced hospital'.[5]

Our care services are indebted to migrants. These are debts and gifts that are easily forgotten in the present, but where history can reveal itself in the teardrop of a life cycle. I have been struck by the numbers of dying people that I have met, particularly older women from Ireland and the Caribbean, who have worked as nurses, carers and cleaners in the NHS as a result of British overseas recruitment campaigns. It is a history that sang and jived its way into public in Danny Boyle's opening ceremony for the 2012 Olympic Games (albeit a romanticized and cleaned-up version).

These care workers who tended to the birth and infancy of the NHS are now ailing. For the first time as patients, some of them will walk through the main entrance of the institutions in which they have laboured. They will be looked in the face. They will be addressed by their names. Some will occupy the waiting rooms, wards and beds that they have cleaned and serviced. The child that they have nurtured will in turn administer to them. What will happen now that the roles are being reversed?

All of this has left me wondering and dreaming about what it means to live life fully. Or as Veena Das has put it 'How does one make the world one's own?'[6] 'The only dream worth having' Arundhati Roy calls back, as if in response, 'is to dream that you will live while you're alive and die only when you're dead'.[7]

Caring for vulnerable strangers remains one of the most urgent challenges of our time. Transnational dying and care are not peripheral concerns. They show the potent economics, demands and the inventiveness of how bodies of all kinds survive with frailty, dispossession and with each other. These are matters that bubble up as eschatological questions that speak to us all. 'Who am I?', 'How did I get here?'

Elephant Pass(t)

I remember sun

crowning my head

in my grandmother's garden when I was five.

Rusty earth on slow-bake, a mongrel on a long chain asleep on the veranda twitching, drooling.

Mynah birds, *kattusas*, dancing butterflies.

Calls of '*Bombai Mutai*' lyrical in the distance.

New Year lanterns brazen in a guava tree

Hari lassanai.

Uda balanna.

Uda balanna.

Caught up in excitement I did not know

I was leaving

forever.

My whole hand would not sink again into

warm chocolate

left on a window ledge to melt.

My mother would stop dancing.

No more dreaming for me

in two languages.

Uda balanna.

Uda balanna.

A bejewelled tusker in the room

whipped and diminished by the day.

Adornment, elaborate subterfuge.

A child's heart senses confused fear

behind his painted eye.

Powerless, ashamed, you watch him disappear.

I forget. I forgot. Almost everything.
Still it lingers. Lumbers somewhere, processing
to the beat of the two-faced *Thammattama*.
Uda balanna.
Uda balanna.

I would return
an orphaned stranger *kalu-suddha*
to gaze at my Grandmother's divided house
through a wire fence.
To feel first love suspended timeless
in fat sounds and tacky rhythms of words
so familiar, now hollow.
Gliding head down through tepid water
in an English swimming pool much later
it floats past me. Out of the blue.
Uda balanna.
Uda balanna.

Word for stuttering word it comes,
the language I am struggling to learn
by heart.
This vocabulary does not lie
waiting anxiously for my return
to be memorised, immortalised,
frescoed into rock.
As Sanskrit's straight lines tore the Ola leaf
Sinhala script branching away
had to bend and curve with its taut terrain.
Somewhere deep within one day,
not trying, just bending, curving,
It comes to me.
Look up.
Look up.

Look Up.

Elephant Pass – gateway to the Jaffna peninsula and the site of many battles

kattusa – small garden lizard

bombai mutai – spun sugar

hari lassanai – very beautiful

Thammattama – two small connected membranophone drums

kalu-suddha – a derogatory Sinhala term for Westernization; a wog

Death and the Migrant – An Introduction

Figure 1.1 Grandmother.
Courtesy: Nela Milic

Feng Dai sits facing his doctor in a clinic at a London teaching hospital. Mr Dai has been told with great care that his cancer is no longer treatable. He seems to take the news with equanimity. His wife is a calm presence beside him. No, he does not have any questions at the moment. There is nothing more that he wants to talk about. Before he gets up to leave, Mr Dai asks for a pen and writes a single word on a small scrap of paper. He tells the doctor that he will look the word up in his dictionary later at home. The word? *Terminal.*

Along with the capacity for mobility, reinvention and resilence required of migrants, there is another side to our world on the move that deserves greater recognition and understanding. Attending to the situation of the migrant at times of illness and death is to open ourselves to the coming together of two of the most radical thresholds of bodily estrangement and vulnerability: the movement across territories and from life to death.

Frank, *A first journey*

Originally, I'm from St lucia. Why did I come? Well, according to the word of God, he say man shall travel to and fro and knowledge shall be increased and shall travel for betterment. Mind you, when I was back home I was my own boss. I had a mini-cab. When I first came here I work in a hotel. Well, I couldn't get a job which I knew about, motor mechanical, and it was cold, very cold, and I said I couldn't do an outside job. I wanted an inside job and I was lucky I had a friend who was working there and he get the job for me, and I was just washing glasses, that's all.

Harshini, *The last migration*

At times there are great difficulties for us. Although she is here, in her mind she always thought that she was back home. She was always talking about India. She would wake up early in the morning and tell me 'I'm going to the fields' and she would open the door and walk out and that was really scary. It happened a number of times that she had opened the door, walked out and got lost. On a couple of occasions we had to involve the police to find her. She had walked about two miles away from home. Then when I was away on holiday my brother took the decision to put her in a care home.

My mother, she was always a very religious person. Without fail she would go to the temple and would do the puja daily, and even today although she is not aware of what she is doing with her hands, without a mala her hands, her fingers, are still working as if she is praying. And the other thing is that she was always very strict about food. Food was not allowed from outside,

Figure 1.2 Hands.
Courtesy: Nadia Bettega

even bread. Now she doesn't know what she is fed on. She doesn't know what she is eating. She just eats whatever is given to her in the care home. She finds it hard to express herself and without the language she is totally in her own world, totally shut down. Day by day she is getting weaker.

Despite the dessimating of state borders by globalization and digital capitalism – e-commerce, telecommunications, biotechnology and the like – the problem of the border most often comes to mind as a problem of spatial movement. Where are you going? Where have you come from? Who belongs? Who can or cannot cross this threshold? In transnational dying, questions of territorial mobility fold into matters of time – into life as a province.[1]

This unique time that is *my* life, that is *your* life, is a *terra infirma*, neither flat nor secure underfoot. It is continually broken up and fissured by events that send the present and the imagined future spiralling off in unforeseen directions. The lives of my mother, brother and I changed on a February morning in 1985 when my father suffered brain damage during coronary artery by-pass surgery. James' life was transformed on a Sunday afternoon with a thrush infection in his mouth (see Dissimulation). Mr Balani's descent into dementia unfurled over a period of years (see Slowly, Slowly in Chapter 11). And June's turning point came on a bus journey to work when her leg suddenly collapsed under her (see Moving On). For the psychoanalyst Christopher Bollas the existential dispossessions of life are even more fundamental than this. 'Moving from the maternal order to the paternal order, from the image-sense world of the infantile place to the symbolic order of language, may be our first taste of exile' Bollas suggests.[2]

When borders are reimagined as a temporality, dying people, wherever they have come from, are already foreigners of a sort, unmoored from everyday worlds and all that is familiar, by the vicissitudes of the body. Who are you when you are leaving your life? Where are you? Who is that strange person that you see as you pass a window or a mirror? 'Well, I was sad because of my shape, I have a horrible shape now' says June Alexander, who has multiple myeloma. 'No waist, an my bottom gone in an everything. If you see me naked you would be surprised. It takes a while to get used to it. I mean, I'm still learning'. As the geographers Dikeç, Clark and Barnett explain,

> amidst all the attention to the negotiation of territorial boundaries which Kant put centre stage and which intensifying globalization has kept on the agenda, what is also always with us are the borders, thresholds, and turning points of ordinary, embodied existence. And these are no less significant than the more concrete figures of mobility and transition. . . .

Illness, destitution, death of loved ones, unexpected pregnancy, love or desire beyond the bounds of communal acceptability, these are all predicaments that 'befall us', exceeding our knowledge and preparedness, carrying with them the risk of a radical de-worlding.[3]

In the debility and the dying of migrants we encounter this shared human susceptibility and also the particular 'de-worldings' that come with the increasing movement across geo-social frontiers that are transforming our thinking and experience of any sense of a bounded national culture or tradition. Claus Leggiwe,

transmigrants live long term in two or more places, constantly speak two or more languages, possess *en masse* two or more passports, and pass continually in both directions through makeshift households, networks of relationships and spaces of communication.[4]

It would be wrong to think about the coincidence of the multifarious border-crossings in transnational dying in terms of matters of scale or of type alone. Mediated by the body and by heightened emotions, the flows between place, economy and culture, are as unruly and paradoxical as they are creative and surprising. Fantasized 'roots' meet up with cosmopolitan 'routes' so that hospice and hospital wards have that similar feel of the airline transit lounge, characterized by long chains of cultural interconnectedness and intergenerational migration.[5] But with illness and disease the interconnections proliferate. Hallucinations, paranoia and hypersensitivities can cohabit with and jostle among prayers, promises, plans, rituals and life-long habituations, pulling the body and self down familiar and new paths (see Dirt in Chapter 4).

'Even today although she is not aware of what she is doing with her hands, without a mala her hands, her fingers are still working as if she is praying' says Harshini. Harshini's mother, a devout Hindu, has dementia. The disease is taking away her mother's memories, her awareness of the religious beliefs that she has lived by and her self-consciousness. At the same time she can walk out of a house in Leicestershire to wander the fields surrounding a village in India that she left many years ago. Her fingers still work the mala 'as if she is praying'. The poet Novalis believed that prayer was 'to religion what thinking is to philosophy'.[6] He was mistaken. Prayer in some of our traditions is the very emptying out of thought. It is a somatization in and of itself, conveyed in the muscle memory of fingers, the voice, the ears, the rhythmic movements, gestures and comportment of the body.[7]

As migrant bodies deplete and unravel with illness, the traces of these other times, places and culturally honed sensorium intermingle with the day-to-day unfolding of diasporic life, post-migration settlements and care in institutions and in homes. The finding of one's ground amid such shifting circumstances is a place-making that even at the end of life spawns practices that are continually produced and discovered. 'You need to be creative and adaptable' says Alex who looked after her mother Olga, who had Alzheimer's disease. 'We got some woollen leggings for her a while back to help her to go to the commode more often. They allowed her to pee without having to pull her trousers down.'

Nadia Bettega, a photographer and researcher, began to photograph Olga over ten years ago – when she was in the early stages of Alzheimer's – until her death in November 2012 at the age of 99. 'My mother is not a vegetable wasting away in bed' Alex says. 'She is an animated lady wishing to communicate with anyone who has the interest, the time, to visit and reach out to her. Looking at her I know that here is a human soul with attitude struggling to live and enjoy life.' Bettega had wanted to tell the story of Olga's incredible life through the objects that surrounded her and that came to take care of her, and Alex too. 'Her whole life was condensed into one room, invisible to the outside world' Bettega explains.

Alex: My mother loved literature and poetry and could recite it for hours on end. She loved music. She liked to dress well and she liked to eat well. I remember with pleasure her reading of Le lac by Alphonse de Lamartine, but above everything she loved people. She loved conversation.

A carer is a someone who provides unpaid care for a person who is sick, disabled or frail.

The number of carers increased from 5.2 million to 5.8 million in England and Wales between 2001 and 2011.

The greatest rise has been among those providing over 20 hours care – the point at which caring starts to have adverse affects on the health of the carer and their ability to hold down paid employment.[8]

With her mother, younger brother and a pig, Olga was among the two million people who fled from the violence that had erupted during the Russian Revolution and Civil War in 1917. During their escape they were forced to scavenge for food 'stealing the odd potato, or two, or more' Alex says. 'This was about survival and a complex set of rules emerged from this life of chaos. They travelled by train when someone was willing to help them, but most of all they walked.' The troika travelled 1,400 miles to Belgium via Lithuania. In Belgium, Olga and her brother were delivered into the care of Catholic institutions, while Olga's mother carried on her journey to England. The children subsequently joined her and were sent to boarding schools in Scarborough.

As Olga's short-term memory began to deteriorate, Alex found that she would journey into the past, recalling happy times and using objects to bridge worlds. A ring passed across and between Olga's fingers could return her brother to her once more. The convent in Belgium came to life when she held her rosary.

For the sociologist Pierre Bourdieu, our everyday worlds are a mosaic of these small 'practices'. Practice, as Bourdieu imagined it, is an improvised, bodily know-how, a sensual capacity to 'habilement' – to skilfully and adroitly navigate through the challenges of daily life.[9] With disability and disease the habitual skill of mundane practice comes under increasing duress from the biochemistry of the body. My feeling is that the practices of living with dying are more analogous to the art forms of music and dance than the rationalities of conscious thought. The philosopher Gilles Deleuze believed that the individuality of the body is

Figure 1.3 Olga and rosary.
Courtesy: Nadia Bettega

ultimately defined by delicate *musical* relationships between inertia, rest, slowness and speed. 'It is not just a matter of music but of how to live' Deleuze asserts,

> it is by speed and slowness that one slips in among things, that one connects with something else. One never commences; one never has a tabula rasa; one slips in, enters in the middle; one takes up or lays down rhythms.[10]

The film Aaj Kaal[11] – translated as yesterday, today and tomorrow – made in 1990 by Avtar Brah, Jasbir Panesar and Vipin Kumar in collaboration with Punjabi elders in West London, is a beautifully rendered evocation of some of the musical embodied place-making practices that I am talking about. The film was part of a participative project at the Milap Day Centre for older people in Southall. By coincidence Milap was also a place where I did my first interviews for a project to produce information for South Asian carers of older people at the same time that Aaj Kaal was being made.[12] The film, in Punjabi with English subtitles, is a heady mix of poetry, song and dance and footage from the life of the day centre, including trips to the seaside and interviews between the elders.

Nirmal Puwar has excavated the little known film in commemorating the work of Avtar Brah and the passing of this first generation of Punjabi migrants. Commenting on the closing scene of the film that features a *gidda*, 'an expressive dance formation that has enabled Punjabi women to air their joys, frustrations and sorrows',[13] Puwar describes how,

> For earlier generations . . . the *gidda* sessions were central to how they settled and made Britain a home for themselves, in an admixture of pleasure, performance and gendered territory. It is in these zones that they made their public lives together. These modes of coming together provide one layer, so far largely unregistered, of migration and settlement in the making of the post-war British front room.[14]

The coda to Puwar's article turns to her 91-year-old mother's sustenance at an Asian day centre in Coventry (subsequently closed due to funding cuts) and recalls her Mother's gidda dancing with a zimmer frame at her ninetieth birthday party in the public spaces of a hall. Puwar's coda seems to sing and dance back to those very different earlier histories recorded by Aaj Kaal, gesturing to the new debilitated spaces of the Punjabi front room. Here I catch a glimpse of the *gidda* entwining with and being extended by the prosthetics of disability and disease, rearranging the furnishings of diasporic and post-migration socialities once more. All of which is to say that *what* and *how* it is for migrants to be deworlded by disability, old age, disease and death is a zone of vitality that even as it depletes cannot be assumed.

And so, as strange as it might seem, *Death and the Migrant* is not primarily a book about loss. My hope is that the stories will show the vitality and musicality of human experiencing right up to the point of death. And sometimes beyond.

Diasporic dying

In the United Kingdom the nature and extents of the overlapping estrangements of migration, disease and dying are in some ways becoming less tenebrous as the cohort of our first generation of post-war migrants are reaching old age and are dying in increasing numbers. Generation Exodus – the nurses, doctors, cleaners, cooks, bus drivers, construction workers and soldiers – leave behind them psycho-geographic trails that began for many with the lure of economic betterment, Empire and personal ambition and which can end in a doctor's surgery, Accident and Emergency cubicle or care home, tinkling with a morbid poetry of words such as *malignant, metastases* and *palliative care.*

History, geo-politics, cultural and religious prescription hover around the migrant's deathbed to pay their last respects, but they do so in strange and uneven ways. There are migrants who because of their marginalization, whether related to their disease, citizenship status or because they queer normative expectations, occupy ambivalent, tenuous positions in the lexicon of transnational life and what Bridget Anderson has called *communities of value.*[15] Struggles over cultural authenticity, who speaks for whom, who can and cannot belong and who is deserving of care continue into illness and death and can even extend into post-mortem 'life' (see Dissimulation).

In following the smaller affects of estrangement that gather weight and grain from the most mundane of circumstances, I hope to derail dominant ideas and narratives about migrants by showing something of our singular differences and our humanity.

I take my cue on this point from vibrant discussions and writing in feminist and queer migration studies.[16] If brutalizing exclusions and contestations take place at state borders, more recent work is also drawing attention to how emotional investments, memory, fantasy and imagination shape the 'multiple and potentially contradictory positions that migrant subjects occupy'.[17]

Ricardo is a recent Portuguese migrant from Brazil. He was diagnosed with advanced cancer about a year after he had settled in London. His is one of many stories that I have heard that express the contrary dispositions of migrants beset by illness. Through an interpreter Ricardo tells me that in Brazil he would have had to sell his house to pay for the cancer treatment he is now receiving from the British National Health Service (NHS). He wants to make it clear that he is a good and responsible patient. Despite the aggressiveness of his disease, he has defied medical expectations. Unlike some others he can think of, he has led a healthy life. He does not drink or smoke. He complies with all the medical advice and guidance that he is given.

Ricardo's repeated affirmations of his responsible determination relegate the inexorable facts of his loneliness and impending death to *crac allure*. Amid talk of seeming banalities – the manioc that he spotted with delight and nostalgia in a local market, his granddaughter in Brazil asking him on Skype when he is going to take to her to McDonalds again – he erupts repeatedly into paroxysms of sobbing. The interpreter and I struggle with our own tears. It is in his account of hospitalization that Ricardo's most immediate and prosaic challenges arc into bigger geometries of his hopeful bargaining of compliance for life.

> Sometimes when I was in hospital I had cheese, but I don't like cheese, and with the language barrier I did not know how to say it. I had to eat it, because if I did not eat I would lose much more weight than I already did, and I think we have to have the will and be stronger when we are in a hospital. Eat your meal and do the right thing, accept the advice, do everything right, and if you do it this way it helps a lot.

For those who die, and for those of us who are left behind, we cannot but pass through the weft between the large and the small in our journeys towards the ends of life. The borders, turning points and transitions in transnational dying feature a familiar human terrain: love, revelation, family feuds, reparation, disappointment, legacy, inheritance and imperfect endings. The relationships recovered miraculously at the death-bed. Those torn apart at the last moment by confessions and confrontations, petty arguments and resentments over who gets grandma's ring, who can come to the funeral or the *proper* spelling of a name.

There is also a layered novelty in transnational dying and bereavement that through the evocation of 'home', tradition or citizenship rights gives some form and musculature to what has been taken-for-granted or never seemed to matter before. Fears of cultural dilution or amnesia can loom large, even for the ethnically agnostic, hopelessly mixed or many times diasporised. The search for meaning so often induced by frailty and dying can take a more down-to-earth turn. There are worries about remittances, repatriation and reputations; the lives and souls of loved ones; the loss of a language or religion, unmoisturized bodies.

The bereaved too can be fearful of the severing of the threads that connected them to other times, peoples and places. Recipes get written down for the first time. Photograph albums are devoured. Oral history is sought out and recorded on mobile phones and webcams. Sometimes a careless utterance cast out from the internal free-wheeling of a morphine haze, where the words *passports* and *tickets* are just decipherable, can turn from metaphor into Mission Impossible.

Dead bodies and plastic hermetically sealed caskets of ashes are flown across the globe in a rewriting of the Homeric script of return. Emptied of any triumph for some, but a homecoming nonetheless. The flabby idiosyncratic bureaucracy of embassies and airlines will be negotiated to get a near-comatose patient onto an arduous flight to a distant homeland. Shafina says it is much easier that way in the long run. When she heard that her father had a week or so to live, they flew with him from East London to Pakistan. He died at eight o'clock in the morning. By three that afternoon they were at his funeral. Nurses and social workers are usually the ones who spend hours on the phone trying to make it all happen, emotionally committed but often mystified by the indomitable compulsions behind these last journeys.

> We once had a patient who had lived in a remote part of Sudan. The professionals that were involved felt her needs were such that she wasn't actually going to make the journey. She was very, very symptomatic. She had a lot of pain. She was virtually constantly vomiting. The family then agreed, perhaps under a bit of pressure, that they would just take her to their home in Tooting and that's where she would die. They'd have twenty-four-hour care, so a lot of time and money was invested in setting all of that up. The family organised their own transport, they organised a private ambulance and instead of taking her home they took her to the airport.

The hospital Macmillan nurse shudders as she tells this story. She does not know how or where the fatal odyssey ended. But she has gone through the various possibilities and outcomes. She imagines a Land Rover waiting at a Sudanese airport to take the family to the far-flung village where the mother was born. She worries that they did not have enough pain control and anti-emetics, that the patient may have died en-route. She re-settles herself and reasons it out. 'It's cheaper to take someone home alive, than to fly a coffin home, which can cost five to ten thousand pounds to fly someone home when they're dead.'

Five thousand pounds is the figure that Brian gives when he talks about flying Aliz home to Hungary to die with her family. Brian, a hospital social worker in central London, has noticed that his younger, East European patients can be resistant to palliative care, clinging to the remotest of hopes alluded to in active treatment or in the abstract odds ratios of survival rates. Brian speaks of the loneliness of facing death away from family and friends, of the heavy burden that can fall onto the most flimsy of contacts, transformed overnight into next-of-kin and who become responsible for momentous decisions and breaking bad news long-distance to strangers.

Aliz chose to die at home in Hungary in the very last stages of her life, resulting in the need for a business class flight and an accompanying doctor. The doctor's fees came close to 2,500 pounds. Surprisingly for Brian, some of the money for Aliz's home death came from a generous donation from a global chain of continental bakeries where she had worked in London for just nine months.

For the Jarrant family, there was no kindly benefactor on hand to help, when 91-year-old (Curt) Willi Jarrant died. Willi's wife and daughter were arrested at Liverpool's John Lennon Airport in April 2010, accused of trying to smuggle Willi onto an EasyJet flight to his native Berlin.[18] They had dressed Willi in a big coat and sunglasses, strapped him into a wheelchair, and told airport personnel that he was sleeping. Both women continued to insist that they did not know that Willi was dead, that he must have died at the airport. Willi's stepdaughter Anke told reporters that Willi had Alzheimer's disease and had not been in good health. He had wanted to go back to Germany to die. The repatriation costs of flying a dead body to Germany at the time were about £3,000.

To be impoverished of life chances, and to feel the pull of a distant home at the end of life, is not the same vulnerability that we all face of not knowing what the future holds. What is distinctive about the stories of transnational dying that I offer in this book is that they move between and reveal these different registers of estrangement. They complicate what we think of as migration, globalization and care.

'To outline the experience of the migrant worker and to relate this to what surrounds him – both physically and historically' John Berger insists, 'is to grasp more surely the political reality of the world at this moment'.[19] The 'this moment' that Berger is referring to was 1970s Europe. At that time migration was largely the province of men. It is a trend that is now reversing with the increasing feminization of transnational migration due to the rising demand for care workers in the global North.[20] Parodying the myth of infinite substitution and the denial of the male migrant worker's susceptibility and finitude in global capitalism, Berger wrote,

So far as the economy of the metropolitan country is concerned, migrant workers are immortal: immortal because continually interchangeable. They are

not born: they are not brought up and they do not age: they do not get tired:
they do not die.[21]

Migrants die. And the increasing prevalence of their debility and dying brings
us to a neglected plane and temporality in migration trajectories. This is a zone
in which the very conditions of migration – movement, improvisation and
uncertainty – meet the demands of one last journey into the unknown.

Hospice-tality and the geo-social

One in 33 people in the world today is a transnational migrant[22] and the number
of working-age people in the United Kingdom who were born overseas increased
from 2.9 million in 1993 to nearly six million in 2011.[23]

I could have chosen to investigate diasporic dying in a number of settings.
The predicament of dying in a strange place is not only about those who are
ill and impoverished. It is the stuff of Greek tragedies; philosophy; imperilled
border crossings; violence and forced labour; immigration detention
centres and refugee camps. It has, and will, continue to befall cosmopolitan
entrepreneurs and elites, adventurers, soldiers, criminals, tourists and those
who fell in love or just wanted a change of climate. As well as the personal
reasons that brought me to end-of-life care, modern hospice and palliative
care, as I discuss in *Eros*, has been most explicitly oriented to matters of
hospitality and estrangement. The *question of the foreigner*,[24] as the philosopher
Jacques Derrida has phrased it, is most acute at times of debility and death,
summoning up the borders and meanings of community and hospitality.
With the idea of community in mind, the philosopher Alphonso Lingis puts
it this way,

> Community forms when one exposes oneself to the naked one, the destitute one,
> the outcast, the dying one. One enters into community not by affirming oneself
> and one's forces but by exposing oneself to expenditure at a loss, to sacrifice.
> Community forms in a movement by which one exposes oneself to the other, to
> forces and powers outside oneself, to death and to others who die.[25]

Lingis's proposition is counter-intuitive. A community is made not by common-
ality, invulnerability and enclave but through its responsiveness to catastrophe,
exile and loss – a theme and existential metaphor that recurs throughout the
Abrahamic religions. These are not abstract matters for philosophers and social

scientists. They come into play in how we think about the extents of transnational hospitality, human rights and our interdependence.

In January 2008, Ama Sumani, a Ghanian migrant with malignant myeloma was taken by immigration officers from her hospital bed in Cardiff in Wales to Gatwick airport and deported. Ama had violated the terms of her visa by failing to maintain contact with immigration officials and to update her details when she had moved home. The prestigous medical journal *The Lancet* described the deportation as 'atrocious barbarism'.[26] There was also the chuntering of disgruntled citizen commentators in the blogosphere and on the airwaves who supported Amma's deportation amid fears of treatment tourism and an already over-stretched NHS.

The BBC's East Africa correspondent, Will Ross, had met Ama shortly after she had arrived in Accra, where she had stayed briefly in a hotel with two British immigration officers. The officers had tried unsuccessfully to pay for Ama's first dialysis sessions at Accra's main hospital. Ross describes how both officers looked distressed. One had given Ama a pair of her own silver earrings. They left without saying goodbye to a bemused Ama who tried repeatedly to call them on their mobile phones.

Ama died three months after her deportation. In that time over £70,000 had been raised by supporters and friends in the United Kingdom for her treatment and drugs. Speaking to the controversy and resentments surrounding Ama's case, Will Ross offered an alternative set of moral coordinates for thinking about British hospitality. Excavating the global transfusions that the NHS is built upon, Ross observed 'Turn up at a British hospital and do not be too surprised if the nurse or doctor who treats you is Ghanaian. With the drain of this exodus on the Ghanaian health service, some here suggest the UK might owe Ghana a favour or two.'[27]

A 2011 study of nine sub-Saharan countries:

The countries lost an equivalent of $2bn through the doctors that had left to work overseas.

The UK benefited by the equivalent of $2.7bn.

The USA benefited by $846m.[28]

Médecins du monde: 'Deportation to a country where access to adequate healthcare is impossible leads to the serious deterioration of health and sometimes death and goes against the European Convention on Human Rights "No one shall be subjected to torture or to inhuman or degrading treatment or punishment".[29]

There is no escape from these global circuits in contemporary care-giving. Dorothy Ngoma, head of the main nursing union in Malawi, believes that the 200-odd Malawian doctors in Manchester outnumber those in the whole of Malawi, a brain drain that Ngoma feels is the cause of the high rates of maternal deaths in her country.[30] For at least four decades, some quarter to a third of all doctors working in the NHS have qualified overseas. And the NHS is the largest employer of racially minoritized workers in Europe.[31] It is more than likely that whenever we have been in need of care, or will require it in the future, it will be provided in some part by migrant and minoritized workers. These caregivers deliver our children, tend to our parents and grandparents, cook our food, clean our hospitals and bear witness to our naked emotional distress.

Others and planetary inequalities are already under our skin, a part of the very bodies we have become rather than something that we can easily isolate and expel.

Neither reducible to, nor separate from these paradoxes and injustices, the dying migrant who wheezes and coughs, walks, limps and wheels herself with me through these pages, is one whose susceptibility I do not want to tether to cultural difference, to a disease or to an overarching sociological category. Nevertheless, her frailty plays out in a world where bodily vulnerability is unevenly fabricated, distributed and defended against, forcing us to think twice about 'the seamless production of abled-bodies' in the global North.[32] Palliative care is increasingly being recognized as a human right, yet at a global level 'A significant number of countries still have no hospice-palliative care provision'[33]

To consider the stories in *Death and the Migrant* with the geo-social in mind is to encounter an interconnected world riven with strange temporalities and *eschatological extremities*.[34]

In the Anglo-American worlds biomedical innovation – screening programmes, DNA testing, prognostication – is creating a foreshadowing of death. Taking cancer as her example, Sarah Lochlan Jain believes that we are 'living in prognosis'.[35] Prognostic time anticipates the future. But it does so through levels of abstraction and chance that simultaneously bring death close and make it impossible to grasp in the day-to-day unique living of a life. As Jain sees it,

> Statistics seem to present us with a certainty, such as '1 in 207 women who are 35 years old will be diagnosed with Stage III breast cancer'. But it says nothing about who will represent the one, so it also carries the counterfactual hint that it might be somebody else ('why me?') . . . Like car-crash deaths or suicides,

the individuated counternarrative folds into the magical inexorability of the aggregate.[36]

The strange logics of living in prognosis time take on another significance in the context of global health. In middle- and low-income nations, cancer can be lived as belatedness. In Julie Livingston's ethnography of an oncology ward in Botswana, the consequences and debris of belatedness are everywhere.[37] We find it in the failure of an international public health agenda to tackle the 'circuits of toxicity' (from food to nuclear waste) that are correlated with carcinogenesis. It is there in the atrophying of African cancer research. It bulges out from the crammed spaces of the oncology ward and its clinic, in the hours and hours and hours that people travel and spend waiting to see the doctor. It is thrown up in the restricted access to analgesics and symptom control – there is a lot of nausea, retching and vomiting in the ward because of the relatively high costs of anti-emetics.

And throughout all of this there is the business of care as improvisation and a deep sociality – care practitioners, patients and their loved ones, tinkering away, trying to bridge the incommensurables, offering each other sustenance, humour and hope at times of great precarity. Livingston is painfully aware of the paradox of how biomedicine can both alleviate and exacerbate health inequalities. 'And yet' she argues 'biomedicine functions as a necessary, vital, palliative institution in a historically unjust world.'[38]

The World Health Organization estimates that every year 5.5 million terminal cancer patients suffer moderate-to-severe pain. [39]

A survey of 76 countries between 2010–12, found that few countries provided all seven of the opioid medications that are considered essential for the relief of cancer pain.[40]

Ninety per cent of the world's morphine is consumed by 10 percent of us.[41]

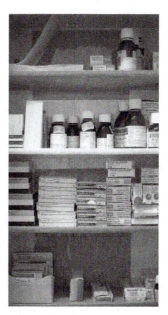

Figure 1.4 Opioids.
Courtesy: Nadia Bettega

In similar ways to Livingston, I am constantly reminded of the global value, histories and the vitality of biomedicine and social care. I have experienced and been affected by good and scandalously bad, inhuman care. The effects of both can spread out far beyond a death and into the lives of a person's loved ones and a community. In *Death and the Migrant*, I am interested in what good care is and in what it might be. And so I work from within the existing terms and philosophies of palliative care and its utopian philosophy of 'total pain' that recognizes pain as being physical, psychological, social and spiritual. Within the domains of total pain the bodily suffering caused by a tumour pressing on the spinal cord and the emotional loss of legs that can no longer dance a *gidda*, are (ideally) both recognized as pain and are administered to. Total pain also gives recognition to pain that gathers over a lifetime.

In 2011 in the UK there were:	The World Health Organization:
220 hospice and palliative care inpatient units	Palliative care improves the quality of life of patients and families who face life-threatening illness, by providing pain and symptom relief, spiritual and psychosocial support, from diagnosis to the end-of-life and bereavement.[43]
3,175 hospice and palliative care beds	
288 home care services	
127 Hospice at Home services	
272 day care centres	
343 hospital support services.[42]	

I have come to think of total pain as being a care practice that tries to simultaneously discover, recognize and become receptive to manifold and unacknowledged situations *as* pain (see Pain). As I go on to explain, the thinking and aspirations of palliative care and total pain have shaped and inspired the methods, writing and stories in *Death and the Migrant*.

Mortal chorographies

Two central themes that recur throughout the book are those of sensuality and space-time, where I see diasporic forces at work in the scattering and redistribution of the senses. I am drawing upon and adapting the insights of the philosopher

Jacques Rancière[44] on political aesthetics here. Rancière believes that the value of artistic practices lies in their potential to intervene in and question existing ways of apprehending and partitioning the world. So in Rancière's notion of politics, life that has previously been 'invisible' or is just 'noise', is given form. At the same time the carving up and ordering of space is questioned as it is rearranged. This giving of shape to what previously was unacknowledged does more than expand the spectrum of everyday sensual life. It interrupts and dissents from what is 'naturally' given.

My approach in *Death and the Migrant* is somewhat different from Rancière's and is two-fold. First, I suggest that the rearranging of sensibility in diasporic dying and care involves exploratory place-making activities that create novel potentials for transnational and multicultural hospitality. Picture a small hospice ward of about 20 beds (see Music). Suddenly, the ululating of an African mother bursts through the ordered quietness. The nurse manager of the ward is in an impossible situation. She tries to work out a just and caring way to respond to and accommodate the acoustic torrent of grief as it bounces and rolls around her. She must also consider her other patients, some of whom are dying and can be hypersensitive to sound. Because she does not know how to respond on this occasion, the ululating continues, filling up the ward. Her disturbance, conflicting fidelities and shock get under her skin. She grasps for the first time the tacit cultural codes of the hospice. She finds herself thinking more deeply about care and the regulation of acoustic space in the ward. The thinking and uncertainty, the holding of unresolved beliefs and sonic impressions, the abeyance of action in relation to this particular family, are all a response.

Whether the hospitality of the ward is permanently extended or not is in many ways beside the point. The reassembling of acoustic space is a disturbance through which a new space is intuited and travels into the future, not only because the issue came up at the ward's next team meeting, moving up from there to the Senior Management Team, but also because the event birthed a new sense of the ward/world.

My second and related point is about method and representation, of how to allude to and trace what can have effects but is non-manifest. The stories that you will read have been produced through an evolving mixed-method approach – mainly narrative interviews, observation and participation – and activism and teaching in palliative care. The research ideas and plans that I started off with in projects have invariably been transformed and recreated out of the in situ encounters and demands of these different settings. There are experiences that I have missed, not only because of carelessness but also because life goes on beneath the world of sensual surfaces and appearance. 'Chorography' is the best term that I have found to describe this ongoing creating and finding of method (and life) by working between the sensible and an orientation to what can defy sensual impressions and rational knowledge.

A quick google search will tell you that chora is an antiquated, now rarely used term. It was first used by the philosopher Plato to connote a divine spirited sense of space and place. Not so much a material place/space (a 'topos'), but a sort of ephemeral milieu that delivers being and is resistant to definition. Julia Kristeva, a feminist psychoanalyst and philosopher, has described chora as being 'analogous only to vocal or kinetic rhythm'.[45]

Chorography then, is an artful practice[46] and as Gregory Ulmer suggests 'has to be approached indirectly, by extended analogies'.[47] The space of chora is evocative. Like the small fish that I played with as a child in Sri Lanka, it slips through the analytic fingers. But the 'problem' of the existential dark matter of chora is very much practical.

To borrow and adapt a question from Ulmer: What might care or research/ writing be when it does not rely upon what can be represented?

I already have some ideas about the chorography of end-of-life care. It is music thanatology and the sonorous embrace of a dying person by live song and harp playing at the bedside (see Music). It is the magical properties of a pressure-relieving mattress for a double bed that brings a couple some last weeks of sleeping together, a time that is unquantifiable (see A Cough).

So my approach differs from Rancière's work on sensibility in the ethical possibilities that I give to choric spaces and to what is sometimes withdrawn from sensibility and superficial appearances. In *Death and the Migrant* you will also come across this withdrawnness with regard to time and the semiotic (how things are symbolized and named by signs/language).

At the time of writing, my thinking is that the withdrawn are realms of existence that are not only elusive[48] but can also never be fully recuperated by careful thinking, a new aesthetic or by a shuffling around of space. I discuss withdrawnness most explicitly in the chapter on researching pain. The point that is relevant to my argument here – and which I also owe to the palliative care philosophy and practical implementation of the total pain approach – is how what is withheld can incite the inventive bridging work of care as a chorographic practice that has to work with intuitive knowledge. This is a labouring that is distributed across all of those who participate in caring relationships – patients, carers and care professionals, spaces and objects such as rings, rosaries or mattresses.

The following story is Eileen's, a cancer Clinical Nurse Specialist. Eileen wrote the story during one of the sessions that I teach on narrative on a postgraduate course in palliative care. With clarity and economy, the story articulates the everyday demands of the withdrawn in caring for others. It was written as part of an exercise that I have been developing called 'A Patient who Made Me'. In this exercise I ask practitioners to write about a care experience that has affected how they care. Eileen's story is about a woman whose pain and short life she had found especially difficult to face. Eileen was organizing the woman's discharge from hospital and she had become preoccupied with the complicated discharge arrangements. She felt that she had been distancing herself from her patient, using the discharge plans as distraction and protection.

> I went to visit a patient on the ward to plan with her her discharge home. She was 31 years of age and had advanced lung cancer with a prognosis of weeks. I remember feeling particularly nervous and sad when talking to her about the practicalities of her discharge.
>
> Suddenly she touched my arm and said 'I have had a life you know Eileen'. I was taken aback as I suddenly realized that I had never discussed her life before her illness. I said to her through my embarrassment 'Tell me about it.' She recounted the most wonderful stories of her travels abroad.
>
> The experience reminded me that people have had lives before illness. There is a whole other person/experience rather than just the illness.

I have had a life you know Eileen is one way of speaking about what is latent, but can sometimes be alluded to. The allusion in Eileen's story might intrude upon the present of her relationship with her patient but it is ultimately inaccessible, a lost place/time not only for Eileen but also for the dying woman herself. How does one ever fully apprehend let alone convey the life that you have had? This is the unknowable otherness within all of us that always has the potential to shock or to surprise ('Where *did* that come from?'). In a way the withdrawn are not unlike vegetative existential metaphors with unpredictable qualities, traits and capacities. And because the withdrawn do not lend themselves to representation or to definition, a rift between lived existence and knowledge or an evidence base opens up. Care as much as research and writing must proceed through inference and extrapolation.

These are complicated matters to think about in the abstract. They recur in different ways throughout the stories in *Death and the Migrant*, where they do not require theoretical thinking.

The book

In bringing together stories informed by my involvement in two decades of transnational dying in the United Kingdom, I am also bringing into the open the taking of time to live with stories and their affects. This is an ethical as much as a methodological stance and context is important. Methodological details and thoughts for those who are interested are in the Appendix.

There have been changes in end-of-life care, demography and social life since I began my research in the mid-1990s that have had impacts for dying people and care professionals. In order to convey something of these developments I have ordered the stories into a loose chronology. The chapters at the beginning of the book provide a context to the development of hospice care and palliative care in the United Kingdom and to the challenges that transnational dying can pose to care regimes. These stories are generally taken from the 1990s when migrants' palliative care needs and service use in the United Kingdom was becoming more widely recognized. It was a time when discussions about hospices as 'white, middle-class and Christian'[49] and the need to 'widen access' to palliative care were also gathering impetus.[50] The chapters towards the end of the book are from more recent projects and draw from my on-going involvement in palliative care education.

There are four relevant changes that I have witnessed in the intervening years, aside from the increased numbers of migrants and racially minoritized people who are in need of palliative care. First is a growing diversity of palliative care staff and hospice volunteers (in the past, the latter were often referred to as 'formidable ladies'). The second has been in the expansion of provision of palliative care by generalists and its extension to those with non-malignant conditions such as dementia, cardiovascular diseases and respiratory disorders. Third is the use of polymedia such as smart phones, instant messaging and social networking sites by patients and carers that is transforming transnational living and dying.[51] And the fourth is in care in the home.

With new opportunities opening up in care markets for 'culturally sensitive' care provision, novel segmentations of care industries along the lines of ethnicity, language, faith and gender are taking place, fortified in the United Kingdom by a social policy agenda of personalization and devolved 'direct payment' care funding schemes. Those in need of social and personal care now have some choice over how to spend their personal care budgets – if they are fortunate enough to have them. Migrants are being employed by migrants and also their long established kin, with the former often living between two countries, producing a convoluted economics in the giving and receiving of care and resulting in care deficits in low- and middle-income nations.[52] Despite care being big business globally it is low-paid, low-status and vulnerable work,[53] especially when it involves hands-on care or what is called 'body work'[54] (see Home). It remains an ephemeral presence in economic and development policies and in the cultural psyche.

More palliative care services are also now employing interpreters, advocates or *cultural liaison* workers to support care to those who do not speak English. And *health promoting* palliative care is using new public health approaches to work with and learn about death from communities.[55] These approaches are subverting the conventional flow of good practice models from high-income nations to those in low-resource countries. For example, the Neighbourhood Network in Palliative Care is a community-led initiative, providing home-based palliative care in Kerala, South India. The service sees over 2,500 patients per week, covering over 60 per cent of people in many areas.[56] It has a simple aim: no one should die alone.[57] A report by the independent think-tank Demos has recommended that a similar scheme is adopted in the United Kingdom so that more people can die at or close to home.[58] Despite such developments, those who work in specialist palliative care are still overwhelmingly white, particularly outside of cities and in senior management. Often in meetings, I am still the only person of colour in the room.

Not so long ago, a hospice in the north of England was planning to relocate its in-patient accommodation and headquarters closer to the city centre. The Medical Director tells me that for all of their service innovations and campaigns, the relocation has had the single most beneficial impact in widening access to hospice care to people from different cultural backgrounds. Before the relocation, she had sent out questionnaires to General Practitioners and district nurses to garner their views and opinions on the potential move. One questionnaire returned by a district nurse was against the plans. It came back with a question of its own 'Who wants to die amidst syringes and mosques?' So please do not take my ordering of the chapters as a smooth narrative of progress.

Body and community' Zygmunt Bauman writes 'are the last defensive outposts on the increasingly deserted battlefield on which the war for certainty, security and safety is waged daily'.[59] Despite social and technological changes, I cannot imagine that the cultural significance of the body will change dramatically. Corporeality may be dispersible and subjectivity immortalized by the click of a finger, so that digital death, bereavement, inheritance[60] and hoarding[61] are now end-of-life predicaments in the global North, but we cannot get around the materiality and symbolic value of the body, even when it is fading. As Margrit Shildrick and Janet Price argue 'Embodiment finds new forms, but it does not disappear'.[62]

I have written *Death and the Migrant* with the hope that it can allow you to read, use and move through the text and images in different ways. You can approach the book as a compilation of short stories about migrant lives and end-of-life care where there is an interweaving of oral history and contextual detail. Some of the stories might resonate with your own experiences or at least stir points of contrast and dialogue. You can also read the book as a fleshy account of geo-social politics from below. A different way of approaching scholarly concerns and debates about the body, transnational lives and multicultural hospitality. The chapters towards the end of the book on pain and the Epilogue are the most sociological. If you are a care practitioner I hope that the book will have relevance to your everyday work and dilemmas, adding other perspectives to policy, pedagogic and clinical initiatives that aim to improve care.

2

Eros

Figure 2.1 St Christopher's Hospice.
Courtesy: St Christopher's Hospice

> . . . *our Christian foundation welcomes people as themselves, with their own*
> *important beliefs and values and underpins a working community of the*
> *unalike.*[1]

On the route of the Network SouthEast train line that connects the leafy suburbs
of Sutton and Caterham to London Bridge lies the unlikely site for one of the
most far-reaching revolutions in twentieth-century health care. St Christopher's
Hospice in Sydenham, south-east London, opened its doors to dying people in

1967, sparking the contemporary hospice movement. The hospice was envisioned in the late 1940s by the evangelical Christian doctor Cicely Saunders and is said to have been inspired by the excessive demands of a dying Polish Jew.

St Christopher's first laid claim to me in the summer of 1992 when my mother had been diagnosed with a terminal cancer. She told Bernadette, her home care nurse, that she wanted a *peaceful, dignified exit*. It was one of those nurse-to-nurse, soul-to-soul exchanges, economic yet profound. Some six weeks later, with a syringe driver pumping infusions of morphine to her intravenously, my mother died without pain in our family home. I knew nothing of the towering cultural significance of my local hospice at the time or of the strange ways in which the work of mourning, which is always searching work, would lure me through a window into the hospice's past.

St Christopher's is a modest building, a hybrid of modernist and utopian postmodern architecture. Alongside inpatient wards there are quiet rooms for contemplation, a gym, and a bright and popular café that is open seven days a week and is used by local residents and patients.[2] The hospice is demarcated at the front from the tree-lined Lawrie Park Road by shrubbery, two driveways and a voluptuous ramp. Crystal Palace Park, with its eccentric prehistoric Dinosaur Court, lies to the south of the hospice, a sight that my father felt compelled to show us as new migrants to South London in the late 1960s. Here, huge cast iron models of the Jurassic monsters, lovingly restored in 2003 with all of their original anatomical errors intact, protrude incongruously out of the greenery in various poses. They have been there since 1852, a part of the Great Exhibition thought-up by Prince Albert to showcase Britain's military and economic might, materializing the Victorian imagining of civilization as one easily purveyed and taxonomical timeline where the extinct rub shoulders with the new.

It seems entirely fitting to me now that St Christopher's should nestle within the domain of the flawed imperial dinosaurs. As the founding story of the hospice goes, St Christopher's revived and reinvented the endangered craft of care for dying people, pioneered for centuries in Europe by monastic medicine. It did so through a blending of multidisciplinary *techné* with Christian ideals. And all at a time when death was akin to medical failure. A hospital doctor at the time remembers 'The surgical Grand Round did not acknowledge the terminally ill man but greeted all the other patients'.[3]

Cicely Saunders' approach to pain at the end of life grew from practices she had observed in early homes for terminal care in London. At St Luke's in Bayswater in the late 1940s, Saunders learned from Lillian Pipkin, a Salvation Army matron, of the benefits of the regular giving of a modified Brompton

Cocktail. The opioid elixir of morphine and other varying ingredients – gin, cocaine, cannabis, cherry syrup – had been first concocted to relieve the pain of tuberculosis among patients in the Royal Brompton Hospital. The St Luke's version Cicely wrote 'omitted the cannabis and, I think, the cocaine'.[4]

At St Joseph's Hospice in Hackney in the East End of London, more than a decade later, Saunders' ideas were further honed by the Irish Sisters of Charity, an order that had established Our Lady's Hospice at Harold Cross in Dublin in 1879. Going against convention and with what Cicely described as a 'compassionate matter-of-factness',[5] the nuns gave their patients injections of morphine at regular intervals to keep their pain in abeyance, inspiring one of Cicely's often-used dictums 'constant pain calls for constant control'.

Karl Marx mistrusted religion as the opium of the people. He had not been able to foresee the revolutionary powers of religious administration as opium *for* the people.

Cicely's fund-raising and plans for the building of St Christopher's came to fruition in the late 1960s, a time when, despite new legislative restrictions, the impact of immigration from the Commonwealth was becoming increasingly manifest. Not long before the Conservative politician Enoch Powell made his potent *rivers of blood* speech, conjuring the perils of a nation close to inflammatory destruction due to immigration, a Statement of Aims for St Christopher's proclaimed 'St Christopher's Hospice is based on the full Christian faith in God, through Christ. There are no barriers of race, colour or creed'.[6]

The honouring of difference by Cicely Saunders in the foundations of hospice care as a *working community of the unalike*[7] was more than philosophical and abstract. Twice she had close relationships with dying Polish men in her care. The first was David Tasma in 1948 when Cicely was working as a hospital almoner – the predecessors to medical social workers. The second man, Antoni Michniewicz, was a patient at St Joseph's hospice in 1960 when Cicely was a newly qualified doctor. Cicely went on to have a long-term partnership with the artist Marian Bohusz-Szyszko whom she met in 1963. Bohusz-Szyszko's Catholicism and an estranged wife in Poland constrained the formalities of the relationship. Only when he was widowed in 1980 did they marry. Marian was 79, Cicely 61.

With others from her privileged class background – the novelist Virginia Woolf and the labour politician Hugh Gaitskell among them – Cicely Saunders' English xenophilia comes close to what the cultural theorist Mica Nava has called *visceral cosmopolitanism*.[8] Alongside the pull towards a diffident insularity in the interwar years, Nava has identified contingent and libidinal fault lines of hospitality and openness to cultural others in British consumer culture, the arts and in politics. It seems that those who have allowed themselves to feel the precariousness of belonging or the dull flatness of sameness can find themselves desiring of, and empathizing with, outsiders.

Such affinities surface throughout Saunders' biography. She articulated them most strongly in her recollections of her parents' troubled marriage and her isolation at the exclusive private English boarding school, Roedean. Speaking of her formative experiences at Roedean – where she says she was sent against her wishes – Cicely has said 'In a sense, I was an outsider there, which was good for me in that being unpopular when you are young gives you a feeling for others who feel like they don't belong.'[9]

From the 1940s onwards, Cicely Saunders' chaste, almost anti-erotic cosmopolitanism, pushed to the limits cultural and professional mores and her own emotional resilience. The facts of these dissident attractions can never be fully known. But the mythic figure of the foreigner in the founding scripts of palliative care is an origins story that carries an ambivalent, if much neglected, symbolic weight.

The theologian Karen Armstrong, among others, makes the point that in modern times we have forgotten that creation myths were always regarded as more therapeutic than factual. They demanded belief or *pistis* – trust, faithfulness, involvement.[10] But in whom should we place our trust? Just what is it that we are being faithful to? What involvement might a creation myth incite for those who are most often the objects of knowledge rather than its subjects? What sort of faithfulness is it when a migrant researcher is drawn to the flickering fragments and remnants of other migrant biographies passed over by others in a cultural archive?

There are parallels here with the story *Rodinsky's Room* told by Rachel Lichtenstein and Iain Sinclair.[11] David Rodinsky, a Russian Jew, was the reclusive cabbalist scholar and caretaker of a synagogue at 19 Princelet Street, Whitechapel. He disappeared suddenly in the late 1960s and his room was left undisturbed for over a decade. For Sinclair, Rodinsky was the man who had become a room, a Vanishing Jew whose enigmatic story would be fodder in the reimagining of Spitalfields by property developers in the 1980s. Rodinsky's hold over Lichtenstein is a story of crossed paths and personal histories, of narrative ghosts passing each other without quite touching on London's streets.

Lichtenstein's grandparents, like David Tasma, had left Poland in the early 1930s and settled for a time in East London. They had a home and a watchmaking shop in Princelet Street. Rereading *Rodinsky's Room* and its descriptions of Jewish businesses and restaurants in writing this chapter, David Tasma began to wander across the pages. Might my David have worked in the Kosher Luncheon

Club in Greatorex Street or bought a watch in Princelet Street, catching glimpses of the young David Rodinsky above the synagogue, on the way? The man who became a room meets the man who became a window; unfinished, abandoned stories reaching out to migrants' children across the archive.

An archive is a collection of historical records and the physical place in which they are located. The archive of the contemporary hospice movement as you will see is more than this. It includes dreams, promises and windows.

With archives we must always work from and read between the lines of the 'real' and the imagined, Rajeswari Sunder Rajan argues. Rajan advocates attention to the spaces and inconsistencies between competing stories, putting these into relation with the disparities within communities, where those who are on the margins are 'more often the sites of . . . contests than participants in them'.[12]

Mariam Motamedi Fraser makes a related but different point. She recognizes that the distinctions drawn between fact and fiction, art and science are at best unstable and shaky. At the least they are not self-evident 'Archival documents, for instance, are "artful" in a banal sense insofar as an archive is, necessarily, a collection of artificially gathered-together entities.'[13] Second, the archive is always evolving Motamedi Fraser argues because archival objects and those who work with them are in the process of quietly transforming each other. Each is working upon, augmenting and moving the other. The affective and methodological terrain of archival research Motamedi Fraser suggests entails 'learning, in part from the materials, what kind of relation we are in. How do I open this letter? How does this letter open me?'[14]

Opening is one word for it. Another is susceptibility. And to the extent that we can be opened up by the archive there is also obsession or 'archive fever', to use Jacques Derrida's term.[15] As I began working with the hospice archive and its founding stories I found myself 'opened', caught up with and diverted by the Saunders-Tasma story and three artefacts: the story of an English social worker's relationship with a dying Polish Jew, a 500 pound bequest, and its accompanying exergue 'I will be a window in your home'.

Come with me.

The promise

The exergue is a citation, a found object or quote . . . a frisson that communicates the intention and the spirit behind that intention in advance of the thing itself. Whether a quotation from a famous philosopher or poet, a tombstone, a snatch from a popular song or an advertising jingle, it sets the tone, maps out the archive in advance of its constitution as such, and delivers a promise.[16]

For some thinkers an exergue – as a citation, theme, or object in an archive – is a historical fragment, a fragile precursor and a sort of promise.[17] And because the archive is populated by contested and incomplete discourses – 'how is it that one particular statement appeared rather than another?'[18] – it can be misleading. So an exergue is always problematic; inheritance and what is bequeathed, always uncertain.

But we need to start somewhere. And in following the trails leading to and from the hospice archives, I have been drawn to David Tasma's ambivalent presence in hospice histories as simultaneously commemorated and neglected. There can be little doubt that David's words – and those of other dying people – in Cicely Saunders' campaigning and autobiographical stories give the narrative arc of this origins story its sense of novelty and progress. This is a break with the past. We are on new ground: discursive territory that in the next decades will be further democratized by dying people writing and blogging pathographies, bad-mouthing and speaking-up for themselves.[19]

At the same time there are the enigmas and omissions in David's story that interrupt the smooth plotline of hospice stories. It is also the case that when an archive and its stories are so interwoven with care institutions, philosophies and practices, as they are in this case, the archive extends like the roots of a tree, across materials and space.

As well as working with documents from the Cicely Saunders Archive at the King's College campus in the Strand, I viewed other materials exhibited at *The Cicely Saunders Institute of Palliative Care* at the King's College campus in Denmark Hill in South-East London (where my mother had also worked as a clinical nurse tutor). The items include books, letters, photographs, inspirational poems and newspaper cuttings that are exhibited in glass cases inside the atrium of the Institute. The atrium ranges over four floors and is encased largely by glass so that it is flooded by light, becoming an exhibit. Also in the atrium is the work of two artists: an audio-visual installation *Birch* by Tania Kovats and Caroline McCarthy's *Light for Cicely* consisting of photographs (and a dedicated website) of lighted lamps in the homes of people that Cicely had collaborated with during her working life.[20] Describing McCarthy's work, Jenni Walwin, Curatorial Advisor to the project, has said that the photographs bring a sense of each person's home into the building,

The notion of 'home' as an antidote to the institution was central to Saunders' concept of a suitable environment for those living with terminal illness – a radical idea in her time.[21]

It was in moving through and between these different spaces and objects in the hospice archives that I first began to wonder if I had been looking in the 'wrong' places for David Tasma, or rather whether it had been my limited understanding of the archive that had restricted my thinking. As I wandered through London and across different spaces and materials, as I read more about Cicely's mission to recognize and alleviate 'total pain', and as I read Cicely's correspondence and the articles and books that she was reading, a new question began to take form. To what extent is modern end-of-life care and its quest to relieve *total pain* a response to the atrocities of the Shoah?

The suggestion is not as fanciful as it might first seem. Numerous innovations in medicine and care grew out of personal experiences of the Second World War (and we must not forget the legacies of Nazi medicine). As well as Cicely Saunders, Paul Weindling in his work on the psychiatrist John W. Thompson, records the work of others.

> Helen Bamber, who was with the Jewish Relief Unit eventually allowed into Belsen, later organized the Foundation for the Victims of Human Torture. After working with the UNRRA in Poland, Sue Ryder devoted her life to caring for survivors. Elisabeth Kübler (later *Elisabeth* Kübler-*Ross*) was moved by the trauma and death she observed at the camp at Majdenek to develop a psychology of dying.[22]

Cicely Saunders drew upon Holocaust stories throughout her working life. Dr Viktor Frankl, survivor of Auschwitz and other concentration camps, whose work Cicely Saunders admired and often quoted, has written in vivid detail about the numerous ways in which camp regimes turned men into objects and until 'the last ounce of his physical resources'.[23] Saunders wanted dying people to be assured of their sacred personhood. 'You matter because you are you. You matter to the last moment of your life, and we will do all we can not only to help you die peacefully, but to live until you die.'[24]

Is the modern hospice movement an allegoric mirror image of the Holocaust, reversing the philosophy and regimes of the camps and ghettos that sought to inflict total suffering and abjection to the point of death? To begin to imagine this other genealogy of hospices, we must turn back once again to the story that began in London in the aftermath of the war and at the deathbed of 'David' Ela Tasma.

David

The love between Cicely and David was a strange love, underwritten by teeming asymmetries, not least the professional-patient relationship. These are matters that hospice histories tend to sidestep. Of her subsequent relationship with Antoni Michniewicz, Cicely has said 'Fools rush in where angels fear to tread. I think love is so important that it doesn't matter that it's vulnerable. When you fall in love you feel that you have no choice, but in a sense it's the freest thing you ever do.'[25] Yet both David Tasma and Antoni Michniewicz as dying people in Cicely's care were quite literally captivated. It is difficult not to question how 'free' each man was to fall in love with Cicely.

The relationship between Cicely Saunders and David Tasma began to flourish at the beginning of 1948 (they had first met in July 1947) as England was recovering from six years of aerial bombardment and the losses and austerity of war. When I first began this chapter I had written 'love affair'. But just as love can take different forms so too can our memories and rendering of love. Cicely talked about her bond with David at different times as the love of eros and agape. What remains constant in her stories is the trope of David Tasma's window. 'David's influence on my life was enormous' Cicely has said

> He was very poetic and when he died he left me £500 in his will and said, 'I will be a window in your home', meaning the Hospice. It took me 19 years to build a home around the window, but the core principles of our approach were born out of my conversations with him as he was dying. His use of the word 'window' led me to understand that we should be open to the world, to all who would come – patients, families and those who wanted to learn.[26]

So 19 years after David's death, and following her retraining as a doctor and extensive public fund-raising, Cicely Saunders had transposed and thickened David's exergue into a real window. Until the summer of 2009, the window lay on the right-hand side of the main entrance to St Christopher's Hospice, providing a bland view of the parking bays and the street.

The window is still there today, even though the main entrance and the everyday hustle and bustle have been moved away from it. The pane of glass that has become synonymous with David Tasma is legendry in the world of palliative care. I had expected it to be more spectacular, obvious at least. For curious historians, sentimentalists or 'psychic tourists'[27] the window does not give up its secrets too readily. I am glad of that.

Figure 2.2 Cicely Saunders and David Tasma's window.
Courtesy: St Christopher's Hospice

The Saunders-Tasma window is a practical window, undifferentiated architecturally from those that flank it, inciting its own effacement and forgetting. Before the hospice was renovated and reorganized as a part of its 40-year Anniversary Project, the window fronted the reception area. Relatives would congregate unknowingly around it, sharing news from the wards upstairs, dispensing tissues and consoling embraces. No matter how close they would draw to the small inscribed silver plaque on the window's sill, few seemed to take in the epigram underneath the exergue, *David Tasma of Warsaw who died 25 February 1948 and made the first gift to St Christopher's.*

What David had in mind for his gift and why he chose the symbol or perhaps the eye-like prosthetics of a window are mysterious. But there is a poignancy to the very ordinariness of the Tasma-Saunders window and how again and again it recedes into the background. Is this effacement of David's volition, the window asks me, a condition of day-to-day surviving in post-war London? Why did only his employer, Mr Biedak and Cicely attend his funeral? Did he harbour secrets or disturbing emotions and memories that intimacy threatened to unearth? Did he face differential exclusions from local communities because of his Jewishness or low social standing?

Archival stories are never mimetic descriptions. And stories always change in the retelling. As the oral historian Alessandro Portelli has recognized, although

Figure 2.3 David Tasma's grave.
Courtesy: Nadia Bettega

oral sources are not always reliable with regard to facts, this is also their strength. '. . . errors, inventions, and myths', Portelli believes 'lead us through and beyond facts to their meanings'.[28] That said, there is something that riles me about the easy verbatim reciting of what David Tasma said and meant in hospice histories. To my biased ears, there is so much that is glossed over, forgotten, excluded.

What has always struck me is how cryptic David's reported speech is. Possibly the result of pain and of speaking in a foreign tongue and/or a quality of the translation of oral accounts into written records. We must also bear in mind Cicely's practice of selecting and using sound-bite type quotes for her campaigning work as 'a propagandist for patients'. 'I was trying to get patients to speak, to be a voice for the voiceless' she has explained.[29] She was adept at this sort of *in absentia* ventriloquism, working creatively and efficiently with patient stories, translating them into unequivocal evidence for the need for more humane end-of-life care.

Saunders' biographer, Shirley du Boulay, reports this story that Cicely told her of another often-cited quotation from David Tasma.

> One day when he was very sad, he suddenly said to her, 'Can't you say something to comfort me?' and she, respecting his Jewish roots, said the twenty-third Psalm . . . He asked her to go on, so she said the Venite (Psalm 95) and then, perhaps running out of suitable things she knew by heart, offered to read to him, as she had the New Testament and the Psalms in her handbag. 'No', he said, 'I only want what is in your mind and in your heart.' So that night she learnt the *De Profundis* – a Psalm pleading for forgiveness – in order to be able to say it to him by heart the next day; a loving gesture, if not quite the spirit of a remark that was to become one of the corner-stones of hospice philosophy.[30]

We know of all these small details because Cicely spoke about them in lectures and interviews and recorded some of them in her diaries. In fact, she maintained a prolific archive of every aspect of her working life, including her appointment and prayer diaries (she recorded 28 meetings with David). And although David Tasma was a recurring figure in Cicely's published writing and in her speeches and lectures, biographical details of David are scant.

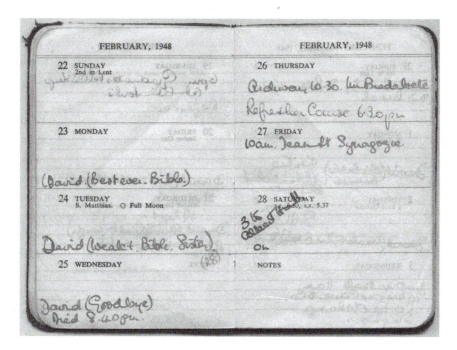

Figure 2.4 Cicely Saunders' diary.
Courtesy: Kings College (London) Archive

In Warsaw he had been called Ela and later took the name David. He had three brothers and his mother had died when he was young. David was the grandson of a rabbi, an autodidact who despite being multilingual and reading widely did not think of himself as well-educated. An annotation in Cicely's diary suggests a verbatim self-description from David – 'only a rude old fellow'. David began his working life early at 14. In London he worked as a waiter in a Jewish Restaurant in the East End, owned by Mr Biedak (in Polish biedak is a word for impoverishment).

We should not be shocked by the exclusions of the archive the historian Carolyn Steedman advises.[31] In form and content, archives show us how power and morality have operated at different historical moments. And they always hold the traces – the 'dust' – of their exclusions.

The face

David Tasma was 40 years old when he met Cicely Saunders. He had inoperable and obstructed carcinoma of the rectum and had received a colostomy. His symptoms included pain and vomiting. In the busy London hospital wards where he was cared for, staff did not seem to have the time, or perhaps the courage, to accompany David in his attempts to make sense of his harrowing short life. It is the circumstances of this abbreviated life that I have found myself drawn to, piecing together and counterposing fragile fragments against the towering events of the Warsaw ghetto and the Holocaust.

What we learn from Cicely's stories is that David had left the Jewish quarter of Warsaw in the early 1930s because of an infatuation with the wife of a friend. So he had migrated before the Warsaw ghetto had been built and before the uprising in 1943. The Warsaw uprising was an attempt to resist the Nazi's last efforts to transport the remaining residents of the ghetto, mainly Jews and Roma, to the Treblinka extermination camp. Although Cicely does not tell us about David's family and how they were affected, it appears that his immediate family lost their lives during the Holocaust. Facing death alone in London, David feared that his own life would be inconsequential, that as the last surviving member of his family he would disappear into nothingness.

We do not know about the journey that David made from Poland to France. Neither do we know how he survived in Paris as a waiter or whether in his second migration to England he was once again escaping from the tightening grip of Facism. As the keeper of David's life story, Cicely was vague about when

David migrated to England 'I believe he reached London before the War' is all she has written on the matter.[32] The timing is crucial in understanding David's situation in France, why and how he was able to leave and also his status as a refugee in London. As we learn from Hannah Arendt's rueful account of Walter Benjamin's 'bungling' fatal decision to leave Paris for Meaux in the winter of 1939[33] – each decision taken, to stay or to keep moving at that time, was buoyed in a current of history where life could be extinguished by a single wrong turning.

To know of David but not about how history affected him sets in train a kind of churning bewilderment and loss. And so it is that I keep coming back to David, asking Who were you David? *How* were you?

The face that returns my gaze is earnest and composed. The hint of a smile, the immaculate hair, the white shirt, tie and jacket, all suggest that this remaining image of David Tasma belongs to the formality and occasion of the photographic studio. It is a comportment that is increasingly out of place these days among the mobile phone and Facebook generation, where images are contrived to display spontaneity. In so many ways the photograph of David Tasma records a lost era, not least because from 1940 until the end of the war it had become illegal for Poles to use a camera. Cicely has said that the photograph was taken just before David left for Paris.[34] What hopes does the photograph capture? What memories and history does it carry and offer?

Figure 2.5 David Tasma.
Courtesy: St Christopher's Hospice

The staging of the image lends itself to what Roland Barthes has called the social game of the photographic ritual: the subject and the spectator know very well that the image is staged but there remains an impossible longing for something of the 'precious essence' of the true self to make itself known. For Barthes there was an unbridgeable divide between the leaden image mortified in the photograph and the sprightly 'myself' who 'like a bottle-imp . . . doesn't hold still, giggling in my jar'.[35] And so it is with the images and stories of David Tasma frozen into the archive and the mythology of modern hospices. The selective dissociation of David from his past and his own story of total pain produces other distances and divides. The longing to see and to know is as enticing as it is ethically fraught.

In an exhibition *Balkanising Taxonomy*, the artist and researcher Nela Milic placed Balkan cultural artefacts in covered light boxes made of black felt, perforated selectively with peepholes.[36] Photographs of Balkan people were bottled in glass jars, preserved and visible but out of reach. Viewing and holding the Balkan other becomes mediated. As you stand on tiptoe or contort yourself into uncomfortable positions to see better, impulses and desires take form, but they are kept in check by the structuring of the installation. And so uncomfortable questions materialize in the craning of the neck, the straining of eyes, the mounting pressure in the balls of the feet. 'What are you looking for?'[37] but also 'Where are you looking *from*?'

Figure 2.6 Balkanizing taxonomy, light boxes.
Courtesy: Nela Milic

Figure 2.7 Balkanizing taxonomy, jars.
Courtesy: Nela Milic

Dust and guts

Arrival is more fraught when escaping from danger. The psyche and the body can protest. Guts seize up or turn to jelly. It can be difficult to make sense of bodily signs and symptoms, to even remember what is normal.

David Tasma's cancer was advanced and inoperable when it was discovered, which means that it had either been overlooked or was misdiagnosed earlier. It could also have grown and spread ponderously over time without symptoms or David's conscious knowledge. Ensnared by the demands of reassembling a life – learning a new language, finding social networks, a job and somewhere to live – it is not always possible to disentangle the physicality of a pathological discomfort from other unsettlements and losses. Social workers are usually closer to such matters than doctors or nurses, so it is all the more surprising that Cicely has said so little about David's biography.

What is apparent is that trust was growing between this social worker and her charge. On 5 January 1948, David collapsed at his home. His landlady Mrs

Spreadborough telephoned Cicely and David's General Practitioner, Dr Ripka, who arranged for David to be admitted into Archway hospital in North London. 'I visited him while he was waiting for the ambulance and he asked me directly if he was going to die', Cicely has written. 'I gave him an equally direct answer, believing that he deserved to face the truth and that I had no alternative. He thanked me and I promised to visit him.'[38]

If the cruel fate of having escaped the Holocaust only to die from cancer was a perverse injustice that could not be spoken, it seems that David could express through bleak humour, lower case torments, 'all my life I've been waiting for a nice girl and now here you are and look at me.'[39]

When David Tasma died he left Cicely Saunders the remains of everything that he owned – money from his life insurance policy (the 500 pounds would be worth about 15,000 pounds today), photographs and his watch. David was agnostic when he met Cicely. She says that shortly before he died he had told a nurse that he had made his peace with God. At David's funeral in the Jewish cemetery in Streatham, South London, Mr Biedak and Cicely read the sublime poetry of the ninety-first Psalm ascribed to Moses, another founder foreigner *Thou shalt not be afraid of the terror by night, nor of the arrow that flieth by day.*

David Tasma brought godlessness and the Holocaust into metropolitan London and into the founding principles and architecture of a social movement concerned with recognizing and alleviating 'total pain'. Yet the dark coordinates of David's life have been lost by the hospice movement, even with Cicely's meticulous self-archiving. There are so many questions. What was said but not recorded? What was expressed and could not be understood? What could not be put into words but became attached to the ordinary matters of attraction, talking, reading, handholding, crying and laughing?

The enigmatic position of the outsider in origins stories is not unusual. It is part of a long history in the symbolic politics of foreignness in Western cultures. In the book *Democracy and the Foreigner*,[40] the political scientist Bonnie Honig reverses the recurring question *What should we do about foreigners?* Instead she ruminates upon *What problems might foreigners solve for us?* For social invention and founding scripts, Honig believes that the foreigner allows regimes to import much needed but potentially threatening qualities and perspectives that they lack. The most useful foreigner founder is the one who makes a timely departure before their foreignness becomes too dangerous or unruly.

So why in giving legitimacy to a new regime would *a nice girl* like Cicely Saunders need recourse to an outsider, and an uneducated, demanding one at that?

Creating something new from within is discomforting, sometimes painful. It means facing-up to lack, insufficiency and the deep injustices of the world in which we participate and from which we draw our day-to-day privileges. Reading Cicely's stories of the origins of hospice care as a foreigner founder script, it is possible to understand David Tasma's symbolic significance as an outsider whose overflowing body and passions expose the limits and the excesses of the modern rationalism of Western bureaucracy and medicine, a rationalism where *in extremis* individuals are reduced to faceless categories and numbers. Through David, violations and inadequacies can be exposed. A break can be instigated with what has gone before. Brutality against the most vulnerable can be confined to another era.

The cost of such a reading is that we can render the social life of power less ambivalent and contradictory than it is. And in turning David into another political conduit, a name and a couple of anecdotes passed on from one unthinking mouth to mouth, we dehumanize him once more.

Cicely Saunders's fidelity to the memory of David Tasma is as much generous as it is generative, serving as a founding narrative of the modern hospice movement. Beneath the rational coherence of this narrative there is another untold story where language falters and 'The story traces the edges of a wound that can only be told around'.[41] If we are attentive to its silences and disjunctures it asks that we think about the stuttering ineloquence of trauma, and of stories as an opening to other demands and conversations.

Part of the enigma of David Tasma in Cicely's stories is that he is a virtual survivor, rescued and betrayed by the randomness of history as much as everyday life. David was someone who in the turmoil of an unforeseen 'ordinary' death, amid monstrous schemes of annihilation – events that were not fully public at the time – lived the reverberations of catastrophe in the fabric of his life even though he did not seem to know, or was unable to tell, what had been survived. With nothing left to lose, David put his trust in Cicely Saunders. It was a canny, risky decision, but trust does not need facts or reasons. And 'every act of loyalty open(s) an opportunity for disloyalty' Alphonso Lingis reminds us.[42]

It matters that David Tasma's life could well have been of little consequence had it not been for Cicely Saunders. And it matters that David's past has been selectively neglected. But neither was David reduced to a victim of Holocaust mythology in Cicely's stories. The Holocaust did not come to define David or his pain. Cicely literalized David's musings on windows and dematerialized his concrete predicaments. Yet she did not sever David from the future. In bringing David Tasma's fractured story with her into the public domain, it has been put into a relation with injustices suffered by other dying people, allowing pain to be many things, weighty in its historical content, but not without company.

The living always cohabitate with the dead Robert Pogue Harrison argues. In his book *The Dominion of the Dead* Harrison investigates what he calls the 'humic foundations' of everyday life.[43] 'A humic foundation is one whose contents have been buried so that they may be reclaimed in the future', Harrison explains. 'The humic holds in its conserving element the unfinished story of what has come to pass.'[44]

This is an unfinished story with a legacy that will not go away. Not only because the archive of contemporary hospices is marked by violence and injustice, but also because in the face of all that has been overlooked, avoided or suppressed, David and Cicely somehow managed to leave a window open to all *those who want to learn.*

3

Thanatos

It is just after two o'clock, a gloomy December afternoon in London. The three hospice nurses have a lot of say. Gill is thinking about one of her patients, a Ugandan mother with suspected AIDS-related dementia. The woman did not speak English. Her family and friends were in Uganda, she was completely alone.

I found it extremely hard to get alongside her, I would say because of the cultural differences, I would think, um, but I'm not sure. There was a lot to her case in particular, but, I feel that with, here, we do get alongside patients, and, and, we're very good at that, very good at getting to know them and caring for them, but this, er, I found it with Ugandan women in particular actually, that I find it very difficult to, to, I suppose read them. You know, I suppose I go a lot on peoples' non-verbals as well as what they say, and when the language is different you go a lot on peoples' non-verbals, and when you're faced with somebody who's Ugandan, who, their very culture, you know, er sort of suppresses facial features, you know, and they've got a very flat face, um. (She takes a long pause.)

A non-expressive face? I offer.

Yes. Yeah. I'm trying to think of the right word, but yes that's what I mean. But that was coupled with slowed mental processes from dementia so it was very difficult, but I found we never really got alongside her. I suppose I view that as a failure of care in a way. But then can you, can we ever, as somebody from a completely different culture, you know that's what I find interesting, is can I, could I ever have done that you know, given more time? Because there was, you know, there, it's in-bred in, it was in-bred in her not to er, divulge much information, which you know, she didn't want us to get to know her. So, you know, I don't know really (she says laughing nervously).

Gill's story is not an uncommon account of intercultural end of life care. Neither are her bold observations and pronouncements on the *in-bred* traits of *Ugandan women*. Yet there is a 'dark diachronicity' to Gill's account as the philosopher Edith Wyschogrod[1] might say where the otherness that she encounters in the flat face that stares back at her is undecided. Its sensual residues evade categorization.

At the end of life, the effects of disease and pain are a continual threat to the settlement of identity categories and schema. To care for cultural others is to be in a position of perpetual uncertainty. How to interpret diseased bodies, their gestures and rhythms as signs? What meaning is there to be deciphered in a *flat face*? Could things be any different with more time? What to make of this ultimate difference?

4

A Catch

When I was about four-years-old we were sitting eating a lunch of red rice ('samba') and curry at my Grandmother's home in Kandy. A local woman, black-skinned and spindly, sauntered into the house from the back veranda and asked for food, picking up some rice from a dish on the table with her fingers. I have never known the woman's name. She was known locally only as 'Kos Amma'. Kos is Sinhalese for Jackfruit. The name Kos Amma is itself a parody of *Kos Mama* the name given to the independence activist Arthur V. Dias, who pioneered a jackfruit propagation campaign in 1918.

Kos Amma was often drunk and liked to smoke beedis, small cigarettes of tobacco wrapped in a brown leaf. It was her habit to carry her Kos knife at her waist, at the meeting point of her faded batik redda (sarong) and choli blouse. The rumour was that Kos Amma had murdered her husband with the knife in a drunken stupor. She had then lit up a beedi and waited calmly for the police to arrive. I am not sure if this story has any truth to it; or how much of it I knew at the time. But when a drunk Kos Amma arrived at our table, I was terrified. The mouthful of rice that I had been eating seemed to stick. I was unable to swallow, caught in deep fear. My Grandmother admonished Kos Amma for frightening me and hurried her out of the house.

That event, the sight and sounds, the smells and tastes, the stilling of peristalsis, attached themselves to red rice. For some time afterwards whenever I ate the rice it would catch in my mouth and throat. I do not think of this catching, the small interruption of a reflex, as a literal regurgitation of a story 'about' Kos Amma. I have come to think of it as a bodily extension of some of the chaotic sensations of that lunchtime. There is so much mystery to percepts and affects. You will know all about this if you play an instrument or swim, or do yoga or tai chi. Different movements, breathing and postures can slow, excite or raise to the surface sublime pressures and flows in the blood stream, muscles or internal organs as well as feelings and memories.

So I do not mean to colonize the unsaid and to suggest that bodies – breath, swallowing or skin – 'speak'. Neither do I want to suggest that it is necessary to decode and translate this speech into a somatic story before we can respond to sensibility and its demands. As the anthropologist Thomas Csordas says the 'non-verbal is precisely not language'.[1] We can miss something vital about the otherness of what is outside of words by treating the body's lines of flight as analogous to language. 'Reality is delicate', the film-maker and writer Trinh T. Minh-ha feels, 'My irreality and imagination are otherwise dull. The habit of imposing a meaning to every single sign'.[2]

Dirt

Family name: Lewis

First name: Maxine

Sex: Female

Religion: Baptist

Occupation: Retired nursing auxiliary

Primary Diagnosis: Bladder ca

Secondary Diagnosis: Lymphadenopathy

Family: 10 children (3 died in infancy)

In the last days of her life Maxine Lewis was a mess. Her face was streaked with the residue of mucus from her eyes, nose and mouth. A rancid musty odour encircled her bed. Professional negligence was not the cause of this neglect. Neither was staff shortages or budget cuts.

> De nurse have time for me you know Yasmin. But I push er away every time she come wash me. She ball at me, an I don't like people frighten me. I'm tired of people proddin an pokin at me all de time.

Prodding and poking is commonplace in the lives of cancer patients where the skin is as much a battleground as it is a protector. Skin is territory. A place of traction between the innards of the self and that which might engulf or save it. It becomes a site of puncturing, marking, impregnation, eruption, seeping, stretching, burning and rotting. Patients can surrender themselves to the routine epidermal intrusions of medicine, giving up ownership of their skin. They offer up bared arms and hands without much thought. Some ready themselves to lift up clothing at the very sight of clinicians.

By the time someone is in need of terminal care, they have usually gone through the medical mill, enduring varying degrees of pain, intrusive investigation and treatment, dependency and disfigurement. They can be worn down, if not defeated by it all. The root of the word *patient* has various meanings connoting grief, need and hunger from which flow the associations of passivity and tolerance. Maxine could never be described as a patient. She was irreverent until the end, still able to find the humourous sides to her predicament. The recordings of our interviews resound with our laughter. The stories themselves were varied and captivating: marriage, arrival scenes, children and work. And between them all the solace, mischief and joy of civil disobedience. The cancer ravaged her body, but it failed to erase her spirit. Twice she had made daring, ridiculous attempts to escape from the confinements of hospitalization.

> I use to walk up an down corridor with dis bag tingy attach to me. An I have it in my mind, I say 'I leave me tings dhere. All I want is key to get in an money to pay cab'. One of de time when I make to run away, two o'clock in de mornin, an de nurses at dheir table with de night lamp. They always notice me, going up an down, up an down. Sometimes they waves at me. So I walkin an I say to myself 'Pity you giving me a nice waving an don't know I'm on me way ome now'. An I reach far, you know. Oh my gosh Yasmin, I nearly reach de gate. I pass de canteen, I get to Casualty an I ear 'Maxine Lewis. Where you think yu going?' Oh my Lord, that urt me so much, I was jus about to get a cab an she say 'Where you think yu going?' An I say 'I'm going ome'. She say 'Home? You lucky you reach ere. Dhere is camera. Dhere is security guard. Come on an get back in your bed.'

Not unfamiliar with violation Maxine had become a warrior of sorts, through habit, volition or through forces beyond consciousness, it is difficult to say. On one of my last visits to Maxine after she had been taken into a hospice, she surprised me with a strange simile. She said she felt like a donkey. When I asked her what she wanted that donkey to do, there was no hesitation in her response. She wanted the donkey to buck and kick its heels in the air. And then there it was again, a twinkling in her eyes.

At the time I was visiting her, Maxine was the only person of colour in her six-bedded hospice bay. She felt the ripples of a disturbance to the sociality and relaxed atmosphere of the bay with her arrival, noticing over the days how the small talk, jokes and exchange of glances and smiles did not extend to her bed. She suspected that the hospice nurses and volunteers had their favourites. She was not one of them.

> Dey ave dtheir favourite an I'm not sayin it for a lie. It's true when dey would say 'Oh Lovie, Darling you wan your bedwash now' an tings like dat. Dat one dhere, from when I'm on dis ward she is working on dis ward. She never one day said to me 'Hello'. Never. An she come and with dat lady over dhere too to get tea, she give her first, 'Hello mi Darlin. Get up. Tea. Tea'. An she give er first.

Wards and bays are places of transit and transition, micro-habitats created by managers, institutional routines, statutory requirements, architecture and equipment. They are continually altered by the movements, leanings and expectations of those who are passing through. The geographer Doreen Massey believes that place is far from a stable entity. It is an event, open and porous, built up of accumulated layers of encounters that create a 'throwntogetherness' in 'the unavoidable challenge of negotiating a here-and-now'.[3]

If the spiky exclusions of the throwntogetherness of what was unfolding in the hospice bay pricked at Maxine, she did not tell her professional carers about what she was feeling. 'I never complain because I fed up you know, Dose girls no repec no black people. You have to fight for yourself'.

To complain or to talk about racism and other injustices goes against the grain of social convention, threatening the fantasy of harmony as a commensurable equality. It also contravenes the expectation that you should keep your troubles to yourself lest your oppression becomes oppressive to others.[4]

When you are vulnerable and dependent, when you feel that the care that you are receiving is relatively better here than in other places in which you have been a patient, it is especially difficult, if not impossible, to say anything about your unhappiness. The risk is that the unhappiness that you show will stick to you. You will be mistaken as the cause of discontent rather than its effect.[5] You risk being seen as 'difficult'. Your care could be affected. Perhaps artificially enhanced rather than diminished, but affected nonetheless. At the end of life, organic pathologies are also at work.

In the last weeks of her life, Maxine's body was becoming more sensitized and unsettled as her disease progressed and she was given more drugs to relieve her symptoms. She began to become anxious when being touched and moved by the nurses. One day when she had been secured into a hoist that would elevate and then lower her into the warm soapy bubble bath that she loved, she refused to keep her hands tucked in as she had been instructed. The hoist, as it raised her off the ground, made her feel unsafe and thingified *like a piece of meat*. In her anxiousness she began to practice a Gandhian satyagraha, non-violent non-cooperation, preferring to remain dirty than to be bathed. Days after the hoist incident Maxine was refusing all haptic care.

Compliance for the sake of making things easy never sat easily beside Maxine's combative will. Not even when she knew that playing nice could be a part of the brokering of small, but vital, survival deals. In exchange for acquiescence you can get things done. Those small extras. The bed-wash in the morning rather than at midday. Someone to comb out your hair or to help you to oil your skin. All of this was important to Maxine. From the photograph album that she showed me in her home during our first interview, I could see that she was a woman who liked to take care of herself. She had been someone who would coordinate a hat with her shoes and gloves, her lipstick with a broach or a necklace.

Paranoia

So why would Maxine choose a dirty death? A disease related hypersensitivity? Have the touches that had kept her clean and comfortable – the swabs that wiped her face, the sponge sticks that moistened her mouth and lips, the hands that turned her – become painful and unbearable?

As the body faces a critical illness or disease state, a normal protective function may be to shunt a larger percentage of cardiac output from the skin to more vital internal organs . . .

Furthermore, the ability to tolerate pressure is limited in poorly perfused body areas.[6]

Mrs Lewis is irritable, showing increased sensitivity to minor discomfort, sound, and touch.

Paranoid ideas?

Maxine's nurses had recorded her heightened anxiety in her last weeks of life, alerting their colleagues of the need to take greater care when lifting and moving her. If she could have seen the handover notes Maxine would not have been surprised at the diagnostic label *paranoia*. I think she would have laughed. We both would have laughed.

Paranoia is a clinical term, whose symptoms include agitation and combativeness. These symptoms can suggest possible underlying organic causes that require monitoring. Living with any consciousness of racism and other social violations is also to live in a 'constellation of delirium', forever bordering on madness. So thought the Martinique-born psychiatrist Franz Fanon, writing in the book *Black Skin, White* Masks.[7] Some racisms you can know and name for what they are. Others are more slippery and shape-shifting, wriggling in and out of substance and language, intermingling and dissolving into other energies and currents.

Maxine had noticed some of the to-ing and fro-ing between her body's intensifying sensitivities and her unsettlement in the ward. 'It's worse Yasmin when I have very bad migraines' she said after a story about how a nurse in the midst of responding to one of her questions had left her abruptly when another patient had called out to her. Not that uncommon in a ward you may be thinking. Not in itself evidence of racism. But small happenings gather meaning through their similitudes and continuities with other felt circuits. And with racism there is always a certain amount of doubt about what you are sensing and feeling. Doubt is the seed of paranoia and 'Our feelings become its truth' writes Sara Ahmed.[8]

Between these worlds of the solid and the ghostly you can encounter aggression, denial, guilt, shame and the most perverse of all: hurt innocence – 'I never meant it like that', 'I don't know what you mean'. Life will become more difficult – 'Why are you making things hard for yourself?', 'Lighten-up!', 'Don't take things so seriously'.

Racism's paranoia is not annexed from disease. Paranoia and anxiety at the end of life are part of a condition known as terminal restlessness. It can include paranoid psychosis or exacerbation of an underlying and unrecognized confusion caused by medication (opioids, anti-seizure drugs, steroids and anxiolytics), decreased oxygen, dehydration or untreated physical pain. The confluence between advancing disease, adverse reactions to psychotropic drugs and compromised renal and hepatic function can alter the chemistry of the body in ways that are impossible to disentangle from more habitual dispositions. And habits are themselves enmeshed in biochemistry, culture, place and their histories. Is that woman being 'difficult' and unreasonable because of her disease? Is she just angry and mean? Might her antipathy be a reasonable response to experiences that we have passed over?

In dying and in caring for those who are dying, there is a complex throwntogetherness of hypersensitivities, unpredictable in their hooking-up and impacts. When somatic life involves violation the task of politics has been to explore, imagine and bring into language the connections between the body and social life, creating narratives that can articulate injustice and summon up new possibilities for living together.

Care practitioners also do this. Sifting through and considering different information and reasons as to why a body might express itself in the way that it does, interrogating care giving and organizational and professional cultures. The hospice social workers offer their insights.

Jo: I kind of wonder about black people who have been in this country for a while, who have experienced racism on and off throughout their lives, that it becomes a kind of automatic response to any situation where they're powerless, which you are if you're being lifted, um, it's very frightening because if your experience is that white people cannot be trusted with you when you're vulnerable [. . .] then I think, your levels of fear must be really quite high, and that maybe, one argument for that would be 'Well then she's paranoid'. Another argument would be 'Well that means we have to be more careful'. But we have to know that when, if we're a group of white people with a black person, that they might have a history about their relationship with white people, and we either acknowledge that or we deal with it in some way.

Jane: I think particularly when you're touching people, you know as nurses touch, and I think for black people who perhaps have never been touched by a white person, or only attacked, I think that must be particularly, particularly er, complex, you know, it really probably needs to be talked about really.

Jo: And I also think that if you work on a shift on a ward for thirty-five hours a week with these patients who are continually dying, that maybe all your top level of tolerance and patience, you know you're up to here with it (her hand goes to the top of her forehead) and then if you take a difficult patient on top-

Jane: Or somebody who lives too long-

Jo: Or somebody who lives too long, or somebody who nearly dies and then lives, and nearly dies, or something's the matter with them going home or not, or else a difficult family. I mean all that makes it difficult for them and which is also, you know, I think that maybe their tolerance levels can get quite low.

In care although bodies are talked about and theorized, they must also be responded to – engaged, touched, listened to, moved and eased. Biographical

stories can help with the work of tending to bodies and their vulnerabilities but lived violation, hurt or trauma is not easily discernible. Good care must learn to work between what can be spoken and the chaotic sensibilities of the body that bypass language.

Comin throu the rye

Maxine's stories always seemed so fresh and unrehearsed to me, suggesting that she was not a woman in the habit of holding forth or of being listened to. Her tales were often pared down, told in paratactic syntax – short crisp sentences without the small conjunctions that help the Western listener transition from one narrative place to another.

> So why I come ere in firs place? Cause of me stupid usband. Im come an ask me Mum an Dad for me marry. Im turn out to be sheep in wolf's clothing. I didn't love im. But you know, if a fella see you back ome an say they fancy you, you cannot court or go out. Im ave to go an ask for you properly. An even when him asks for you, you not to be fin out in the square, stan up talking to you.

Maxine did not want to leave Jamaica for London, but her husband had threatened to cut off his remittances if she did not join him. He was a cruel man who beat her and she could not bear to face his violence in a strange place, without family or friends for respite. But Maxine's parents were old fashioned. They had felt powerless to protect her, deferring to a husband's ultimate authority over his wife.

> It's dem that put pressure on me to come. 'Dat is your usband. Where you bound, you mos'. You know, dey jus put it dat way. Back ome in de country, dey lif usband igher than God. I say to me Mum, me Granny, everybody, I say 'Would you like to be out ere an get a telegram dat he beats me to death?' Dey say they're praying. So I say, 'It doesn't matter to you if he beat me seven days a week'.

So Maxine found herself on an aeroplane bound for England. She wept her heart out during the journey. The other passengers must have thought that she was scared of flying. Her anxiety at flying for the first time was nothing compared to the fear of her husband's violence. What she did not foresee was the care that she would receive from the most surprising of places.

On one Saturday morning, after a brutal beating, Maxine went to her doctor's surgery. Blood was pouring from her nose and mouth. She told the doctor that she had fallen down the stairs. After examining her and tending to the injuries, Dr Robinson agreed that Maxine could indeed have fallen down the stairs, injuring her mouth and nose like that. She suspected however that this was not the case. She did not lecture or interrogate. She gave Maxine a letter, instructing her to take it to Tower Bridge Court on Monday morning. The bold kindness of Dr Robinson seemed to touch Maxine. She did what she was told.

When her husband was summoned to appear in court, the judge asked him what kind of a person his wife was. Mr Lewis said that he could not find a better wife or mother for his children. He had never had to wait for his meals. The house was always clean and tidy. The judge noted that Maxine took her children to three different schools everyday, fitting in the school run and childcare around her night shifts in a factory, packing sandwiches.

Maxine felt that she got justice that day in court. But all was not well in London. Things were different then. Racist violence and abuse was at home in the streets. Twice she got licked. Once when she was seven months pregnant with Marcia. It was during the heavy snowfall of 1963. She had been with two of her husband's cousins when some boys in Rye Lane in Peckham threw a huge snowball at her chanting, *Go home monkey. Go home*. She would often hear the locution *Go home*. Today it was the word *monkey* that enflamed her. Today, she had had enough. Leaving the two men behind, Maxine ran after the perpetrators with her big belly and a fierce battle cry. The boys ran into a shop and cowered like the puppies that they were. The memory stings, yet Maxine's eyes sparkle with the small victory that has forever transformed the now vibrant polycultural spaces of Rye Lane – a street that has been a familiar feature in the lives of successive waves of migrants.

> Every time I pass dat shop, an I'm in dis country from 1961, every time I pass dat shop, I stan up an give a lickle laugh, cause I remember dat's where dey run.

There are more and more studies that are turning to the exchanges of the urban street to understand how everyday encounters can have 'a bearing on how we test and learn with respect to one another' in the living out of multiculturalism.[9] What is less amenable to multisensory notation and inventory[10] is how the ghosts of the past can linger on street corners, at bus stops and in shops, intervening in the evolving feel of a place and its meanings.

Violent racism on the street was not unusual in 1960s London, Maxine says, but, do you know what?, it was black people who also did you down. A Jamaican co-worker at Dulwich hospital where Maxine used to work as an auxiliary nurse would wind her up everyday. Even though the work of auxiliary nursing was demanding, Maxine enjoyed it. After two weeks of training and under the supervision of the matron, an auxiliary nurse was responsible for keeping patients and the wards clean, emptying bedpans, boiling eggs, cleaning patients' lockers, washing and polishing floors, emptying bins, cleaning toilets, clearing away vomit, urine, blood and faeces. Despite the job title, it was mothering work. Invisible and dirty, but often done with care and affection because back then you got to know the patients and their families.[11]

One morning Maxine had suggested to her colleague that they take it in turns to clean out a blood stained area of the renal unit. The woman refused. She did not need the job or the money. She had two big houses in Brixton that were rented out to Jamaicans. Her husband collected the rent every Friday. The colour tax that local landlords charged new migrants had opened up opportunities for some of Maxine's countrymen. They had bought up properties and then rented out the dilapidated rooms to the new desperate arrivals.[12] One day, the woman's boasting and condescension got too much for Maxine.

> She tell me 'You mos ave alf starving chilren for you to do dis work. I don't have to do it. My usband quarrel every day dat I going out to dis dirty job'. So I say to er 'Don't call me chilren names in your mouth.' 'But dem I've seen alf starved' she say.

Maxine punched her colleague in the mouth and split her lip. Violence at work was a sacking offence, yet Maxine did not lose her job. The young manager who knew her was sure that there must have been history behind the assault '*I say "Mr Baker, you can sack me now. I don't care. It's best I'm sack dan I ave to be wind up*'". Maxine was given a warning and returned to her post. She remained at the hospital until she retired.

Patience

Maxine may have worked in a hospital for most of her adult life but she did not like being a patient. The nurses did not behave like proper caring professionals. They could bully people. They did not bully her of course, perhaps because several of the nurses in the local teaching hospital were from Jamaica. Sometimes they would all make jokes about Jamaicans together. They used to get along. But Maxine took offence when a nurse overstepped the boundaries. Sometimes a nurse would rouse a sleepy patient by peeling back the sheets and telling them to get out of bed, observing loudly that the patient liked bed too much. Maxine did not like this sort of behaviour 'Yu in ospital cause you tak sick, in dere to be care for. I mean it make a lot of people jumpy'.

If the lack of care in hospital was discomforting, Maxine was also growing intolerant of the tests that she had to undergo. Sometimes she would be eating a meal in the ward and a porter would arrive with a wheelchair to take her for a test. She had had several MRI body scans. Not that she was complaining about the scans. In Jamaica to have a scan would cost a lot of dollars. She had been through the scanner three times and had had a bone marrow test. She remembers every detail of the extraction of her bone marrow.

> Imagine me, pure skin an bone, an dey didn't even give me an injection to kill de pain. Dey come with dis trolley, a doctor an de needle. The mistake I mak is to look on trolley, cause the syringe is so big. Di man jus pull the screen roun an two nurse sat down, 'Can we watch doctor?' 'Yes' he say. 'Yes'. An nurse say 'Maxine. Maxine you can old us for support.' So I was dis side. They stand dere. Ooh, I ave so much chilren, but I can't remember one of dem pain ever feel like dat, Jesus, an they going down. I could ear di needle you know, an it going down an it still urt you know. Yes. An it going down. Den a bit of scraping, it going down an I hung on to de nearest nurse to me. When I finish with dose two nurse dey don't have on no apron. Their apron was on de floor. Dey was sweating, panting an huffin, cause dey say dey never know a likkle person like me could grab anybody dat way.

Insight: Fully aware of her disease and the potential prognosis.

Over the months that I got to know Maxine, she did not speak directly about death. Her move from curative to palliative care was talked about through a change of tests, institutions or nurses, so that dying was somehow displaced from her body. During one of her hospitalizations, a staff nurse had asked Maxine if she knew anything about Macmillan nurses who have specialist skills in cancer and palliative care.[13] Maxine said that she did not know what the nurses were called but she had seen them around the hospital.

> I see dem, but I use to say 'Funny init? Ow comes dey don't wear uniform you know?' To me dat's better. Uniforms scare de daylight out of me, especially dem doctor white-coat. I ear about de ospice before, but I don't know where it is. I was scared because white people, black people, everyone saying to me 'You mosn't go up dere.'

So Maxine was left wondering and pondering about what a hospice would be like. Then Kathy, a hospice nurse, came to visit her at home and arranged a visit. A volunteer driver picked Maxine up from her home and drove her to the hospice. She was pleasantly surprised. The day was refreshing. She met and talked to new people and had a bit of a singsong. What she appreciated the most was the chance for some pampering.

> I ave a lick – what's it called? Lickussi bath wit all de bubbles an I should ave had me nails done de following week when I took sick. I got ague fever[14]. It make you shake and you ave dis fire. What you don't know ague fever? It come from back ome, especial in de country. You will ear like someone aving a talk with me Mum an say 'Oh Lord, Mrs Campbell, Jesus! The girl ave ague fever'.

The onset of the fever marked Maxine's deterioration. When I visited her at home after the fever had set in, she was weaker and frail. She was admitted into the hospice a week later. She did not return to her beloved home.

The last time that I talked to Maxine at the hospice, she was sedated and woozy. Her thoughts drifted between the confines of the hospice ward – and whether other patients were eavesdropping on our conversation – and her father's last words of advice to her before she left Jamaica.

> When I was coming away, me Dad call me an say 'I know ow you's stubborn an I know you onest.' An I tell him 'Yes'. An I said 'Papa why you keep telling me dese foolishness?' An him say to me 'Now you remember, you my biggest child. You going to Englan. Dat is a long journey you going on. I'm putting down good prior for you. If you in Englan an hundreds of you pack up into a room an dey give you one bottle of milk, don't ask dem where they get de milk to give you alone. Don't ask no question. Take de milk giving away, say "Thank-you very much." Dat's it.' He was trying to tell me not to go an catch any trouble.
>
> But trouble always seems to fin me.

Assessment and Guidance for Lifting and Handling Patients: Mrs Lewis is extremely anxious when being turned, needing gentle re-assurance as to her safety.

Syringe driver commenced.

Reduce BM monitoring to once daily.

Mrs Lewis's restlessness has subsided. Move only for comfort.

It is always difficult to know how and where to begin a story. It is harder to know where it ends. It is the same with responsibility. And so I talk to a friend. The writing is not going well with Maxine I say. I explain that there could be organic causes in her resistance to care. But what if restlessness, paranoia and hypersensitivity are a body's testimony to its past and not only a recent past?

I was beginning to wonder about the ways in which the body's activities can bypass subjectivity, reason and knowing, how sensibility can make a body into a work of art[15] so that care must also become artful in its responsiveness. 'But', and then there was a hesitation as I searched for the words. In the end I just say – 'But, there was this twinkling in her eyes when she told me her stories, even the stories of violence. I just can't seem to convey it.'

Then tell them about the twinkle she says.

Never Mind

There is no such thing as balanced indifference. There is no center or axis; it cannot be found, or is absent.[1]

Violet is unbalanced.

A series of strokes, left-sided hemiplegia and a growing cancerous breast tumour have left her noticeably lopsided. At times when we talked the old woman would slip away from me, her eyes drifting off somewhere to what lay beyond the top of my left ear. Our first interview felt like a disaster. With the coming and going of her attention I rushed into the silences and pauses with stupid, unnecessary questions, my way of trying to restore some tempo and convention to the interview. She did not seem to hold my foolishness and anxiety against me. When we next met in her home, I was greeted with some affection 'There's my friend Yasmin!'

Over the three months that I got to know Violet, she trained me to say nothing during her absences. I learned to wait for her to return and in the waiting to pick up on my own leanings.

'How can the right-handed person be described?' the left-handed philosopher Michel Serres has asked, offering,

As a severed organism . . . Hot and supple, one side of the body and its extension lives, trailing behind it a sort of cadaverous twin, stiff and cold, contemptible and impotent – in short, unconscious.[2]

Serres' point is that we are all inclined and out of kilter, dragging behind us a neglected forsaken side. Serres' sense of sensibility is that it operates as a fluctuating, directional pull, a tugging of the eyes, mouth, ears, nose and skin that is helplessly open and skittish.

The conjoined twins of disability and disease pull Violet in different directions. The left side of her body is leaden and icy, drooping downwards in a yogic hyper-relaxation. Her upper-right-side skewered by the tumour, lists feverishly away from the left in a new growing compulsion. Between these divided fidelities, any autonomy she has demands other forms of asymmetry. As a patient-in-residence, Violet is always dependent upon others. She can pour water from her jug only if it is half-filled and in close reach, at a certain height and angle on her bedside table. She makes constant, seemingly petty demands upon the nurses, micromanaging the positioning of bottles, tissues, newspapers, biscuits and fruit.

For some patients bedside tables are small recreations of home,[3] transplanting elements of bedroom, kitchen and bathroom.[4] A small brass tazza, hot pepper sauce or a bottle of Bay Rum can bring instant domesticity and comfort to an institutional space.

Violet's bedside table is her lifeline. It is a rope of plaited duties and favours tossed towards the right of her body, bringing cramped opportunities to potter and to feel about. In the economy of a restricted life-world trivia have an inflated value that can baffle and infuriate outsiders. For the nurses, Violet is a *difficult patient*, one of those people in the ward that they are reluctant to pull up a chair beside and to talk to when they have a few minutes to spare.

Violet resents her increasing dependence. 'I don't depend on my family or friends. I wasn't dat person before I took sick, so is very difficult for me. I jus don't like to give people trouble, bother no-one. I don't like it.' What Violet does lean on is her Pentecostal religion. It gives her suffering direction and purpose. It brings her closer to Jesus.

When she was diagnosed with breast cancer, Violet refused to have the tumour in her right breast operated on, choosing to be treated only with radiation and chemotherapy.

> From de time I saw dis lump in my breast, I discover dat it would be someting like cancer, so when dey tol me, it wasn't strange to me. I said 'Well if I go an dey tell me it's cancer, I'll accep it', which I did. What dey wanted was to hoperate an I said 'No. No. I don't want de hoperation. I don't want no hoperation on it'. I stan against dat very much. I'd rather die wit it dis way. I don't believe in hoperation. There are some times when dey hoperate on you an den you could live a few more days longer, but because of dat hoperation you can also go quicker. So dat's why I'm not keen on it.

Without surgery Violet's tumour has continued to grow, forcing itself through her skin into a malignant fungating breast lesion. Fungating is the medical term for an open rotting wound. Fungating wounds are painful, seeping and malodorous, a constant reminder of a progressing fecund disease. Fungating lesions lure senses to the interior of the body, to a secret world of carnal life and sensations devoid of referents in modern Western cultures. Among the Anlo-Ewe people of South-Eastern Ghana there is a basic perception verb *seselelame* that refers to both sense knowledge and to sensations. It is the sensing of sense. It can be used to connote the tingling of the skin, hearing, smell, sexual arousal, intuition, kinaesthetics and balance. Seselelame is translated as 'feel-feel-at-flesh-inside'.[5]

The lively density of Violet's tumour transported through seselelame gives her little respite. Every movement – to stand or to turn, to pick up a glass or to readjust the blanket over her knees – can strain and pull at her body's fraying edges. Sleeping is what she finds most difficult. There are few comfortable resting places, only *pain, pain, pain.*

As a cancer develops, it can explore outwards like a curious, awesome infant, an evanescent energy of mass, fluid, rhythms and pressures that is a distinct presence, even as it suckles from and merges with blood, muscle, bone and skin. The slow birthing of malign matter into the outside world through fluids and odours perforates what the French psychoanalyst Didier Anzieu has called the *skin ego,*[6] a containing envelope of skin and psyche that marks off the self from others.

Every breath for Violet and those around her is an inhalation of decay and death.

Silver lining

The topical application of a sugar paste and honey, or dressings with charcoal or silver nitrate can control the growth of bacteria in a wound and absorb offensive smells, temporarily sealing off an effusive body. Returning it to the present, to visitors, to a home. A body that has been bound, quieted and made private is a body that is less menacing in Anglo cultures, even though all bodies leak.

Among hospice patients whose bodily surfaces could not be restored, the anthropologist Julia Lawton has observed that some patients began to retreat into an inert existing, even when they retained the capacity to communicate with others and to be mobile.[7] They were moved around the hospice, often into single rooms. Other patients and relatives complained about the smell. As the putrid insides of a body flowed outwards, Lawton found that personhood could withdraw in a psychic 'switching off'. Like strangers in the night, the outgoing body and the retreating self could pass each other by.

Those who care for Violet have noticed her lack of presence. They interpret it in different ways according to whether they are thinking about her stroke-induced impairments or other biographical coordinates. A hospice inpatient nurse writes 'Her concentration span is very short, ? dementia'. Violet's hospice home-care nurse, Janice, who has known Violet for some time, finds her stoical, one of her older patients who would never make a fuss about her symptoms. Janice shudders when she recalls seeing the dressings on Violet's breast lesion being changed by her district nurse.

> You know it's hard to imagine that that wasn't a terribly painful procedure for her. She clearly was in pain. She would wince you know. And you felt that she was having a lot more pain than she would acknowledge really.

Whether she is helping with wound dressings, taking blood or listening to stories about the grandchildren, Janice maintains an acute openness to the rich textures of body and soul that rain in on her on a daily basis. A new smell, a change in posture, some play of hue in a complexion, an unusual dilation or constriction of the pupils, a snide exchange between family members are all taken in and registered. With each new symptom, surprise or misunderstanding her palette of care grows a little and becomes more dappled with each patient.

It is a form of body work somewhat akin to that found in the training of 'noses' in the perfume industry, where a novice must learn to identify the subtle chemical distinctions within and between odours: the nuances of amber, hay and tobacco in Clary Sage. The warmth of civet musk or the vanilla-almond of a heliotrope. The philosopher Bruno Latour has dubbed this unfolding of the world with the body as a lively process of *learning to be affected*. Once amateur noses have gone through a weeklong training session Latour observes how,

> . . . the word 'violet' carries at last the fragrance of the violet and all of its chemical undertones . . . words finally carry worlds. What we say, feel and act, is geared on differences registered in the world.[8]

And so it seems that by listening to Violet and her family, and by smelling, touching and observing, a world of tonal contrasts and accords also emerges in Janice's apprehension of her Violet. As always with auscultation there is uncertainty.

> I think Violet's life was hugely compromized when she had her stroke, because of course she wasn't mobile, she wasn't independent and in many ways the breast cancer was almost an incidental because it wasn't actually incapacitating her

because she was already immobile. But I am only surmising and I suppose I felt that Violet was a lady who had been a victim in her life, and this is more on an emotional level, but you know we shouldn't just sort of cast that aside as not being important. I think she had always been a victim, and I think she remained a victim in a way. She was a vulnerable lady. She was disadvantaged in many ways. She wasn't particularly an articulate lady, and although she was demanding in some ways, she was also accepting in others. It was, you know, a bit of a mix there and she did seem to accept her disease on the surface with this sort of equanimity, but I don't think, you know, I think at times, although she seemed to be accepting, you know, at the end of the day who wants this dreadful thing, the thing that every day she was witness to? And yet she had refused treatment. You know, there was a strange mix there really, that I, I never, and I don't know whether anybody ever did, get to the bottom of really, because you know she had to have her dressing changed everyday, so that was a daily reminder that she had a nasty, horrid, painful lesion there.

This backstory of Violet had been prompted by a disclosure from Violet's daughter of the violence her mother had endured during her marriage. Frustrated at her own complicity with the pretence of a happy marriage, Janice nevertheless respected Violet's opacity 'I suppose one has to work with what you're able to'. And Janice did this work by managing Violet's dressings, pills, patches and creams and by risk-taking and stealth. She would encourage and gently coax Violet into saying more about herself. Hoping for a spark of something, knowing that it might never come.

On a home visit, Janice talked to Violet about a recent change in her pain control. She crouched down onto her haunches so that Violet did not have to look up to her. She lowered her voice for discretion 'Violet I can see that you haven't been taking your Oramorph tablets that the doctor gave you for the pain'. Without any signs of an emerging dialogue about Violet's refusal of the opioid analgesics, Janice moved into multiple-choice questions and possibilities 'Did you forget to take the tablets, Violet? Do you not like taking tablets? Would you prefer to take a liquid instead?' Each inquiry or suggestion was met with a blank stare or an *I don't know Dear*. But Janice kept going, searching gently for reasons and possibilities until Violet said that she was not taking the tablets because she did not want to become addicted to the drug. Janice was reassuring about the safety of prescribed morphine, but she knew that this standard script would not be enough. She persuaded Violet to try a synthetic analgesic, Fentanyl, absorbed into the body through a patch stuck to the skin. A small, but not insignificant result.

Yvonne, Violet's eldest daughter, appreciated Janice's insight and her perseverance. One day, after we had finished a home visit and were on the way to Janice's car, Yvonne came out after us. Standing on one of the many communal paths in the housing estate, Yvonne told us against grey skies that her parents are of a generation that is deferential to authority and to professionals. Violet is someone who would not find it easy to ask for more help and support 'You'd have to drag it out of her' Yvonne tells us.

For better or for worse, Violet is not entirely deferential. As Janice recognized, to go against medical advice – the weight of statistics and clinical trials, the case comparisons, the ticking clock and the poised pen – takes courage and strength. Non-compliant patients, who remove themselves from the conveyor belt that moves seamlessly from diagnosis to treatment, test the authority and moral fibre of medical and nursing staff. Treatment does much more than cure, exorcise or manage disease. It is the means by which medicine measures and validates itself.

In the contemporary ethos of *partnership working* and *the expert patient*, doctors must accept and honour a patient's decision. A referral letter from Violet's hospital is non-judgemental, to the point. 'Mrs Lawrence is firmly of the opinion that surgery spreads cancer and has therefore declined our interventions'. But there are striations of resentment and frustration among some of the professionals who care for Violet. A doctor 'I would imagine that she can present as socially pleasant, but in reality, I think she has little insight into how to look after herself'. Other members of Violet's inpatient hospice care team point to her indolent introversion, her excessive demands on their time and personnel. Because of her disabilities it takes two people to move Violet. She is what they describe as 'well-covered', making her heavy and cumbersome to assist. Violet can spend up to an hour on the commode trying to pass urine, a nurse half-complained, half-described to Janice.

Talking to Violet was hard work too. I found her laconic. Our conversations would often stall or be batted off-course with a perfunctory *I don't know Dear* or an out-of-the-blue chuckling. *I don't pay it no mind* was an apt, often used part of Violet's vocabulary, recurring when she talked about difficult situations. I heard it for the first time when she told me about her efforts to find a job as a new migrant to London in the 1960s. 'Well you know dey used to call us names', Violet said.

I mean you go for a job and ting and dey see you coming, then say 'We don't want any blackies . . . We haven't no job for no blackie. Go back to where you come from', and ting like dat. When you go to work they skin up their face agains you. But we learned dat you know, we just pay dem no mind really, and we didn't pass back no word at dem, nor nothing, because being we weren't brought up dat way. And we have white people in the West Indies and we treat dem very good. We work with dem. We do everyting for dem. So it was strange for us coming here, an dey treat us like dis, like wasn't like at home. The white people in de West Indies were very nice. Nice people.

So how did you actually feel when you went for a job and they would say things like that ?

Jus don't pay it no mind, Dear. I just ignore everyting. We ignore everyting.

This observation of the strange behaviour of white people on their home turf compared to the *nice* white English people in Jamaica was still a puzzle to Violet and one in which *paying no mind* was the superior moral response. Jamaica Kincaid's memoir *A Small Place,* that records the colonial presence in Antigua, suggests that the English could be just as 'ill-mannered' in the Caribbean.[9] An Antiguan response – very much like Violet's – displaced recognition of racism with a moral rhetoric 'We felt superior, for we were so much better behaved and we were full of grace. . .'.[10]

Such moments of lively story telling from Violet, of being curious and puzzled by life, were rare during our conversations. With Violet there was a sense of a withering of connections with others and what was outside herself. The external world was becoming more distant, receding and being nudged into the background.

As her disease advanced, Violet took to spending most of her day when she was at home, living in two square metres of space. Her confinement and domestication were not far removed from parts of my own daily life (when I am not teaching) and the dislodged reality of millions of cyber-addicts and workers in cities across the world, tethered to screens and simulacra in what the writer Paul Virilio has described as an uncanny 'spastic immobility'.[11] Although Violet's imposed captivation is without the sociality that cyber space can offer, it was somewhat softened by a circle of her most precious and utilitarian objects, including a bible, clock, television remote control, a pack of cards and an aerosol air freshener. The citrus-vanilla undertones of the air freshener would momentarily deodorize the fetid air in Violet's sitting room. Ultimately, the functional fragrance of the spray with its soapy tonality would be recruited into the animalic base notes of the cancer so that it became nauseating and oppressive.

Violet said that she chose not to have friends to visit her during this time. She said that she tired quickly. And she did not need to go to church because healing can take place anywhere. But visitors were also staying away, ashamed and fearful of being so directly assaulted by the stench of illness and death.

Theorizing the revulsion caused by such *dirty dying*, Julia Lawton suggests that over-spilling bodies pose a double threat. They terrify and threaten Anglo-European ideas about personhood as enclosed and privatized, and they undermine distinctions between order and dirt. Making sense of her observations of the lonely deaths of hospice patients who were avoided by other patients and their own families as their bodies unravelled, Lawton writes

> The smells, and other fluids and matter emitted from the unbounded body, extended the boundaries of the patient's corporeality, such that the patient's body 'seeped' into the boundaries and spaces of other persons and other places. . . . In effect the other participants in the hospice were trying to maintain the integrity of their own selves, by avoiding having their bodily boundaries breached by the corrosive effects of the sick person's bodily disintegration.[12]

'What does cancer smell like?' is a recurrent topic in the blogosphere, with patients and carers exchanging their experiences and suspicions about the meanings of cancerous scents, likened to vinegar, Swiss cheese, stale sex, mushrooms or sweets. One woman noticed a smell around her that was most pronounced when she used the toilet. A man picked up a scent near his partner's left breast, that he recalled from his mother's breast cancer, 20 years earlier. Another could smell a sour-wine odour on her husband that lingered in the bedroom and on the sheets. He was subsequently diagnosed with inoperable colorectal cancer. Most of these people seek reassurance that they are not mad to trust in the contact they have made with the body's aromatic ghosts; a contact and participation in an olfactory world that is also made by dogs and is being used to develop electronic noses that are able to distinguish between healthy and malignant breath.[13] The leap outside of reason brings these courageous apprentices in the art of *seselelame* full circle to a rendezvous with cutting-edge medicine and to an intimate attunement with human vulnerability that clinicians have mostly forgotten. Or at least have tried to forget.

To smell is to feel and also to remember. Scent receptors at the back of the nose are connected to the limbic system, the most primitive part of the brain that is responsible for the processing of emotions and memories.

Les Fleurs du Mal

With the smell from her wound becoming more difficult to disguise and manage, Violet would only venture outside of her house for medical appointments or admissions. Even then, with the privilege of hospital or hospice transport, she had little direct contact with the streets. For this she was grateful. The pace of life in the London suburb where Violet lived had become too fast, too loud, too scary. On her last journey outside she felt wrong-footed and enfeebled by the shakiness of the ground underneath her. Recoiling from the world in infirmity is like learning to walk in reverse, a tottering regressive immobilization in which confidence, balance and bearings are slowly lost. The body tightens. Temperature soars and plummets. The jaw clenches, shoulders rise, the heart races, the gut churns. The world wobbles.

The pitching, rolling loneliness of an ever-increasing drift while all the time staying put is an inner migration. Yet Violet's solitary journey beneath the skin was more than the encumbrance of her disabilities, the lethargic heaviness of her movements, the tense asymmetries of an upper body curved around its open, stinky wound.

Frailty bends time and space. It had changed Violet's sense of her place in the world, of being in synchrony with herself and with others.

The nineteenth-century French poet and lover of all things urban, Charles Baudelaire, understood so well this metaphysics of infirmity. In the poem *Recueillement*, we find the poet wandering through the town at dusk with his *douleur* – his pain/sorrow.[14] The anxious douleur is addressed and consoled as an indulged child, with the poet reframing and humanizing fearful nocturnal presences. Lost years are personified as old women looking out over their balconies. Regret is beneficent, emerging *smiling from the sea*. Restoring a fragile calm to all which threatens to overwhelm, the poem culminates with tender and wondrous expectation: *Listen, my Dearest, hear the sweet night march.*

I did not get the chance to say goodbye to Violet. I hold onto a fantasy that she had some sense of peace before her night came – that her douleur was comforted and reassured.

A month or so after my last visit to Violet's house, she was admitted into a nursing home for long-term care. Her husband was not able to cope with looking after her at home and Yvonne feared that Violet might once again become a victim of her father's violence. Less than a week after being admitted into the nursing home Violet suffered a haemorrhage from her vagina. She was taken as an emergency to her local hospital where she was found to have a large undiagnosed pelvic mass. She died without regaining consciousness.

It is difficult to imagine that Violet could not *feel-feel-at-flesh-inside*. That she was somehow unaware of the weight of the gestating mass bearing down through her. It is more distressing to think that she was prepared to accept and endure quietly whatever fate bestowed upon her in a slow, passive suicide. Difficult probing questions were asked about the robustness of the protective membranes of care surrounding Violet. Plausible explanations were offered and interrogated. Without a post-mortem examination there was no evidence that the haemorrhage was cancer-related, Janice told me. Violet also had uterine fibroids that could have caused the bleed.

In the end the turbulent outpouring of Violet's life remained beyond Janice. She was utterly devastated by what happened and felt in some way responsible. She should have been more attentive, more pushy 'Violet wasn't always able to say what her problem was', Janice said. 'She really didn't make a fuss about the things that were causing her the most discomfort and that strangely was it seems, the cause of her death.' For anyone who cares, responsibility metastasizes, spreading to small crevices and tucked-away places that are not easily perceived or accessible. Techniques and protocols of care can be examined, evaluated and refined in the hope that future catastrophes can be avoided, but there is always an excess that cannot be put into words, that demands to be felt and to be remembered.

'Wild honey has the scent of freedom, dust of a ray of sun, a girl's mouth of a violet', wrote the poet Anna Akhmatova 'but we have found out forever, that blood smells only of blood.'[15]

6

Dissimulation

Each day throughout the warm summer months he has put on a thick woollen jumper and nurtured a hot water bottle at his chest. He feels cold. Whatever he does, he cannot seem to get warm. He finds it difficult to concentrate at times, losing the thread of his thought, 'I've lost myself' he tells me apologetically mid-sentence 'I don't know whether it's the medication that makes me feel this way, because I am sort of dazed'.

James is soft-spoken, beautiful and dying from HIV-related cancers of the throat and lungs. James did not want anyone, including his estranged wife and two children whom he lived with, to know that he was seropositive. 'I just thought that the moment I mention this kind of thing, the whole family is going to shatter.' In the hospice where he had been admitted for a two-week stay for symptom control, James was passing himself off as someone with terminal cancer. So let's just say that James – he chose the pseudonym himself – is Kenyan and that he had lived with his secret for about 18 months before I met him.

London is the epicentre of the United Kingdom's HIV and AIDS epidemic. Nearly half of all HIV diagnoses are made in the city. The retrovirus HIV has hit Black African communities hard. For a decade or so they have accounted for over a third of those who find out that they are HIV positive. Despite advances in antiretroviral drugs (ARVs) that suppress the virus and stop the progression of disease, Black Africans are one of the groups least likely to access the drug regimens. Fear of stigmatization and insecure migration status are said to be some of the barriers to HIV testing and access to health care services.[1]

To benefit from ARVs you need to have an HIV test. You should take the test early on in the disease when your CD4 cell count – white blood cells that are the backbone of the immune system – is *higher than 350 per cubic millimetre of blood.*

Those who are diagnosed late have a tenfold increased risk of death within one year of a diagnosis. In 2010, an estimated 50 per cent of those adults diagnosed in the United Kingdom were at a late stage of infection with a CD4 cell count of less than 350 cells/mm3. Late diagnosis was highest for Black Africans.[2]

Faces, numbers and surreal dreams can haunt you when you think of taking the test that will help you to access ARVs and the possibility of a longer, healthier life. In those moments, months or years you can find yourself drawn to the fates of those who are sick and dying around you, and in the city, hometown or village that you have left behind. You will try to develop immunity to the virulent gossip and judgements 'This one is infected, can't you see how slim she has become? She will die and no one will attend her burial.'[3] You must be certain that the rumours that a seropositive diagnosis will lead to deportation are not true. And you should not be an undocumented migrant who may be refused National Health Service care or who will have to pay substantial hospital bills. If symptoms emerge, you will ignore them for as long as you can. When your condition gets worse, you may send for herbal remedies, perhaps bark powder or leaves from the Neem tree. Only when you are desperately ill will you seek emergency care.

At the end of 2011 an estimated 34 million people across the globe were living with HIV, about 30 million were living in low and middle-income countries.[4]

Sub-Saharan Africa accounts for 68 per cent of the global prevalence of HIV, with women and young people being disproportionately affected.

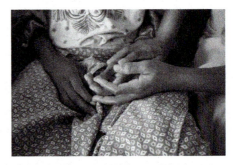

Figure 6.1 HIV, sub-Saharan Africa.
Courtesy: Nadia Bettega

Population based health surveys suggest that less than 40 per cent of people who are seropositive know their HIV status.[5]

Shock

James was diagnosed as HIV positive after noticing a thrush infection in his mouth. He thinks that he contracted the virus about four years before he took the HIV antibody test. His memory of the test is vivid. It all began on a Sunday afternoon. Because it was the weekend, James could not consult his General Practitioner, so he had travelled by bus to the Accident and Emergency department of a hospital in the city centre. A nurse advised him to take an HIV test the next morning.

How did you feel when you found out?

> I think the person I saw was quite nice, but it's such a horrifying experience being told that [. . .] yeah, I, I didn't know what to do [. . .] with myself or [. . .] whether to actually scream or cry or what. It was a terrible experience [. . .] because, you know, you are there, you are alone and here you are presented with this massive answer [. . .] which you didn't even want to know [. . .] and that's it. I just sort of froze [. . .]. I just thought 'It can't be me.'

To freeze like this is to be in the lure of simultaneous and opposing chemical impulses. Underneath the immobilization of shock, waves of adrenalin drive forward a movement from one state to another, from thinking *It can't be me* to a resolve of *It will not be me*. For James, this leaving behind of a self, who is somehow caught-up and at the same time is in flight, is a disturbing premonition and something familiar.

Some 20 years ago, he had left Kenya in pursuit of a better life, rising to meet each new demand, turning from one occupation to another, continually reinventing himself. Ultimately, he says, he found himself stuck, in the grip of another epidemic. It is not only viruses that cause a fever.

> You get caught up into a certain syndrome and you remain in the same position. You come here thinking that you are going to make a fortune. You are going to study and after studying, you will find a job somewhere. Everything we think of is as if it is really made up for you. It's waiting. When you're in Africa thinking about Britain and all these big, you know Super countries. You always think that everything is there for you and that you can't fail because you hear the newspapers talking about countries of dreams, dream countries and say for instance in my position, when I came to Britain I thought as soon as I finish my education, I'll get a job. I'll buy a car. I'll buy this. I'll buy that.

> That's not how it is. Things are completely different. You find yourself struggling to make ends meet and you get caught into a situation whereby you don't have enough money and yet you can't progress yourself. You cannot do anything to progress because you are trying to make money to survive. So things just stay there.

If what is *right* becomes more discernible when things go wrong, then the morality of James' hindsight[6] as he evaluates his life, is one that is intruded upon by the cannons of cultural tradition that have not let him forget how things *should* have been.

> I felt caught because I didn't want to go back to Kenya and by then I had a wife who I was also trying to make work so that I could increase our revenue, and things were very difficult because you can imagine, you're a new person arriving in Britain, just to start working, whereas you should be treated in a different way, because she has just been newly wed and all those things were hurting me, because that's not the way it should have been. It should have been that I should have been set up and then when she comes I've got a house. I've got all the money really to look after her. It never happened that way.

The rub between the demands of tradition, disintegrating life-plans and what you are prepared to do in order to survive in the diaspora are never straightforward. Which customs matter? What can you let go? Which path is right for you? What might other people think?

If James found that money could eat into self-esteem, cultural tradition and family relationships when it was scarce, in times of greater plenitude he also became aware of how it could bestow and disperse social significance and standing. In London, when he had money, James was able to donate to cultural events and to funeral costs. In the 1990s, when the epidemic was at a peak, there seemed to be a funeral or more every month. James' beneficence was his emergence as a Somebody in both continents, maturing into an investment that doubled his sense of jeopardy. Practical matters loom large when James thinks about his family in Kenya.

> I don't want to use the wrong words, but to my brothers and sisters I am an important person because I keep sending them money and if that disappears, it is a tragedy to them. So that is the fear within themselves, if this person dies, what will happen?

> Officially recorded remittance flows to low-income countries are estimated to have reached $372 billion in 2011, three times the size of official development assistance. The growth rate of remittances was higher in 2011 than in 2010 for all regions except the Middle East and North Africa, where flows were thought to be have been moderated by the Arab Uprisings.[7]

There can be cynical master plans behind faking an identity, but imposture in illness can be incremental, a day-to-day journeying where self-interest and a sincere concern for the good of others co-exist. Substituting one persona in favour of another requires courage and skill. It is also disease- and medicine-dependent. Some diseases, like skin colour or facial features offer more room and materials for masquerade than others. And some drugs, such as ARVs, can be so efficacious in controlling symptoms that it is entirely possible to mask and to even 'forget' that you have a disease.

But at the end of his life, the virus and its bodily devastations are only a part of James' problems. The stigma that surrounds this disease and how it might affect his family, preoccupy James, driving him away from others, into a lonely phantom.

> So it feels, just from what you've been saying, that this illness has been quite a lonely time for you.

> It is, yeah, because it isolates you completely, and you don't want anyone else, because it is like a taboo illness, because once people know that, you know, that you are this ill, the way they see you is confused. Completely different, I think, you know, people are too ignorant in such a way that, you know, they don't understand properly. It makes me angry that people behave in such a way of ignorance that they don't actually understand that it is just another disease.

> Like cancer?

> Exactly.

In the world of illness taboos and disease imposture, one person's cancer is another person's HIV. For Nusrat, a Pakistani Muslim, the decision to be open about her cancer was fraught. She knows from experience how quickly news can ricochet between London and Lahore and how in a matter of hours it can afflict generations of a family. Nusrat remembers those acquaintances that she now suspects were dying from cancer and who were hidden away behind closely guarded doors, excuses and half-truths – 'We've come to see Aunty' – 'She's sleeping'. They were made to disappear so that cancer and its threat of infecting and blighting the health of the heteronormative family could be deflected. 'People feel that if others come to know about their illness, they won't be able to marry their children off. Or people may think if the mother had cancer, then the children will also have it.' Stigma, like culture and cancer, can be sticky and tentacular. It can also have an after-life, threatening the lives and the futures of others, so that the need for imposture can extend beyond a death. Louise, a hospice nurse,

We had a young Indian boy die of AIDS on the ward . . . I remember the father, they hadn't actually known he had AIDS, he, he had chosen to keep it from his parents and they had inadvertently found out from the ambulance crew um, who, who had berated them really for not telling them that he had AIDS. It was a terrible sort of chain of events, um, but they were also really distressed when he died because they couldn't have the coffin open at the, in the church, and, and they just really didn't know how they were going to explain that to all their extended family, er, it was just,um, they were, um that was a major hurdle, hurdle for his parents to overcome, 'What are we going to tell people if there's a reason why we can't have his coffin open?' It was, for them, that was like a very, very big issue [. . .]. I'm not actually sure how they resolved it though. I mean they basically told everyone that he died of skin cancer, um [. . .], and I think used that as a reason why they wouldn't have the coffin open, because it's, it's so distressing to look at, you know, and he would have been in a body bag and everything.

Barbara Browning, an academic, novelist and dancer, predicted some time ago that the progress made by white gay men's tactic of announcing their seropositivity was unlikely to translate in a future global context. '. . . the strategy of volubility (Silence=Death)' Browning wrote 'was predicated on a fact of early AIDS demography in the US: the impacted community had a considerable economic, and so political base'.[8] The politics of volubility has been limited cross-culturally, but the heroic figure of the proud HIV positive subject has also been recast by pharma developments, particularly the use of Highly Active Antiretroviral Therapy (HAART), impacting upon HIV activism among gay men and in how disease identities can be taken up, 'forgotten' or bracketed.

In March 2008, Cass Mann – *one of the world's then longest surviving HIV positive diagnosed gay men* – posted a video on YouTube *With Antiretroviral Drugs (ARVs), Does HIV Still Matter?*[9] The film brought antiretrovirals into discussions of the increasing rates of HIV infection and sexually transmitted diseases among gay men. The implication was that the promise of longer life and a pharmacologically mimed asymptomology had impelled new illness identities leading to a decline in safer sex practices, denial of the risks of HIV infection, non-disclosure and new resistant mutations of the virus. Cass Mann's lilting Indian accent on YouTube does not temper his stark message. He tells his audience 'another danger of barebacking is if the person you are having sex with infects you with multi-resistant HIV. You are fucked. In more ways than one.'

As the sociologist Marsha Rosengarten has pointed out, what HIV is and its effects are informed by the unceasing 'traffic' of information between biology, medical treatments, culture and how HIV is lived.[10] HIV, Rosengarten argues, is not a single entity, but becomes the performative effect of value enfolded into evolving matter. What it means to be HIV positive – and therefore what it means to pretend that you do not have the virus – is constantly shifting and being reconfigured.

So HIV disease impostors and their accomplices walk through emotional and biopolitical minefields every day, surrounded by threats that are always regrouping. The danger is highly contagious, spreading out through social encounters, relationships and interviews. Impostors are difficult people to engage in conversation. They tend towards evasion, obfuscation and fast-talking, moving topics on before they become too close. Their sentences, straining at the seams with other things, kink and trail off. In my interview with James I tried to pick up on the clues and to fill in the blanks. But when there is no freedom to name or to tell a story I am not sure that there can be rapport or reciprocity.

Body heat

During my interview with James, I became entangled with his anxiety and nervousness. I felt small rushes of adrenalin and pinpoints of heat igniting in my face as we moved towards and then around incriminating words and topics. Our conversations became encoded. We talked about his *illness, the disease, the terminal condition.* This shared lacy language made a mockery of the recording of the interview and my assurances of confidentiality and anonymity. As the ethnographer Norman Denzin has recognized 'Nothing is ever wholly private, and much of what occurs in public presumes confidential (private) understanding and agreements'.[11]

'Nothing is ever wholly private'. Yes. We both knew that. So we talked, and I now write, with non-synchronous shadows, labouring between what can be revealed and the husks of what must not be said, between the potency of this almost story and the forces that strangle it.

In my first attempts at making sense of what James was trying to tell me, I was too engrossed in the immediacy of the interview, too beguiled by the Western preoccupation with personal freedom, autonomy and reason. Potent contexts went missing. African masks that vanquish demons.[12] The trickster tradition of dissimulation and indirect criticism in Kenya as a response to national regimes of repression that flavours the work of writers such Francis Imbuga, John Ruganda, Ngugi wa Thiongo and Wahome Mutahi. And whole swathes of British colonial secrecy covering-up the sanctioning of torture, castration and rape in Kenya during the Mau-Mau uprisings between 1952 and 1960.[13]

There is never only one secret. And we all have secrets. Some are so enduring that they are seemingly without origin, a part of the cultures and households that we were raised in. The unspoken presence of something withheld. Other secrets we acquire later, a response to the discrepancies and constraints that press in on us. And when someone wants to talk about their secrets but does not want to talk about them directly, we are in the world of secrecy. In secrecy there can be fear, but also what the British psychoanalyst Donald Winnicott has called 'play', an inventive intermediary space in which realities can be brought into the world of make-believe and can be experimented with – real/not real, me/not me.[14]

And although James often chose to talk in the third person and adopted the passive voice that erased the pronominal 'I', he was neither entirely silenced nor submissive to his secret. There was something more artful going on. Amid the ordinary conversational moves and turn taking, the densities of silence and hesitation that hung in the air were spooky and provocative. These demons forced me, and continue to push me to feel and to wonder about how things could feel so dangerous.

James' omissions and innuendo corroded the distinctions between what is made public and what is withheld, what is safe and what is risky. And yet, despite all of the constraints, his muted story articulates and touches. It reproduced poetically in its silences, stuttering and slinky U-turns, the effects of dys-ease in his life, demanding a different empirical attentiveness and imagination. I have grown to think of the heat and pulses of adrenalin that I felt when listening and talking to James as fleshy text messages, small bodily interruptions and abbreviated inscriptions that forced me to feel how even the most ordinary and basic of human exchanges can become potentially catastrophic and life-threatening.

For a long time, I used to feel the pressure of thinking that to cover-up something of who you are because of fear and shame is to die a little; that being honest is wholesome and liberating, good for the soul. That was abstract thinking and Western reason. I was spending too much time with my head in the wrong books, ignoring what I know about the complicities of the heart and flesh, of living and dying in a morally buckled heteronomy, enmeshed with the warm needs and weight of others. So with James something unexpected tripped me up: how mimicry and passing can be their own palliative care, an intervention in suffering that can alleviate pain.

The word *palliative* is derived from the Latin noun *pallium*. There is some tension and play in its first meanings: to cloak, cover or protect.

This is not to overlook the damage caused by injustice, hatred and ignorance. Or to romanticize the lonely and insecure existence of disease impostors and the painful contradictions that they live with; how at one moment James tells me how proud he is to be a Kenyan, how he carries that pride deep within, how he will always regard Kenya as his home,

> I still love it. I am going to go back, even if I am dead.
>
> Can you tell me something about that?
>
> I think it's just that I feel that I belong there, and I think that's a general consensus of most of us. We feel that we have no place here, that every person who is able must be taken back, buried back.

Then in the next breath when I ask about his relationships with Kenyan people in London, the ethnic identifications, the *we* and the *us*, fracture and dissolve, I receive something altogether more menacing: community as barbed and dangerous, predatory and two-faced.

> I don't want to have anything to do with the Kenyan community here. With this disease they tend to actually prey on you, because as soon as people find out that you know, you have actually contracted this thing, they spread out rumours to the rest of the community which is quite damaging. So that's why most Kenyans don't want any other Kenyan to know about it.

Shortly before he died James told his estranged wife about his HIV. His fantasy of being buried in Kenya as a proud Kenyan was made impossible because of the medical administration that is required to repatriate bodies with HIV infection. At the time of James' death, several African countries were also refusing to receive the body of a seropositive person.

Community, like home, is an idea wrought from and too often squandered on life-long illusions. The fantasy and solace of Kenya as a final resting place for James could have been a last homage to the authority of cultural prescription. Or perhaps something entirely more visceral: a yearning in the blood to feel the caress of red earth, the smell of warm rain, to hear the *work haar-der, work haar-der* call of the ring necked dove. But I wonder whether I have been missing something. Whether in the journeying between the fissures of an idealized homeland and the bite of community, James was gesturing to a different space of belonging for some of us. Home not as birth right, continuity or safe enclave, but a condition sculptured from displacement and ambivalence, of that which falters and fails. *'Home is our first real mistake'* the poet Ann Michaels[15] has written in her haunting novel *The Winter Vault*, 'It is the one error that changes everything, the one lesson you could let destroy you. It is from this moment that we begin to build our home in the world. It is this place that we furnish with smell, taste, a talisman, a name.'

As I remember James sitting with me in that sun-filled room, holding tight to his hot water bottle, I think again about why he felt so cold and could not feel the warmth surrounding us.

Moving On

A 159 double-decker bus rolls majestic through the early morning streets of South London. The route the bus takes is a part of the city's post-bellum superstructure. The 159 first voyaged from West End Green in North West London in November 1947, passing the Houses of Parliament and Brixton en route, to terminate at Thornton Heath clock tower in South East London. Nine months after the 159 was inaugurated, the former German cruise ship the *Empire Windrush* made its way up the river Thames to Tilbury Harbour. Some 500 passengers from Jamaica disembarked to start a new life.

When June Alexander talks about her life as one of this cohort of migrants, it is buses not boats that are a recurring setting in her stories, attesting to the power of mundane habit in the sedimentations of memory.[1] And conveying something of the migrant experience itself. Not simply of journeying – the stopping and starting, being immersed, heated-up, diverted, carried away, jostled – but the hopeful waiting and faith.

June remembers bus journeys when some passengers would get up and move somewhere else if she sat next to them. Others would alight and wait for the next bus. The enclosed spaces of buses with their singular sensations, rhythms and interred 'passing propinquities' can be especially prone to the excitement of conviviality as much as buried intolerance.[2]

Sitting or standing in lines, bodies are forced into encountering each other at tangents but within simultaneities, moving, vibrating, resting and swaying as one. Visceral intensities build and move quickly. The leaning away of a torso, the turning of a face, the sharp gathering-up of a coat, are small cramped gestures expansive in their injuries. All through those times June did not show her anger, hurt or disappointment. She was to become adept in the masking of hurt and of self. As the cold shock of hostility turned to hotness in her cheeks, she had learned to focus her attention on another horizon. This network of contrapunctal[3] allegiances and distant reference points, lifted her out of the present, redistributing and scattering space and time.

Perseverance was everything.

Well you ave to press through. You're in this country an you have your families bac ome looking to you. You can't go back. You have to try an do something that will let you press along. Yeah, you press along hoping that better days will come. Perseverance. An because of perseverance, ere I am. A lot of condition ave changed. The prejudice still goes on, but people are realising that we are not animals. They realize that we are people like themself, only from a different background. But then it was hard.

'It were rough. Very rough', June tells me when I ask about this time in her life. She recalls going to a church on that first Sunday in England. She had put on her best dress, a hat and gloves and had walked two miles to the nearest church. After the service, the minister had approached her. June was unprepared when he said 'Please, don't come back. It's nothing personal, believe me, but if you keep coming, some in my congregation will go elsewhere and I will lose them'. It would be months before she went to church again. June got through those times with a quiet dignity. And as she says, conditions changed.

Faith

June used to make her daily journey to work at St Thomas' hospital, on the Southbank of London on the 159 bus. She was a hospital cleaner or 'domestic' as she called herself. On a Thursday morning in February, the 159 took June on a wayward journey.

I was on my way to work in de mornin. I was standin at de bus stop. I was there for about an hour, waitin for de bus. It was very cold an as soon as de bus come, I grab onto de rail an my lef knee went in, but I eld on. I never turned back, seein that I was going to de hospital anyway. I knew that I would be seen at de Casual Department, so I continued with my journey. At de Casual Department, they have my knee x-ray. At firs they diagnose arthritis. A few weeks later they said it is something greater than arthritis and I would be requested for another x-ray. When I return an they had my x-ray, they said it was myeloma. I never understand what myeloma is so I ask them to write it all down on a bit of paper so that I can take it ome an explain it to de family. Well my usband was quite shaken, but I know that de Lord is able. I tol him not to worry, it is in de hand of de Lord an I jus continue like that. But I was a bit shaken because once cancer has been diagnose, it's frightening because not many pull through. But I respond to de treatment. I have transfusion. I have chemotherapy. I have radiotherapy. An ere I am today.

And even after numerous visits to St Thomas' as a patient, June can still feel out of place when going into the hospital as a patient. She does not complain about the tests, therapies or the continuing struggle with pain and fatigue. The changes in her body are described almost dispassionately. She has always been diminutive but suspects that she has shrunk some inches since the onset of the disease.

> I was much taller than this. An now I am lopsided, so I ask de head doctor if it is a stroke I had an is why I am lopsided an have decrease in height. She say no it's not a stroke I had, but is because de bones in my body collapse. They're not in de same form as they were an I will never be back to my normal shape. I was worried at first, but from when she make mention to me about that, I jus accep it. Well, I was sad because my shape, I have a horrible shape now. No waist an my bottom gone in an everything. If you see me naked you would be surprized. It takes a while to get used to it. I mean, I'm still learning.

June ascribes her ability to live in a relatively peaceful co-existence with her disease and her changing body to the power of prayer, fasting and healing, described by a Pentecostal pastor as 'instruments of humbling'.[4]

Over the time that I knew her, June came to outlive her prognosis by over 13 years. She is one of the 12 per cent or so of people in England and Wales to live at least ten years after being diagnosed with multiple myeloma.[5] June is vaguely aware of the statistics. She is neither overwhelmed nor taken in by them. Open to the divine work of a *deus absconditus*, June has always been receptive to mystery as faith's infinite gift.

> One evening I was coming ome from working at St Thomas. I was carrying my baby, but I never know that I was pregnant at de time. There was a lady, I didn't know her but in my distric back ome there was a woman like that. An when de lady come up on the bus, downstairs was full up, so the conductor say to her to go upstairs. When I look at de state of her condition I thought 'My God, can a woman like this go upstairs?' She was very handicapped, her foot plaiting an everyting. An it's the second person I ave seen like that. The one I left in my

distric an de one that I have seen on de bus. An I get out of my seat an I say 'You can have my seat' an I went upstairs. When my child was born, he was normal, but de symptom was there. That day when I went ome I said to my usband 'Recall the woman Hatshepsut in our country?' He said 'Yes'. I said 'I have seen a lady today coming from St Thomas de same way'. An when I had de baby I went out to pay a visit to two friends. When I come back, my husband said to me 'You remember de lady you was telling me about? Mathew is going just like de lady'. You know, I stan there an I watch de baby. He was wriggling all over. It is difficult to explain. You would ave to see de person yourself an then you would understand. In de early stage of pregnancy you ave to be careful because if you see things an you are sorry for it, you can spoil your baby, mark it. So I said to my husband 'Give me three days unmolested' An that's what he did an I remember de Lord speak to me. He said 'Go three days of fasting an on de last day take de child down to de church an let de elders an ministers lay hand upon him an he will recover.' An that's what I did an within de space of that time Mathew return to normal. I have much to thank God for.

Opened out to the register of the divine, to life as a journey to a glorious destination, June says that she is not afraid of dying 'It must come one day. And when the rapture come, I won't die. I will only be changed'.

Music

In September 909, William the Pious, Duke of Aquitaine, was moved by end-of-life contemplations to deed a sizeable tract of land in the verdant valley of Cluny to a Benedictine monk, Berno. William stipulated that the monastery – in the Burgundy region of France – should be free to pursue its spiritual life without interference from his family or local bishops, being accountable only to Pope Sergius III. The philosophy and web of devotional practices that evolved at Cluny was unique in four respects: the recognition given to the human need for beauty, skills in conflict resolution between feudal groups, the tradition of commemoration of the dead and monastic medicine.

In the Cluniac infirmary, manuscripts or *customary* record that dying people were tended to body and soul. The most sublime care was administered by the monks through music and song, in a discipline that is now called music thanatology. The acoustic anointing of dying people with live music at the bedside – usually singing and harp playing – is said to weave 'tonal substance responsorially over, around, and above the physical body of the patient, from head to toe'.[1]

This description comes from the pioneer of music thanatology, Therese Schroeder-Sheker, a musician, clinician and educator in the United States. Schroeder-Sheker traces the inspiration for her work to the 1970s and an encounter with a man she remembers as 'sometimes vicious, often brittle and selfish'.[2] The man was dying from emphysema in a care home. He was in pain and unable to swallow. The thick rasping sensuality of distress and foresakenness that engulfed Schroeder-Sheker when she entered his room displaced rational thinking. Therese climbed into the old man's bed and propped herself up behind him midwife-like, relieving some of his weight. In this intimate cradling, with heads and hearts aligned, Therese began to sing and sway their bodies in rhythm. 'I made my way through the entire *Mass of Angels*, the *Adora te devote* of Thomas Aquinas, the *Ubi caritas*, the *Salve Regina*, the *Mass of the Blessed Virgin Mary*', she recalls.

> For all I knew, he could have been Eastern Orthodox or Jewish, because all the residents were Russian émigrés, but I never knew the details of his life. The chants seemed to bring him balance, dissolving fears and compensating for those issues still full of sting. How could they do anything less? These chants are the language of love. The repertoire had become the chalice that held him up into true repose. Long after his heart ceased to beat, I was allowed to hold him.[3]

There is always mystery in the alleviation of another's suffering. The play of unseen waves and vibrations across skin, bone, hair and muscle that is hearing is believed to be the last remnant of our sensory connection to the world before we die. For the philosopher Gilles Deleuze music is the spiritualization of the body.

> When music sets up its sonorous systems and its polyvalent organ, the ear, it addresses itself to something very different from the material reality of bodies. It gives a disembodied and dematerialised body to the most spiritual of entities.[4]

We have yet to fully understand the chemical structures and circuits that underlie hearing, but the molecular biologist Ching Kung has found that for both hearing and touch it all seems to come down to 'a single physical parameter – force'.[5] To hear is to be touched and to receive. To take in and to resonate with the ambient and sublime presence of others and the world around us. And to do so whether we like it or not.

Noise

As much as the spiritual embrace of music and song can be a repose from the loneliness of dying for recipients of music thanatology, the feral intimacy of sound in the noises of dying and grief can be unwelcome and disconcerting, leading to censorship and control. The earliest European laws that we have recorded knowledge of – the laws of Solon described by Plutarch – suggest that in sixth-century Athens and in other Greek cities 'everything disorderly and excessive' in women's funeral rites was forbidden.[6]

From the ancient societies of the Mediterranean and Near East to pre-modern Europe, public mourning was a responsibility given over to women, some of whom were hired professionals such as the Roman *praeficae* or the *mekonot* women of the Hebrew bible. Women sang dirges, loosened and tore at their hair and clothes, beat their breasts and scarified their faces. Lamentation marked personal loss. Nevertheless, the academic and musician, Gail Holst-Warhaft cautions that 'even when performed by women familiar with the dead, the lament is a formal genre intended to arouse an emotional response in the listener. Skill is demanded both in the structuring of the sung poetry, and in the gestures of affect that accompany it.'[7] As a cultural genre of its time, lamentation could also be used to express a community's cosmology, its injustices and grief.[8] The Romans believed that the secretions of women in mourning could nourish the dead in a sonorous enclosing of the circle of life. In the Greek plays of Aeschylus, Sophocles and Euripides, lamentation was dangerous, resurrecting past violations and inciting violence and murder.

In early modern Ireland the poetic ritualized keening at the graveside by barefoot, wild-eyed women hid social critique and subversive messages from the colonial power of the church. 'This licence was allowed in part', the literary theorist Kathryn Conrad notes, 'because the women acted out their grief as if mad'.[9]

The bodily manifestation of grief and loss, then as much as now, can pit women against authority and stoke cosmological and institutional insecurities, even in places of loss. I will tell you something about the difficult side of my work says Camilla, a hospice nurse, before she describes finding herself and her patients unnerved by noisy mourning.

> People from Mediterranean countries express emotions much more overtly and that can be uncomfortable. I mean I can think of many families here who have, you know, expressed their grief really, really, rawly and how demanding and challenging that is for us and how nervous it makes us. I remember a Greek man dying and his family were clutching his body and screaming and lying on the floor and you know, were just expressing their grief very, very rawly which we tend not to do and in the context of a bay, that's quite shocking for other patients and other families. I mean there's no denying it, it's not easy for us to

contend with because anybody who expresses their grief really rawly, makes huge demands on our attention.

We all have ideas about what makes a good death don't we? For some, the sensuality of dying well and of grieving is laid out in rites and rituals: chanting from the Buddhist scriptures, Quranic verses recited softly into the ear, anointing with oil or sacred water dropped into a mouth. In institutional settings the rites and rituals that are most readily sustained are those that take up the least space or which do not contravene growing health and safety regulations. Small bells can be rung. Holy Water can be sprinkled. A Tulsi leaf can be placed in a mouth. A dying person can be dressed in an ancestral garment. The burning of incense or candles tends to be prohibited. And for Hindus, for whom being close to the earth at times of death has spiritual significance, mattresses in hospitals are not usually allowed on the floor.[10] Some people, feeling the constraints of institutional dying, tone down or edit death rituals and customs. Through bodily signs – lowered voices, silent tears, synthetic smells – they absorb the 'somatic norm'[11] of what is not put into words but which enters and corrals the body: to die well and to mourn *here* is to do so quietly: contain your turmoil and your excesses.

A statement of the *Aim and Basis* of St Christopher's hospice – the first modern hospice – written in the 1960s, asserts that 'dying people must find peace and be found by God, quietly, in their own way'.[12] Peacefulness and quiet are not silence. Yet noise is incongruous, if not antithetical to Western ideas about dying peacefully and with dignity. This is why in hospices and hospitals there are many small routines that attempt to enclose, if not set apart, invasive bodily emissions.

Single-bedded rooms are used to cordon-off noisy mourning and to sequester patients whose bodily surfaces have been eaten away by disease, causing the seeping out of organic matter, waste and smells. Nurses use aromatherapy oils, electric diffuses or air-fresheners to cloak the smell of necrotic wounds or excreta from fistula. Doctors administer anti-cholinergic medication to suppress the death rattle in a dying person, even though the noise of air rattling accumulated mucus in the trachea seems to cause no distress to the patient. The drugs are given to palliate the pain and discomfort of those around the bedside.

World Health Organization:

Acute exposure to noise, particularly for those who are physically vulnerable can be harmful to health. The World Health Organization has found that noise can activate nervous and hormonal responses; blood pressure and heart rate can increase. So too can levels of stress hormones.[13]

Figure 8.1 Air diffuser in hospice ward.
Courtesy: Nadia Bettega

If the battle to stem and control the leaking of sensory matter out of bodies is not always a medical necessity, what is it that is being struggled over? Eve's gripping story provides some insights. Taken from a group interview with hospice nurse managers, it is full of latent knowledge as much as bewilderment.

Eve: In England when people die, we are quiet, or cry occasionally. We do not scream and ululate. We do not, we do not. There's so many assumptions about how to behave and one of the most traumatic things for me was watching a, from the West Coast of Africa, I can't remember the country, um, a young woman dying of HIV and her mother going absolutely bananas and spare, you know with the grief and although I felt very frightened and felt out of control, I remember thinking 'I expect she gets this out of her system better than we do', just because there was a feeling that it was just (makes whooshing sound and sweeps both arms up), you know, it looked, it was so different. It just looked different from our situation and thinking 'what part do we have here?' Not because I'm a white British, but because we're staff and this is a professional situation for us.

Yasmin: Um, can you explain a bit more about that? What's the sort of tension for you about being staff?

Eve: I think that it's, the fact that you're staff seems to imply that you should be in control of the situation and that we should be dictating, however subtly, or directing how the situation goes. And very often that's not a problem, but when their experience is so very different from ours, the expression for instance, the physical expression and the distress and the levels of vocal expression are so different, um, it's certainly, we realize we're completely superfluous, which is, you can get, you know with a white English family, but it was very, very highlighted it was completely about their needs. Do it their way. You know-

Diana: Which in a ward situation can be at times quite awkward when you've got-

Eve: Yeah.

Diana: to balance the needs of the ethnic minority family-

Eve: It was upsetting-

Diana: against the needs of the other family.

Eve: It was upsetting other families who did not obviously perceive this as the way to do it and all they could hear was the screams and they didn't know whether it was somebody in pain. Well, it was somebody in pain (she laughs), but they, they imagined many things because it was such an unusual thing to happen, um, and what would normally be a very short period of time i.e. viewing the body, coming to see it, being quietly upset, you know um, we put our judgment on what is appropriate sorrow or not, turned into three days of almost festivities, and er, filming the death and playing songs and sort of a mixture between extreme grief and extreme, um merry-making, in a sort of way. I found it deeply disturbing.

There is so much reverberating in this exchange. Not least the compelling urgency of a story that has been waiting to be told, a compulsion where form and content, story and voice, converse with each other. To ululate – from the Latin *ululāre* to howl – is to sing out your grief from the heart lalalalalaleesh. The rhythmic dissonance of sound comes from the throat not the mouth. And this story spilled out of Eve, animating not only her voice but her body. Leaning forward as she spoke – with arms gesticulating, both hands at one point holding her head, fingers raking back her hair – there was a palpable sense of the unresolved, full with a shimmering, guttural confusion. If we listen carefully, Eve is telling/showing us something about the meeting of two carnal orders.

What happens when our bodies, public spaces and cultural expectations are breached? Just how much room can we allow others to take up in our communities? What is the right balance between my needs and yours?

Where do grief and loss belong?

Hospice-tality

Hospice buildings are relatively small compared to most hospitals. Those with inpatient care tend to include a mix of shared bays of between four to six beds and single en-suite rooms. In the bays, when someone is nearing death, the dying person and their loving ones, will often be given privacy, should they want it, behind a curtain. I am not sure whether the West African family that Eve is talking about was in a single room or in a shared bay, but I am familiar with the ward and the hospice in which she worked. The cries of the mother would have bounced off the cosy architecture of the building, amplifying and extending the sound. The usual serenity of the ward, like a calm sea, would have been overtaken by a tidal wave of distress. Grief after all, is believed to be a primary force in human vocalization.[14]

For those who have been accustomed to noise in life, silence in illness and at times of death can be unsettling. For others, the noise of dying or grieving can be the future coming closer, whispering in the ear and breathing down a neck. It can jangle the nerves and turn the stomach, especially in English cultures where quietness runs deep into the authority of the church and so many national institutions.[15]

In late December 2007 and in January 2008, a story about plans by a mosque in Oxford to seek council permission to 'broadcast' the call to prayer using loudspeakers, made the national news. The newsworthiness of the story centred upon threats to Oxford as an idealized site of Englishness, a city of 'dreaming spires'. Articles in the tabloid newspapers *The Sun*[16] and *Daily Mail*[17] used comments garnered from local residents to suggest that an amplified call to prayer would disturb children's sleep, undermine community cohesion and turn the area into a 'Muslim ghetto'. Dr Allan Chapman, who lives close to the mosque, was quoted as saying, 'If this is allowed to go ahead it will be intrusive and distasteful. People will have no choice but to have this message rammed down their throats'.[18]

There has been similar disquiet across the globe to the sensual extents of multicultural living, from noise abatement campaigns in Singapore directed at the Islamic call to prayer, funeral processions and church bells, to the support for a referendum proposal to ban the building of minarets in Switzerland in 2009.[19] The threat posed by the sensory evidence of cultural difference is a salutary reminder of what Étienne Balibar and Immanuel Wallerstein call 'differentialist racism', 'a racism which, at first sight, does not postulate the superiority of certain groups or peoples in relation to others but "only" the harmfulness of abolishing frontiers, the incompatibility of life-styles and traditions'.[20]

Racism will always don new clothes. But Dr Chapman and his confused anatomical metaphors make an important point. Because we do not have ear-lids, there is relatively little choice over what we hear. And because sound is forceful, it fills not only the ear but also the core of the body. The ear is in effect a mouth. We ingest and swallow sound through an aural alimentary canal that travels from the ear and head, through the neck and throat, down into the labyrinthine gut where the distillation of an outside pushes at us from our insides. In those moments when another's sound knocks around the body, the artifice of human boundedness and self-possession dissolves. We are forced to feel our interdependence, our inescapable susceptibility to others.

The Australian philosopher, Rosalyn Diprose, has named this openness of the body and the relentless exchange between us *corporeal generosity*. The term *generosity* in Diprose's thinking is laden with ambivalence and asymmetry where 'the generosity and the gifts of some (property owners, men, wage earners, whites) tend to be recognized and remembered more often than the gifts of others (the landless, women, the unemployed, indigenous peoples, and immigrants).'[21]

This theorizing is helpful in understanding why the grief sung out by the African mother and other relatives is so perturbing for Eve. It is so unsettling in fact that the painful grieving that is the source of the weeping and wailing is almost forgotten. *They didn't know whether it was somebody in pain* Eve says of the other patients in her ward and then has to remind herself *Well it was somebody in pain*. The ironic laugh that accompanied this almost-forgetting touches, as humour often does, something deeper and uncanny: how is it in a place that aspires not to sequester death, pain and grief away from life and the community, that the sound of maternal loss can be so out of place? *Going bananas and spare* and *being on the edge* are forays into the wild. And at the same time, the feel of such dispossession appears to arouse envy as much fear 'I expect she gets this out of her system better than we do'. It brings to consciousness the tacit sensory regime of the ward – all that *controlling, dictating and directing* – and its continuity with Western ideals of personhood as self-controlled and privatized.[22]

But there is more going on here than cultural difference and the matter of how as the ward manager Eve must regain control of the cacophonous environment. In situations such as this 'We realize we're completely superfluous' Eve says. She continues 'which is, you can get, you know with a white English family'. That some English families can also render staff superfluous begins to rock the solid *we* of Englishness, opening out Eve's story to the demands of what might be heard as 'other-others' – noisy, working-class English families perhaps, or those suddenly overtaken by the visceral force of grief and loss? Let's return to the story at the point at which we left it.

> Yasmin: So what was disturbing about it?
>
> Eve: I think the fact that it was so raw. So, um, it felt very frightening because I felt it was on the edge and I guess that feeling is often there, but we're often spared from it because people culturally determine a way to behave and these people are saying, 'No. This is how we want to behave. This is how we would behave. This is how we are behaving.' And that is very frightening if it's different from what, what you perceive as normal.

What hits me time and again with this extract is the 'it was on the edge . . . but we're often spared from it'. Being spared is a curious musty turn of phrase, reminiscent of sacrificial scenes from the Abrahamic religions – of sheep, fattened calves and beloved children. Such scenes have inspired philosophical writing on the ethics of the gift, where gifting has been imagined outside of economies of recognition and reciprocity. Real gifts, some philosophers believe, must go unrecognized on both sides, so there are no expectations. No gratitude. No indebtedness.[23]

And what if we start to think of this acoustic mayhem as a gift for Eve? A gift that because it is *so different* in its form and non-compliance – *No this is how we want to behave. This is how we would behave. This is how we are behaving* – brings to the surface the wreckage of the confusions and paradoxes of multicultural living, dying and caretaking: the compromises; the impossible demands and conundrums; the times when routines, rules and convention go out of the window and you find yourself being, doing or thinking something out of the ordinary. Jacques Derrida calls such singular moments 'absolute responsibility'.

> Absolute responsibility is not a responsibility, at least it is not general responsibility or responsibility in general. It needs to be exceptional or extraordinary . . . it is as if absolute responsibility could not be derived from a concept of responsibility and therefore in order for it to be what it must be it must remain inconceivable, indeed unthinkable: it must therefore be irresponsible in order to be absolutely responsible.[24]

This Derridean version of responsibility institutes a simultaneous division and a binding between an unconditional and conditional hospitality, between an unlimited openness to others and the need for laws and regulation as a means of adjudicating between competing demands. The impossibility of accommodating the needs of a competing array of others is for Derrida the very condition of the capacity to be moved by singularity, so that for one reason or another, routines are sometimes transgressed and *this* mother, *this* family now has the space to mourn, to belong temporarily.

Spontaneous transgressions do not guarantee greater justice or freedom in the future, although they may inspire the pursuit of more workable, conditional solutions or on-the-spot improvizations.

Some hospices have responded to the 'problems' of noisy mourning by accommodating grieving families in rooms away from the main wards, so that noise is contained. Grief is annexed. Difference is put in its place. I am not sure what Eve would have made of these developments. And I am not sure how an acoustic refuge from suffering honours the aspiration of the unconditional hospitality of hospices as a *community of the unalike*.[25]

The monks at Cluny believed that the architectural organization of sound in a place could allow for epiphany – a heeding of the richness and splendour of life and what lies beyond it. Therese Schroeder-Sheker feels that 'If particular sacred music is sung by a prepared community of liturgical singers in the most appropriate way, an epiphany can occur'.[26] The choir space at Cluny is said to materialize this belief. The monastery is renowned for its intricately carved eight capitals – the upper aspects of the stone columns – that surrounded it. The space was called the *deambulatorium angelorum* – the walkway of angels.

Take a look at the ordinary

Don't need to look at Paradise

You could be next to

an angel in disguise

So sings Corrine May.[27]

'What makes me think?' Rosalyn Diprose asks, 'Something gets under my skin. Something disturbs me'.[28]

The Prince and the Pee

Intent concern accompanied the glinting blade
That sliced from hip to hip.
A tributary
Meandering down into dry recesses of manliness.
A cut so deep, so low
Folds of distinction reopen.
Hard layers. Moist untouched spaces.
Shiny black skin. Striated muscle,
prowess
flow into tired sinews of a pure new
softness.

He has a story to Tell.
He doesn't know how.[1]

'Eighty-eight year in August' Edwin declares. 'An de way I look at it, is a lot of over-time I been doing. I one lucky man. From when I was a youn man comin up in de world, I was free, appy-go-lucky. I go and I drink when I want to drink. I eat when I want to eat. I sleep when I want to sleep. I was free like a bird. I was very free. Even when I get ill, I never worry bout nothin. Even when I get marry I never worry about nothing.'

Edwin has advanced cancer of the prostate that is leaching out to his bones. He is a man of solid build, who moves slowly and with purpose. This sense of purpose is etched into his face. His skin is without a blemish. His eyes, nose and mouth are so clearly defined that they seem to allow no room for hesitation or second thoughts. Edwin's upright posture and comportment, his formal dress and rhythmic speech are a mix of influences and idiosyncratic invention. Born in Jamaica, in the early decades of the twentieth century, Edwin's views on ageing and death have much in common with the Stoic tradition of philosophy associated with those such as Cicero, Marcus Aurelius and the slave Epictetus who is believed to have said 'I must die, but must I die groaning?'[2]

Cicero, writing in 44 BC, regarded the weakening of the body and a decline in bodily pleasures as advantages of old age, freeing-up the mind and the intellect. In his treatise on ageing *De Senectute* written as an imagined dialogue, Cicero opines 'carnal pleasure hinders deliberation, is at war with reason, blindfolds the eyes of the mind, so to speak, and has no fellowship with virtue.'[3] Death offered just two possibilities to Cicero: nothingness or everlasting life. In either case he reasoned, there was nothing to be gained by worrying about it.

The futility of worry is an enduring, recurrent theme in Edwin's lay philosophizing. Worry was a terminal malady without resolution. 'There no cure for worries', Edwin states. 'No cure. So I don't let things worry me, cause I wouldn't benefit by it, by thinking an worrying. Providing you're not feeling dat nasty pain. Nothin bother with me.'

Edwin is one of a growing number of older African Caribbean men struck by prostate cancer. The disease affects three times as many black men as white.[4] It took a couple of years and several visits to his doctor before Edwin was diagnosed with the condition. While on the waiting list for an operation to remove his prostate, Edwin had what he called 'stoppage of water' and was taken to hospital for an emergency operation. Complications of surgery for prostate cancer, and the radiotherapy that usually accompanies it, can include incontinence and impotence.

A report, *Hear me Now*, by the organization BME Cancer Communities, produced in 2013, has highlighted an 'uncomfortable reality' of prostate cancer for men of Caribbean heritage. Black Caribbean men in the United Kingdom are 30 per cent more likely to die from prostate cancer than are white men. They are also more likely to be affected by the cancer at a younger age.[5] The report discusses multiple causes behind the statistics, including a lack of ethnicity-related cancer research, geographically uneven service provision and culturally insensitive health promotion and care. It also highlights how prostate cancer, its diagnostic testing, treatment and effects, can pose a particular cultural threat to black men.

For the Trinidadian writer and political activist, Darcus Howe, diagnosed with the disease in 2007, prostate cancer is the silent killer of black men. A TV documentary *What's killing Darcus Howe?* – aired in 2009 – charted Howe's attempts to raise awareness of the disease among British Black men. Howe says that he found a machismo-related resistance to acknowledging vulnerability to *The Beast*. Set against historical representations of black masculinity as hyper-masculinity – physical, potent and über sexual[6] – prostate cancer, Howe suggests, is a culturally loaded disease. But changes are afoot.

Older men, like Edwin, may say little in public about the disease and its effects, but younger patients in their fifties and early sixties are stepping into the discursive void that surrounds black men's experiences of the cancer. At one mixed-sex group meeting that I attended in South London, where hospice patients were being asked for their views on improving services, a Caribbean man in his sixties stood up among the other seated patients. He talked about the difficulties of coping with his treatment for prostate cancer, particularly the drug Zoladex that is administered by a large injection into the abdomen. 'I've had eight-inch needles thrust into my belly where I could feel them tickling my metaphysics' as Anatole Broyard once described the procedure.[7] The injections deposit a slow-releasing, rice-grain-sized pellet of the drug underneath the skin. Zoladex is a chemical stun gun, a narcotic remote control for men-on-pause. It lowers testosterone levels and can cause feminized symptoms of hot flushes, night sweats and mood swings.

There were nods of sympathy for the patient's story. Cancer and palliative care patients are a part of a culture of affirmative disclosure. *It's good to talk* is the unwritten mandate of modern illness cultures, where patients can speak in evangelical narratives that ratify *thinking positive*.[8] Everyone's experience is acknowledged and in principle no topic is off limits. At this group in South London, the supportive exchanges were entirely predictable until the man with prostate cancer stopped describing his treatment and said with great intensity 'I can't make love to my wife any more and I miss it'. There was a graphite silence across the room, then a shuffling of bodies and chairs. It can be difficult to find a sincere and appropriate response when hit by the interlacing of modern taboos such as sex, illness and death. And even as men resist dominant versions of masculinity, their rebelliousness in talking about sex and sexual losses can end up bolstering the sexualized attributions of black masculinity that they seem to be undercutting.[9]

Those men who are fortunate have supportive family and friends to fall back on. But many will find themselves in circumstances similar to Edwin, living out their last days alone.

Tings

Edwin lived in a large one-bedroomed council flat in South London. The kitchen, bathroom and bedroom led off from the living room. In the front right-hand corner of the living room there was a settee, an armchair, a Formica coffee table and four chairs, a telephone and a television. All were contained within the boundaries of a well-worn rug. The settee had two large pink pillows on top of it and a bucket beside it. At the back of the main room, tucked into the far left-hand corner was the bedroom, its door ajar. There was not much more.

Edwin's home was austere. Like Edwin, it came across as phlegmatic. There were no photographs, ornaments, books or pictures on the walls. Artefactually abstemious, the domestic environment offered itself to contradictory readings. On first entering the home it could appear uncared for and neglected. But sit for a while with Edwin and the stillness choreographed by the absence of things, intimated an attentive accommodation and hospitality towards loss and transition. 'I quit life as if it were an inn, not a home', wrote Cicero. 'For Nature has given us a hostelry in which to sojourn, not to abide.'

I could not tell whether Edwin liked his home and living arrangements, whether he had chosen a minimum of affective decoration or whether he lacked the motivation to give time to domestic aesthetics. 'Well I have no complaint', he said raising his eyes from a cup of tea and allowing his gaze to wander around the room. 'Some people complain, but I haven't got no complaints. I satisfied wit what I got. I'm able to jus go aroun an do my own tings. I don't business with people. You get what I mean?'

The irony was that the very sparseness of the furnishings and adornment in Edwin's home carried an elemental force that did business with people. Space curdled and time slowed when I was there, so that the air became thick and muscular. His home felt like a waiting room that was withdrawing from worldly concerns. A space untethered from the overwhelming predicament of consumer choice that is the legacy of the late twentieth century. It was a space in which a person could move unhampered by the illusory security and static of relics and mementos. It was also an arrangement that carried a social story.

Single-person homes are a growing phenomenon in the United Kingdom. One in three British households now consists of a person living alone. Although older women are more likely to live by themselves than men, it is estimated that by 2020 the percentage of men over the age of 60 living alone will be about 30 per cent.[10]

Edwin's wife had had a stroke a year before I met him. She lived in a local nursing home, with Edwin visiting her when he could manage it, two or three times a week. From his accounts the visits were as pared-down as his home, a time of minimalism and silent accompaniment. 'We don't have to sit down an talk, talking every day, every day. We been around for a long time so all the talking finish.' I wondered if it was difficult since his wife has not been at home, having in mind the pain of loss and of being alone after 50 years of partnership. 'Oh yeah, Oh yes', Edwin said wryly, continuing without a pause 'But I get meals-on-wheels and um, food, and I got de home attendance people they come an see me in de morning.' If there was more to the topology of marital separation and what it is for an old man to live alone with a failing body, it was there in Edwin's home as much as in what was said or not said during our conversations. 'The person in that living-room gives an account of themselves by responding to questions' the anthropologist Daniel Miller has observed from his ethnographic research with 30 households in one street in south London. 'But every object in that room is equally a form by which they have chosen to express themselves.'[11] One of the most poignant portraits of domestic life in Miller's study is George's flat. George, after a life-time of living in hostels had found himself with his own home at the age of 75. Here Miller describes the disorientation of being in George's flat,

> What I can barely ever remember encountering is a habitation entirely devoid of any form of decoration. There is a violence to such emptiness. Faced with nothing, one's gaze is not returned, attention is not circumscribed. There is a loss of shape, discernment and integrity. There is no sense of the person as other, who defines one's own boundary and extent.[12]

The emptiness of Edwin's home was different. Not so much the material manifestation of an empty life, more like an emptying-out and gutting of attachments, a sort of simulated dementia of things, expressing and controlling loss.[13] The desensualizing of Edwin's home took on added pathos because it was far-removed from the locality in which he lived, a place typical of those on the outskirts of central London that have generated their own fast-flowing ecologies. Despite the grandeur and history suggested by its Victorian and Edwardian buildings, it is an area of fluid, fast-running socialities. It is home to people from the Caribbean, West Africa, Albania, Cyprus, Turkey, Ireland and Portugal.

At some time in the past Edwin was caught up in the vibrant social setting that surrounded him. He remembers meeting up with friends for a drink and a game of dominoes. But since his prostate cancer metastasized to his bones, restricting his mobility, he rarely sees his friends. Some have died. Some have grown frailer. Others have returned to Jamaica. Once in a while a friend may visit, but these are rare occasions; so his locality is moving on without him.

The neighbourhood is not the only thing that is moving on. Edwin's four children have their own lives. His two daughters are in North America, the two boys are somewhere in London. He does not say where. He rarely sees his sons these days, rationalizing their absence without any outward signs of rancour or resentment.

> They have to work for dem living an tings like that, ain't it? You have to go to work, an you have to hustle to go to work an dem have wife an kids to look after an de time right now, if you don't go to work, you don't get your money, so, dem have to look after demselves an dem kids ain't it?

Edwin has not made a will. He gave what money he had saved to his children some time ago. He does not want the government interfering in his affairs. That is all he has to say on the subject of a legacy. He has a visceral suspicion and distrust of institutional authority that seems to extend from the government to the researcher sitting in front of him, asking him to talk about his life.

Our conversations, like Edwin's home, are devoid of adornment and require a clearly set out structure. Edwin tells me that he wants me to ask him questions, and when I do, it is the factual questions that are most readily responded to. Questions that come close to his emotions and feelings are batted away with curt answers. He is diffident and prone to watching his back. When Edwin talks about migrating to London from Jamaica during the 1950s, he is dismissive when I ask whether he encountered any racism at the time.

> It don't bother wit me. I don't know bout it. It don't bothers me. I jus go around an do my tings. I don't business wit people. Whether they want prejudice or not, dat is their business, it has nothin to do with me. You get what I mean? I jus live my life. You go your ways an people go their ways.

Edwin has also left cancer to its own business, particularly in the early days when he was not so much affected by the pain. He says that he did not take the disease seriously, even when he was given his diagnosis. 'I never really think of it. Dat's de hard way. You know, I jus break my min to de condition, an jus say "Come what may. What ever will be, will be?" So I never really take it down. Maybe if I had take it serious and worry about it I would be gone by now'. With some further questions from me, Edwin goes on to tell me about how the disease has affected him. The 'number one' effect was upon his sex life. 'It's sad, but what to do?' he muses, before continuing 'Well it never change my appetite. I can always eat my food'.

Soldiering on and accommodating whatever life throws at him makes sense. The unused double bed that lurks in the background seems to tell another story, unencumbered by language. It is an interruption and protest that flares up against the rationality of the philosophy that connects Edwin to the Stoics. So when we talk about what it is like to spend most days alone in this energetic city, it is the enigma of the bed that is the point of contact between different worlds. The words tumble out of Edwin, suggestive yet ambiguous. For reasons he cannot fully explain, Edwin has not slept in the bed since his wife was admitted into the nursing home.

> From my wife gone to de ome, I never one day lay in dat bed inside ere. An she, the woman, never one day lay in de bed. I stay out ere all de while, I don't know why. I don't sleep in de bed.
>
> Not even at night?
>
> No.
>
> Really? Since your wife's gone?
>
> Yeah (he pauses briefly). I don't know why, I jus prefer to stay out ere.
>
> So does it remind you of her?
>
> Umm (and then he laughs at my suggestion), dat is one reason too, but de reason, mos of my reason is because, you know, through dese tablets I ave, I taking water tablets an I pass me water very often an to get up and walk, to walk de bed, is a longer movement. But when I sleep out ere I use a pail an I jus come off de settee ere. It's easy. I jus roll off an ave a pee an put it dere in de morning an take it out. You see, dat's why, why I don't, dat's one of my reasons too for not sleeping in dere. An yu know, de bed is wide an when I sleep out ere, I can make me foot up, you know comfortable.

As Edwin says there are good practical reasons as to why he may choose to spend his last days sleeping in the restricted space of a settee rather than in the marital bed. I understand his point that the architecture of the settee helps to keep his foot elevated, allowing excess fluid that has accumulated in his legs to drain away. The low centre of gravity of the settee is well suited to helping him urinate in the night with a minimum of disruption and effort.

And from the vantage point of his couch Edwin misses little, especially at night. Shards of the polyphony of the street pass him by in all their timbrel range: drunken rants, loving exchanges, the new-nawing of an ambulance, urban foxes raiding bin bags, the tinny engine of a moped delivering a pizza. Even if these passers-by do not know that he is there in the darkness, their liveliness nips and tugs at him. He feels accompanied, a small part of something. On his good days, the sound track is a trusted friend that entertains and distracts him. Sometimes it provides the lullaby that soothes him into a wave of sleep. At other times it is a reminder of life without the heaviness of pain and infirmity.

And should he be awoken by a sudden quietness, or an eruption of distended memories, Edwin's small circle of furnishings and his routines provide a terra firma that contains the panic.

In the shadows of nightfall
He feels the knife.
This time in his heart
quivering, shimmering.
In this place of dislocation
contorted emasculation
He marks his loss. Silently,
with truth.
Rolling saltiness around his mouth
he leans forward slowly
pisses into the bucket.

Relieved.[14]

10

Failing, Falling

About ten or so years ago, Denise Brady, the librarian at St Christopher's Hospice, showed me an extraordinary article. The paper, by Margaret Clarke, Illora Finlay and Ian Campbell, published in 1991 in the journal *Palliative Medicine*, is a compelling, short account of the end-of-life care of a recent migrant to Wales. The article opens with a salutary warning, insinuating discomfort in the palliative care reader from the offset 'It is easy to develop a complacent smugness about our caring' the authors write; the implication being that the acute vulnerability of dying can render patients and their loved ones overly grateful and uncritical.[1] For these wounded healers, it is the failures of care that are the most instructive.

The story, told in just three pages, is about a Korean family that spoke some English and where the mother, who was the patient, spoke none at all. She had undergone a mastectomy in Korea four years previously, but there was no paperwork from her doctors so it had not been possible to establish what the mastectomy had been for. The woman had had one dose of chemotherapy in the United Kingdom, which was presumed to be for a recurrence of breast cancer. She appeared to have refused further treatment or follow-up care.

When the hospice consultant visited the family, on the request of the patient's General Practitioner, the woman 'was lying flat on a board on the base of a single bed. She looked frightened and had obvious pain on movement'. Her husband did not believe in Western medicine and had been administering faith healing. This had included the whole family fasting over the preceding three months. They ate fresh fruit, no animal products or vegetable carbohydrates. The three children aged five, 11 and 13 had been allowed bread and boiled vegetables. The husband consented to a hospice admission on the condition that the fast continued and that his wife would not be given any drugs.

An image of the woman's chest X-ray on admission to the hospice is included in the article. It is described as showing 'multiple cavitating lesions with apical scarring consistent with advanced pulmonary tuberculosis'.[2] Analysis of the mother's sputum was negative for acid-fast bacilli and for malignant cells. 'Her country of origin, the lack of documented histology of the mastectomy and her clinical state suggested a possible diagnosis of TB', the authors tell us. During the early days of her hospice stay, the husband had continued to refuse analgesia on his wife's behalf. He subsequently agreed to one mg diamorphine intravenously every four to six hours and to liquid vegetarian dietary supplements. Communication with the family was impeded by language differences, further compounded by tensions with local interpreters whose help they had rejected on previous occasions.

The woman was given antituberculous therapy and improved during the first four days of treatment. She collapsed suddenly on the sixth day 'becoming rapidly shocked, clinically comparable with a Herxheimer reaction' (where a body eliminates toxins at a fast rate). In the last hours of her life the family sang hymns. When close to death they tried to revive her 'by rubbing her arms, hands and legs and shaking her body vigorously'.

> The doctor and duty nurse remained with the family as much as possible during these last hours of her life. Both were weeping silently. When this was noticed by the eldest daughter a few minutes after the mother's death, she ceased screaming, allowed the doctor to hold her hand and the three children and father together with the doctor and nurse sank slowly to sit on the floor around the dead woman's bed.[3]

A post-mortem examination showed extensive cancer in the woman's lungs. There was no evidence of tuberculosis.

Confusion and chaotic distress saturate the account of this death as the authors retrace and question their clinical decisions and actions and the effects of differences in culture and language. It is in this episodic reliving of the technicality and phenomenology of care that cultural difference takes shape. It gathers form in the clinical investigations undertaken, in the diagnosis making, the negotiations about pain-relief and nutrition. It emerges in beliefs about health, medicine and pain, food, family relationships and death rituals. And it is there at the time of death, when words and professional protocols fail, drawing together in distress the family and the care professionals.

As the opening of the article forewarns, the storying of this death speaks to the very meaning and purpose of palliative care. Departing from the standard structure of academic journal articles, the paper ends with a 'Comment' rather than a 'Conclusion' section suggesting that this experience could not be neatly rounded off or assimilated. The inclusion of the woman's chest X-ray was perhaps a way of supporting and evidencing the team's preliminary diagnosis of tuberculosis to the wider palliative care audience. But with the accompanying narrative, the image is more poignant than technical, bearing witness to a life, suggesting layers of submerged meaning.

Inklings

Radical doubt and uncertainty are not unique to cross-cultural palliative care. They can surface in situations where routines of care become ineffective, where trust and communication breaks down and professionals have to work out and improvise not just what to do, but also what kind of care they want to create and be a part of.

Feelings of jeopardy and failure in transcultural care – especially when there are cultural and language differences – can produce corrosive insecurities. These insecurities do not seem to have changed in the years since Clarke, Finlay and Campbell first publicized their experiences. How to judge the appropriateness of your care? What changes should you make to care protocols to accommodate different beliefs and values? Should care augment men's authority in the name of cultural sensitivity? How do you know whether your care is oppressive or violating?

There are objective measures and care plans against which professionals can begin to judge the quality of the clinical aspects of their care. Pain and symptom alleviation, for example, or improvements in breathing, movement, bowel function or appetite can tell you if you are on the right track. With culturally responsive care, judgements become more subjective, sometimes visceral. 'How do you know when you are providing good care?' I sometimes asked care professionals in the *Stories That Matter* project.

'It's very intuitive'.

'You kind of try and tune into what's going on'.

'You might have had an inkling'.

In one multidisciplinary group interview in a hospice there was laughter and nods of recognition to the phrase 'We're in' from a social worker describing moments of connection with his patients. 'I think sometimes we come out of, say a first visit and say "We're in" . . . and whether it's body language, I don't know what we're picking up'.

And of course when you do not know what you are picking up on there is uncertainty. Professionals are able to tolerate and explore the unknown of intercultural care giving. Sometimes they need more. Joyce, a white British nurse in a community palliative care team, believes that good care can be better achieved with patients who are 'open and honest with us about their culture'. Joyce made her point with a story about an Indian, Hindu grandmother who was dying at home. For some Hindus, lying on the floor to be closer to the earth is a part of death rituals.[4] It was a practice that Joyce was unaware of at the time.

... when she [the patient] was very poorly, the nursing profession wanted to get her into a bed, but she insisted on sleeping on the sofa and the background to that actually was that the sofa was very much nearer the floor than her bed would have been, which is where she needed to be, but none of us knew that and that caused horrendous frustrations and difficulty. If we knew that from the beginning, we could work with her.

Yasmin: How did you find out about that?

I think it was the district nurses that established that in the end. But who told them or how they got it out of the family, I don't know. It was probably the granddaughter who's actually involved in the care as well and who was very Westernized, so she might have, I don't know.

Nursing With Dignity,[5] (an online training unit produced by the Nursing Times)

Hindu religious belief begins with the assumption that all living things have a soul, which passes through successive cycles of birth and rebirth

A dying person is placed on the floor on a clean sheet or mat, symbolising closeness to Mother Earth, freedom from physical constraints and the easing of the soul's departure.

Cultural difference in Joyce's story is animated through the practical activities and demands of home care, where space is restricted and interpreters are not always available. You come into a house and you see a dying person on a sofa and not on a bed for the first time in your nursing career. How do you respond using your personal and professional knowledge while remaining open to other perspectives and values? How do you communicate with a patient and their carers, about the conditions that you feel are most amenable for the setting up and maintaining of syringe drivers and catheters that can help to alleviate symptoms, while not imposing these conditions upon them? What happens to the partnership and 'working with' aspirations of contemporary care that aim to promote enlightened patient choice?

There is a moral high ground in Joyce's story. Dying on a sofa designates this body as different. The difference is charged. It becomes an obstacle to care routines and expectations. Having a body at a more elevated height, with face, arms and legs accessible and not burrowed into crevices and corners, facilitates but certainly does not preclude pain and symptom control. Joyce's third-person distancing (*the nursing profession wanted to get her into a bed*) authorizes a technical rather than an arbitrary rationale behind the expectation of where patients should do their dying. It is a rationale that for Joyce includes the logic of the nurses needing to have knowledge of different cultural beliefs and practices in order to provide culturally sensitive and competent care.

But what if the patient or their carers do not know what you need to know? Or they do not know what you do not know? The answer for Joyce is 'horrendous frustration' turned against the family as the keepers of the Holy Grail of cultural knowledge that she thinks she must have in order to provide good care.

The high wire

That an ill person and her carers should be *open and honest* about their culture/religion in order to receive good care is another way of saying that some people are to blame for bad care.

Joyce is not alone in her belief that cultural knowledge leads to good intercultural care. This is a pervasive logic that informs policy recommendations and training resources on 'cultural competence' where professionals are encouraged to increase their awareness of different cultures and faiths. Although there is little agreement as to what culturally competent care is,[6] a common theme in the literature, debates and training resources is the need for practitioners to have some knowledge of the beliefs, traditions and practices of different cultural groups. 'I think we do need more information about cultures', a hospice nurse says, 'so that we can relate to people even more than we're doing at the moment, so we are really trying.'

This confidence in group typifications as a way of understanding the individual characterizes modern knowledge systems that operate through categories, codes and statistical probabilities. It is an approach that informs the science of epidemiology and public health, risk assessment and the prognostications that are made about our lives and deaths. In increasingly sophisticated and digitally augmented forms, the coding of human life into bio and geodemographic data is proliferating under information capitalism. Data from surveys and commercial sources are routinely used to get a sense of the *kinds* of people that we are[7] – perhaps at risk of diabetes or breast cancer, or more banally 'Affluent Greys', 'Aspiring Singles' or 'Struggling Families' with certain consumer and lifestyle habits.

Typifications generated by different software are already prevalent within medicine and are stalking intercultural care. There is now a tool used in the commercial sector called *CultureGPS* – a menacing but ironic homonym. The tool claims to help users 'to analyze visible behavior differences in intercultural encounters and to predict to a certain degree, which interactions evolve when people from different nationalities meet'[8]. The app does not actually use GPS technology (Global Positioning System). Its five-dimensional model of national cultures is based upon survey research and not satellite navigation technology. But how much the naming of this little app says about how cultural difference as distance and as an unknowable, dangerous terrain is imagined and sometimes felt.

Over the years I have become accustomed to hearing a recurring metaphor of intercultural care as what I can best describe as intuitive, precarious footwork.[9] 'We're walking on a bit of tightrope' a hospital-based social worker says. For a specialist palliative care nurse working in the community it is the walking of 'a fine line' between knowledge and nescience. As he sees it,

> you don't want to offend, but you don't want to appear ignorant either. So it's a fine line you walk actually and sometimes it's just a gut instinct that you're in there and sometimes you get a window opening of something and you just go with it . . .

And if something does not *open* up for you, there is the immobilization of fear to wrestle with. A hospice social worker says that not making assumptions about cultural beliefs and practices and asking questions 'just frees up the whole thing, there's less of a sense [of] . . . treading so warily that I'll jam-up completely'.

Intercultural care as tightrope walking.

A sensual moment-by-moment balancing of

uncertainty   faith

knowledge   risk   skill

intuition

An insecure unfolding of care as a 'thinking on one's feet',[10] and all the time underwritten by the risk of absolute

and spectacular failure

that can come with a

f

a

11

As reassurance, hope, a balance pole or a safety net, cultural competence has the qualities – with an anthropological and postcolonial twist – that the sociologist Anthony Giddens has described as an 'abstract system'.[11] Abstract systems, for Giddens, are a consequence of modernity's drive for control amid accelerated social and technological change. They offer a quixotic fantasy of dominance over the unceasing churn of social life by promoting routinized practices. Abstract systems are a 'protective cocoon' excluding, deferring or dissolving difficult moral and existential questions.[12] Do not use up your energy thinking, questioning, fretting and worrying; just follow the protocol or tick the boxes. Giddens calls this giving away of moral responsibility the 'sequestration of experience'.

Not-knowing

In the rationale of cultural competence, situations such as those described by Clarke, Finlay and Campbell could be avoided or at least could be less devastating if practitioners had knowledge – or now more likely profiling information – about Korean cultures. But what useful information or aggregate statistical probabilities, however merticulously gathered and assembled, could practitioners receive from books, pamphlets or their smart phones that could have enhanced the care of this family?

As Clarke, Finlay and Campbell suggest although cultural identity and practices are often approached as a constant – assumed to be continuous across time and space, shared by groups and by families – as experiential knowledge and day-to-day living, culture is more disjunctive, pragmatic and feral. In relation with disease, the process that is lived culture not only resists, but can escape from the indexical clutches of culturalist knowledge. And no more so than at times of fast-moving crisis. Over the course of caring for the mother, the practitioners' understanding of what was happening, what was causing what, unfolded recursively, The effects of cultural and language differences became shifting simultaneities alongside the advancing disease, clinical practices and palliative care beliefs about what constitutes good care and a good death. And so in their commitment to learn something from the family and the temporary collapse of professional expertise and authority, they end up with more questions than answers.

> . . . was it right to admit her to the hospice rather than obtain a domiciliary chest X-ray at home in an attempt to clarify the diagnosis? If this had been done would it have altered our action? Should we have attempted to contact Korea . . . to obtain details of her histology? Can the hospice team insist on trying to provide analgesia against the family's wishes when the patient cannot express her own wishes? How can we prepare the family better for the death without language or similar culture? Knowledge of a country may not represent the subculture and religious denomination from which a patient comes.[13]

Care practitioners, educators and policy makers are not dupes. They know about the dangers of reductive thinking, of seeing complicated effects as the result of a single cause, or of taking culture at face value. They often talk about the importance of taking time to get to know each patient and their carers, of being open to the idiosyncrasies, cultural hybridities and the paradoxes of the living out of culture and faith. A doctor says that he tries to put himself in the position of his patients when it comes to intercultural care.

> I think most of us choose to step out of our cultural context. I do . . . I deviate wildly and if I was in a country or I didn't speak the language and somebody from my culture came along and said . . . 'this is how we do things in our culture' that may be very, very different to how I would have chosen in that situation and I think we need to assume that other people in cultures with which I'm not familiar may choose to do the same thing . . . I don't want to work in a way that doesn't allow them to make that choice.

'I think we need to guard against "I've read the Ladybird book of religion and therefore I know what Muslims want"' says a hospice social worker, parodying transcultural training resources as the books that introduce children to reading. She continues 'Everyone lives out their faith differently anyway, so in some ways it was better not to read the book at all and say "How do you want this done for you?"'

Asking a sick person and their carers 'How do you want this done for you?' as I understand what this social worker was saying in the context of the wider conversation, is the beginning of a process and not what the Dutch philosopher AnneMarie Mol has dubbed a 'logic of choice'.[14] The logic of choice is ubiquitous in contemporary care systems in the global North where patients have been reimagined as customers and consumers. The neoliberal logic of choice does not recognize how disease, depletion, fear and anxiety can make it difficult to choose or to be an active partner in care. Which is why palliative care doctors are not so easily unsettled by the injunction 'You decide, doctor'.

'Choice' Mol insists 'comes with many hierarchical dichotomies that are foreign to care: active versus passive; health versus disease; thinking versus action; will versus fate; mind versus body'.[15] The trouble with dichotomies is that some people will always end up on the wrong side. In contrast, the logic of care, Mol tells us, arises from responsiveness to the ongoing practical activities and constantly changing demands of living with disease and caring for diseased bodies.

A clear message from Mol's research is that good and responsive care involves the public telling of rich stories about care, including stories about mistakes and catastrophes. It also demands the creating and nurturing of spaces where bespoke care approaches are allowed to emerge and critical thinking and resilience can be supported when care fails – as it inevitably must.

> improvement begins with the recognition that something needs to be improved. That not everything is as it should be. It fits with the logic of care to attend to frictions and problems. To acknowledge that some things do not work well, no matter how well intended they may be. This suggests an entirely different accountability practice.[16]

We failed this patient and her family Clarke, Finlay and Campbell say to the palliative care community. We do not fully understand what went wrong. We do have all the answers. But we will keep trying to understand. And so must you.

The accountability practice that begins to figure in the story of this case partially inverts the rationale of cultural competence. But it does not decentre the cultural values of palliative care. Cultural difference is produced as a strain and stress, an undermining of seemingly universal ideals of good care. When 'ideal standards cannot be attained because they do not correspond with the wishes of the patients and family' Clarke and colleagues write 'respecting the patient's autonomy puts a greater emotional stress on all members of the team'.[17]

Such a stance is truthful in its ambivalence. It is also silent with regard to its normalizing: how the privileging of autonomy is itself a cultural value as indeed are ideas of a good death as being pain-free, if sometimes insensible. It says little about how care can become complicit with myriad oppressions within families, or of how competent care might sometimes entail intervening in a status quo. At the same time there is a tentative questioning of care as an active doing and fixing[18] and a pointing to the singularity of the situation that demanded a responsiveness that the practitioners felt unable (perhaps, 'incompetent') to provide, rendering them in many respects passive.

Sayantani DasGupta, a physician in the Program in Narrative Medicine at Columbia University, has named this vulnerability to the singular demands of patients as 'narrative humility'. For DasGupta, narrative humility is antithetical to cultural competence approaches that can become 'a sort of cultural mastery of marginalized communities'.[19] In contrast, a disposition of narrative humility, for DasGupta, can help a practitioner 'to place herself in a position of receptivity, where she does not merely act upon others, but is in turn acted upon'.[20]

The psychoanalyst and social work educator Margot Waddell has thought of the negotiation between activity and passivity in care as a difference between 'servicing' and 'serving'. Waddell believes that the ability to offer a receptive presence to evacuations of distress, anger and pain requires the negative capability of 'serving' rather than the frenetic activities of 'servicing'.

> 'Servicing' urges itself as a substitute for 'serving' because the not-acting of serving brings us in contact with feelings: feelings which are very hard to bear – the conscious phenomena of unconscious psychic pain . . . It may be more comfortable to be doing something, whether it is writing a prescription, making an interpretation, arranging a visit, than not doing so – although *not doing anything* does not constitute *doing nothing.*[21]

In the writing of the philosopher Emmanuel Levinas, passivity in encounters with the Other is an ethical relation in which Otherness always exceeds total knowledge and understanding. In a reversal of the logic of cultural competence, a vital feature of the ethics of the self-Other relation for Levinas is that it is not dependent upon understanding or shared experience as the foundation for responsibility. Passivity in a Levinasian schema involves something more than simply being the opposite or absence of activity. As the capacity to be moved, touched and affected by the predicament of an Other, it becomes an opening to new ways of being with/for Others – without which it might be said there would be no desire or impetus for new forms of practice or indeed the pursuit of 'competence'.

Approaching caregiving with humility has repercussions for technical knowledge as much as for interpersonal relationships between clinicians and patients. As Julie Livingston's ethnography of an emerging cancer epidemic in Botswana has shown, what cancer is crystallizes between clinical interventions, resources and practices, the patients' own bodily experiences and beliefs about disease and pain, and public discourses about the disease.[22] The molecular, cultural and emotional event of one person's cancer is not the same as another's. Each will require a different care.

Recognizing the vitality of disease and of patient experiencing, reinstates care as an adventuring, my colleague, Monica Greco, argues. It includes holding the tension between knowing and not-knowing, or more accurately as Greco describes it 'knowing that you *can* give, without knowing the positive content of the aim of that giving'.[23]

In the skin of a lion

Matters of cultural difference in care are difficult to raise in the manner that Clarke, Finlay and Campbell have articulated them. It is even more difficult to talk about racism. Racism is the monster in the room in British palliative care teams and institutions.[24] Racism is an 'unhappy' signifier for the feminist theorist Sara Ahmed. It is a toxic, miserable little word that threatens to undermine the good feeling within institutions. It is far easier, much nicer, to talk about 'diversity' and 'good practice'. 'But what if the good – good feeling, good practice, positive stories – is what keeps our attention away from the bad' Ahmed asks, 'from what hurts, from what gets under the skin . . .'[25] For Ahmed, it is the black woman who voices her anger at racism who is the iconic killjoy, contaminating teams and organizations with bad feelings.

In palliative care it is social workers that are the killjoys. They most often interrupt the 'complacent smugness' that Clarke, Finlay and Campbell describe so aptly, that can run through palliative care cultures. Professional training in Anti-Oppressive Practice[26] means that social workers can be more cognizant of social inequalities and of how histories of racism and other injustices can affect care. They talk about racism more. And they talk about their feelings about racism more, making explicit the feeling work or emotional labour of multicultural caring. When they are white and Anglo it can be this acute awareness of racism that can impede good care. 'I feel so ashamed and guilty', they say. Or 'I fear triggering rage and fury about white people's history of treatment of black people'.[27]

Racism and cultural insensitivity as bad, sub-optimal care can be stark. More often than not it is blended into other deficiencies in organizational resources, disciplinary cultures or care protocols, so that it is felt in the mortar as much as in the architectures of care. Care practices may not look so different, but they *feel* different; the connective tissues can be weaker or more electrifying. Care is still administered, practitioners say, but it is more pared down, less holistic. If you are anxious or fearful you become less daring, less willing to take risks in case you get things very wrong and fall off that tightrope. 'I was thinking of a black family and the mother who's ill and she's very closed down' says a hospice social worker.

> I don't think that I challenged that in her. I couldn't take the risk. I feel very aware around black, Afro Caribbean culture, around respect being very, very important as well as not being clear about the rules and boundaries and the cultural etiquettes around that. But I wonder if that's also me being frightened of actually saying 'Look you're very phlegmatic. You're very philosophical, but I actually don't believe that you aren't sad about the prospect that you are going to die and you're not worried about your son'. So I do wonder if I would have been different with a white person.

Even when ethnicity and language is shared other differences can adversely affect caregiving. 'I wouldn't even dream of asking a question about sexual intimacy' a bilingual health advocate reveals to the surprise of her colleagues, 'that would be one of the disadvantages (of shared ethnicity) . . . going to see an elderly Asian patient with prostate cancer. If you had a particular list of questions you're supposed to ask, I couldn't ask the question about his sex life.'

High-quality and innovative care involves risk-taking; trying something new and different; challenging patients, carers, colleagues and one's self; following intuitive hunches, wandering/wondering outside of established pathways and routines. Palliative care is a specialty that seems most hospitable to creative and quirky risk-taking, and professionals are not averse to making public their experiments. A French psychologist writes of playing Shubert's *Ave Maria* sung by Jesse Norman for a patient during a painful procedure.[28] A Japanese doctor shares his not uncommon practice of writing personalized traditional Japanese poems (tanka) for his patients.[29] A British palliative care social worker who after years of trying very hard to acquire expertise through established protocols, is open about relaxing her desire for structure and certainty. 'I am now comfortable to work with mystery, to wait for the unspoken to emerge, to work with image and metaphor.'[30]

One of the ways in which I think racism operates in palliative care is through a constriction of these adventurous spaces of caregiving. It is not just that migrants and racialized others can receive the worst forms of care, although I have little doubt that this can happen. It is also that some of the most vulnerable and the most 'different' of patients – recent migrants, those with limited English or without a family advocate[31] – can be the least likely to benefit from practitioners tightrope walking their way into innovation and risk-taking. This can happen without consciousness. And it can happen through a twisting of very different ideas about unbridgeable differences. In what has been described as the 'new', 'cultural' or 'second degree' racisms, a fundamental incommensurability of lifestyles and experience that closes down the possibilities of relating to others.[32] In the ethical philosophy of Emmanuel Levinas, it is the desire to bridge what is incommensurable that is the opening up of an ethical relationship and a new undetermined future. Dikeç, Clark and Barnett elaborate,

> What Levinas reclaims and makes central then, is the very receptiveness of one person to an Other, that capacity an embodied self has to take its inspiration from what it perceives as the needs of an other self, an other body. His hospitality, we might say, proceeds from that *vertiginous moment* when one feels *bound to the other* – the moment that makes possible that ever risky tipping together of unfamiliar lives.[33]

This is another perspective and recasting of the fibres and textures of the tightrope of intercultural care.

Elspeth, a hospice social worker, has a story about this sort of tightrope walking. 'I feel my knowledge is not as good as it could be' she began, prefacing her story of an Afghani patient who had told her 'terrible things' about his life and flight from Afghanistan. He had talked about himself as a lion, responsible for protecting his family from danger. At the same time he had felt guilty about surviving and leaving Afghanistan to come to the United Kingdom as an asylum seeker. Talking about all of this with Elspeth had been distressing.

Later, Elspeth was confronted by the patient's angry son 'You don't understand our culture. You mustn't talk about these things', he told her. 'You brought up things which should never be brought up.' Elspeth tried to reassure the son that she had not been the one to bring things up. 'But he was very angry' Elspeth said, 'although interestingly, he then asked me if he could come to counselling, feeling that it would be more helpful to him, but his father shouldn't speak.' Elspeth felt so bad after this encounter that she did not return to see the father who was deteriorating and died shortly afterwards.

Elspeth's two social work colleagues responded to the story at this point. One spoke of the complicated family relationships that are involved in such cases and the difficulties of working across generations with different views and values – which also happens with white British families, she reminded them all. Using sexuality as an example, Elspeth's other colleague acknowledged how working with threatening topics and offering opportunities to talk can be particularly difficult at the end of life when sensitivities are heightened. So difficult, she suggested, that 'it can sometimes make you scared to offer those choices. Is that going to be imposing?' This conversational and imaginative pacing backwards and forwards between the familiar and the strange, the comparing and the contrasting, the recognizing of how fear and anxiety can affect all care encounters, shifted something in the conversation. When Elspeth next spoke she was more able to articulate some underlying fears.

> I think we have all been trained . . . to ask questions [but] . . . there's still the sense that we are white and British and that . . . can take away our voice . . . because . . . we're holding guilt that we have abused people in the past. I mean racism. I mean . . . when you are sensitive to other cultures, it can actually have the opposite effect of making you so sensitive that you have no voice anymore. And I think there's something about having to take risks, both being curious about what's going on for that person and asking the questions, but being careful as you do it.

That awareness of history, of social differences and of racism should derail care in this way is a tyrannical underside to some transcultural care pedagogies, where a lack of knowledge and awareness is what is thought to stand in the way of responsive care (as it sometimes does). Elspeth seemed to be getting at and demonstrating something more: how in social work the capacity to be undone by the weight of postcolonial guilt and related feelings of fear, shame, anger and inadequacy – the capacity to be rendered incompetent as it were by a heightened political sensorium – can become an emblem or perhaps a side-effect of a certain racialised professional integrity.

Such twists and turns in the emotional life of racism have been themes in black feminist scholarship and activism where guilt and unexpressed anger are recognized as the stuff of deflection and defensiveness, impairing the creation of a meeting point across differences. 'Guilt and defensiveness are bricks in a wall against which we all flounder' Audre Lorde wrote in her pioneering essay *The Uses of Anger*.[34] For Lorde, it is anger that is transformative, an affective terrain that 'implies peers meeting upon a common basis to examine difference, and to alter those distortions which history has created around our difference.'[35]

Care is a face-to-face, body-to-body encounter. It is without doubt supported and enhanced by science and rational knowledge. The trouble with care is that it is also stubbornly non-rational. Emotions, feelings and sensibilities for all involved can ruffle the surfaces of an interaction, resisting, betraying, inflating, colliding with and burrowing under everything that has been learned in a training room or from reading.

I often find myself thinking about the emotional costs of the patriarch as lion for both the father and the son in Elspeth's story. How both men seemed to express the pain and pressures of breaking from the constraints of this version of invulnerable masculinity in the last days of their lives together. Their desolation and loss, their different ways of trying to bring some order to tragedy, were possibilities crowded out in Elspeth's narrative by her guilt and feelings of inadequacy. She did not seem to consider that it might have been the very differences of age, gender and culture that brought the father to this thoughtful and sensitive young woman, and that helped him to prise open the 'things that mustn't be talked about'.

That evening after the interview, I received an email from Elspeth. She says that her head has been full. It was good to talk and to listen; they do not often get that opportunity. The issues are so complicated. She knows there are no short cuts, that failure, mistakes and difficulties must be faced, not run away from. She wants to learn more about racism and about her own feelings and responses to racism as a white woman.

The fragile missive suggests other textures and worlds in walking a high wire. Jeanette Winterson

> I live in the space between chaos and shape. I walk the line that continually threatens to lose its tautness under me, dropping me into the dark pit where there is no meaning. At other times the line is so wired that it lights up the soles of my feet, gradually my whole body . . . and I see then the beauty of newly created worlds, a form that is not random. A new beginning.[36]

Home

Those of us in post-industrial economies will die relatively slowly in old age, probably from cardiovascular disease, cancer, respiratory disorders or the 'prolonged dwindling' that is dementia and frailty.[1] As our functional abilities decrease over time, it is likely that we will receive at least some part of our care in the home. However, the proportion of home deaths has been falling. It is estimated that if current trends continue, fewer than one in ten of us will die at home by 2030.[2]

Care at home is a complicated business, described by the think-tank Demos as sometimes being a 'blizzard of disconnected services'.[3] This blizzard of care is spread out across the public, voluntary and private health and social care sectors, among personal assistants, General Practitioners (GPs), Clinical Nurse Specialists and district nurses, social workers, health advocates and occupational therapists. Current government policy aims to encourage more home deaths and to provide palliative care to all those who need it, regardless of their diagnosis.[4] Yet evidence suggests that there are numerous problems in accessing palliative care. These include local variations in what palliative care services are able to offer and a lack of awareness of palliative care services among those from socially disadvantaged groups.[5]

Unlike the care that is provided in institutional settings, care in the migrant household not only rearranges the time and space of what is private and what is intimate[6] but also what is *here* and what is *there*. 'In the aggregate, the global household produces and distributes a large quantum of social wealth in the form of unpaid household labor, household-based business income, monetary and in-kind remittances, and gifts',[7] the feminist economists Mahila Safri and Julie Graham have pointed out. Alongside these hidden relationships are small revolutions and redistributions in domestic power between carers and ill persons.

Body work

Figure 11.1 At home.
Courtesy: Nadia Bettega

A blade of sunlight makes an incision into the darkened room, illuminating the Hindu gods Shiva and Khrisna who are keeping watch over him.

For the past year Mr Gupta, a Bangladeshi Hindu, has been confined to his bed. The ecstatic language of his grunts and rasps is unintelligible to me. To his wife, and two home carers, the distilled sounds are heard in Sylheti as concrete interjections – 'He is asking where his wife has gone', 'He wants to go to the toilet'. This call-response relation is peeling itself away from the parochialisms of language and culture. Mrs Gupta feels that she is the only one who is truly fluent in this evolving sensuous dialect, the intricate gestures of face and fingertips, how his eyes listen, talk and touch.

Each small communication is a resounding sign of Mr Gupta's continuing being in the world. Perhaps this is what the philosopher Jean-Louis Chrétien meant when he wrote of the soul's appearance at the skin's surfaces, of how the human voice can be gripped by the 'superior force of a bidding that nonetheless would never materialize without its vivid deficiency'.[8]

Sahab and Iqbal, Mr Gupta's home carers, visit three times a day: one hour in the morning and in the evening and for 30 minutes at lunchtime. This is the amount of care that Mr Gupta has been assessed as needing by the local authority. In these two-and-a-half hours they provide 'personal and social care' that is means tested. It includes some cleaning, lifting, washing and 'bottom cleaning' as Iqbal explains to me through an interpreter. This type of care has been called 'body work': 'employment that takes the body as its immediate site of labour, involving intimate, messy contact with the (frequently supine or naked) body, its orifices or products through close proximity.'[9]

Sahab and Iqbal work with little verbal communication between each other. They are accustomed to the tacit rhythms of this body work: who will do what, when and in which order.

Figure 11.2 Shakti.
Courtesy: Nadia Bettega

The carers don plastic aprons and latex gloves, using a red plastic bowl of warm soapy water and a small red flannel, to wash Mr Gutpa. Sahab and Iqbal alternate between facing each other and working side-by-side. They use the mechanical bed to raise and lower Mr Gupta's upper torso. Sahab will hold one of Mr Gupta's arms in the air, gathering in the fingers and supporting the wrist while Iqbal washes Mr Gupta's armpit.

The colour red is significant in the Hindu religion. It is an auspicious colour. The colour of *Shakti* (prowess).

In washing Mr Gupta the carers need to work with sensitivity to what they see and to what they can feel, hear and smell, which can change daily, and also within the same day. As Mr Gupta's disease progresses, his body has become more heavy and lifeless. He appears as someone caught in a deep and irreversible woozy state, somewhere between sleep and awakening. To Mrs Gupta, her husband is still very much present though locked in.

To wash their charge thoroughly and to minimize any discomfort for an interred subjectivity, the carers must learn to work on, with and around the idiosyncrasies of each disabled body and its prostheses. They do this by applying and then modifying the skills that they have been taught, and in accordance with the body wisdom and preferences that are passed onto to them by each of the people that they care for. These are relatively small things, perhaps how a person likes to have their back rubbed or their ankles elevated so that they do not rub on the sheets.[10] Ultimately, they must learn the sensual terrain of each body in situ, working with its resistant forces, varying sensibilities and dispersed weightiness, building up an intimate hands-on knowledge as they go. At times 'corporeal anticipation'[11] – of flailing hands or of a body's habitual listing to one preferred side – will take over; a firm steadying arm is extended across a body just before it crumples or falls.

All the time that they are tending to him, Sahab and Iqbal watch Mr Gupta's face and body for signs of distress or discomfort. They talk to him in Sylheti, moving between a regard for corporeal surfaces and an interior life where cultural decorum and deference to elders must also be attuned to. Only as the flannel moves downwards does Iqbal break eye contact, fixing his gaze on the flannel, a civil inattention and emotional middle distancing that is practiced in intimate medical examinations,[12] minimizing embarrassment for all parties.

The red flannel that moves over the vulnerable body is charged by a delicate *Shakti* where warm water and multiple sensibilities wash over Mr Gupta.

The care provided by Sahab and Iqbal is paid for through a 'personal budget' allocated through a direct payment scheme from the local social services department. Direct payments are part of a care agenda of personalization that in this case was further mediated by a local non-profit Bangladeshi community organization.

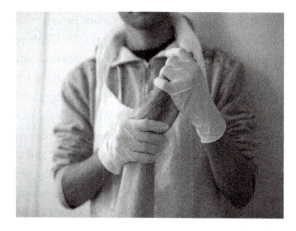

Figure 11.3 Washing bodies.
Courtesy: Nadia Bettega

With each visit Sahab and Iqbal do much more than personal and social care. They bring with them freshness and temporal rhythms, a breeze from the outside world where clock-time and tempo still have meaning. Both men are recent migrants from Sylhet who have left rural villages and families to marry British Bangladeshi Muslims in the East End of London. Iqbal says that his caregiving is not like a job. Despite their religious differences, he feels a part of the family of this childless couple. It is as if he is fulfilling a son's duty to his father.

This tendency to align or to naturalize care work as a kin relationship is a double bind. It contributes to the devaluation of the work – it is not 'real', skilled work – and it can compensate for low wages. On his day off, Mrs Gupta tells us, Iqbal sometimes does the shopping for them, as well as other small extras, such as picking up a prescription; tasks that are not included in the rationalized economics of their care plan. Iqbal is more like a nephew she says.

Nobody in the room speaks English, except of course Mr Gupta. Mrs Gupta had been a nurse in Bangladesh but she was too ashamed of her lack of competence in English to try to re-qualify and to practice her profession in the United Kingdom. Instead she took up unskilled jobs, often sewing with other Bangladeshi women in the East End factories that are the hidden powerhouses behind the high-fashion designs worn by celebrities across the globe. Without children or extended kinship networks, Mr Gupta was to become her only means of contact with life outside of the Bangladeshi community in East London.

As Parkinson's disease has taken away his mobility and strength, the more intensive care that Mr Gupta needs has brought with it unforeseen, if precarious, opportunities. It has revivified Mrs Gupta's world, while providing a vital livelihood for Sahab and Iqbal. The reciprocal dependencies that characterize the emergence of these new segmented linguistic and ethnicized markets within the global economy of care are another facet of the ambivalence in home care. The intimacies of body work, together with shared social and linguistic exclusions for both care recipients and caregivers, spawn and encourage the kinning of paid care. Yet the very nature of care within the home, its physicality and emotional labour, a resistance to seeing it as a job with specialist skills, choices, boundaries and career development, contribute to making it a vulnerable, low-status occupation that is especially difficult to unionize.[13]

The care workforce in the global North is increasingly made up of migrant women. According to the United Nations, women now constitute half of the international migrant population. They are a part of what is called the global care chain 'where migrant women from poor countries fill the gaps in care activities in richer countries in order to send money to other women left behind in the country of origin who take care of their family members, often through unpaid family labour.'[14]

As first-generation migrants age, the demand for same-sex personal care for some cultural and faith groups is opening up economic opportunities in the care sector for men like Sahab and Iqbal who tend to be employed by community, consumer and advocacy groups. New unforeseen opportunities are also being created for women in the households of declining patriarchs.

Slowly, slowly

Mr Balani is a Gujarati from East Africa, living in the Midlands. He has diabetes, cardiovascular disease and dementia. He is cared for at home by his wife, with help from his daughter Pavita. Our interview took place with the three of them together. I speak neither Gujarati nor Hindi. Even though Mrs Balani speaks English with fluency, she thought she might not be able to express herself fully without her daughter's help. Around this crowded interview the circumstances of everyday home caring encircled us, where bodies as much as objects – wheelchairs, walking frames and commodes – become conjoined and herded into small spaces so that it is difficult to avoiding bumping into things and each other.

Mrs Balani began by describing her husband's *day-by-day* descent into incapacitation over a period of ten years and how his dementia had eventually led to the ruin of the family's small business and the loss of their home. The story was interspersed and supplemented by Pavita, so that each narrative spoke to and modified the other, producing something new.[15]

Mrs B: After the stroke he was OK a couple of years and then he started day
          by day-
Pavita: He started with a walking stick and loosing his memory and not
          recognizing people and his speech slowed down. That's it, slowly,
          slowly and now his complete care is actually twenty-four hours.
Yasmin: So is that what you have now, you have twenty-four hour care?
Pavita: Well she doesn't have twenty-four hour care. She's the carer, it's
          just that they live on their own and they've got a day centre in the
          morning. First thing in the morning actually somebody comes to give
          him a bath, then he goes to a day centre and then he comes back like
          at four o'clock and between five-thirty and six Chirag comes again,
          because every time he needs to take the medication, somebody's got
          to be there, otherwise he can get quite aggressive.

As the story was unfolded, passing back and forth between the women, moving between three continents, and all the time across a mute Mr Balani, the dialogue began to dovetail with the rehabilitative equipment surrounding us, an apparatus and aid supporting a faltering, and at times painful conversation about the reshuffling of power within a debilitated household. Interviews can sometimes be used in this way, as a space from which people can voice and explore difficult topics, apparently for the benefit of the interviewer. More often they are talking to each other about what has not been working, what has never worked.

Mrs Balani was married at the age of 15, leaving her family home in India where she was treated like a 'little princess' to migrate to Nairobi and a small household where everybody worked very hard; 'I never had a rest, I'm just working, working, working.' Before his stroke Mr Balani was a workaholic his wife says. He took control of everything in the household, including her. This was his modus operandi. His own father had been an alcoholic, Pavita tells me. At the age of 13, Mr Balani had become the family breadwinner, making small toys and trinkets to sell at the roadside and helping his mother to care for his eight siblings. After his migration to the United Kingdom in 1961, he continued to support his family in Africa, eventually paying for the passage to England of his parents and six of his brothers and sisters.

Even though she had worked full-time in a factory after their migration to the United Kingdom, Mrs Balani had not been allowed to shop for the groceries or to know anything about the household finances. 'Now, it is all upside down' she says about her life after Mr Balani's stroke. At first it was family members who took her out of the home and to do the shopping. More recently it is Chirag, the home carer, who is a new migrant from India.

When the Balanis' lost their home after their small business went into bankruptcy they had gone to live with one of their sons. The arrangement did not work out. Mrs Balani felt as if they were a burden. So the couple moved on to another son's house. Again she felt that they were in the way. Her grandchildren were not used to having their grandparents around. They resented her authority. After a couple of years of moving between her sons, the Balanis moved into a council flat by themselves. Their large social network began to wither away. 'When you are down and out even your family does not want to know you. My family never came into my house – no, perhaps three times in one year.'

Before her father's illness, Pavita says that they were visited almost every weekend by relatives, who looked upon Mr Balani as a paternal figure. Now it is all different 'the relatives have moved away because it's like "Oh it's not fun going down to their house anymore"'. 'They are coming back slowly', Mrs Balani reminds Pavita.

This happens several times during the interview. As difficult stories or emotions begin to surface, Mrs Balani tries to cancel or retrieve them before they do any damage, like a grandmother scooping up a unruly infant. Of the time spent moving between her sons' homes she asks 'Is this a life?' responding quickly to her own question 'We've had a good life, really'. At this stage of her life Mrs Balani says that she will not blame anyone. It has to be 'forgive and forget'. 'You can't demand from anybody, I know this. Love. Love each other. That's it.'

Love is a refrain for Mrs Balani. At times it was seemingly unconnected to the conversation, not requiring context, just needing to be said out loud. Here we had been talking about the difficulties of bathing Mr Balani.

Yasmin: Did you get any support for yourself as a carer?

Mrs B: I love my husband. I can't live without my husband.

Pavita: I think that's her biggest nightmare thinking 'I don't care what he's like.' She dreads the fact of what will happen if she looses her independence completely and has to go and live with somebody.

Intermingling with the hardships and drudgery of caring – Mrs Balani cannot remember when she last had a full night of sleep – there have been new freedoms; a liberating redistribution of familial power that is usually unrecognized in social policy and campaign narratives of family care that pivot on simultaneous tropes of the victimization and romanticization of both carers and disabled people. That illness has been empowering for Mrs Balani by incapacitating her husband, loosening his power and control on family life, is beyond doubt.

For Pavita, the love that Mrs Balani declares for her diminished husband, is most readily acknowledged as a heartfelt valuing and commitment to her own newfound independence. It is a reading that is bittersweet, opening up webs of incapacitation and care across generations of women in the family. A very different rendering of the feminized global care chain. Pavita says that in Africa her mother had always been dominated and 'repressed' by her grandmother.

> But even then, dad was quite a dominant partner. The reason why she didn't go out was because she didn't have a choice, you know. So all this time he was quite a dominant character and 'You do as I say' and that was it, you know and all of a sudden now, she takes over the role and it's a huge personality change for mum, absolutely completely, because I've never seen my mum even speak up for herself and that's why I'm the way I am, because I refused to be like her when I was growing up, thinking 'I'm not going to be like you. I'm going to be outspoken and ambitious', because I wasn't allowed to study as well. At eighteen, I got married, because that's the norm in our family, you know, the woman aren't [...] and that's how mum was treated as well, but as she said, you know, working and everything, but we didn't know any different, so you just do it and my grandma was like in charge.

This time, Mrs Balani does not add anything to what Pavita has to say. She seems to understand and accept the assertion that illness and infirmity can be beneficial when it is the power of a family despot that is eroded; that illness, disability and care have many different sides and outcomes. It is a testimony to the character of both women that they do not say anything about the delivery of Karma and the fairness of Gods who will ultimately see that you get what you deserve.

As we exchange small talk at the end of the interview Chirag arrives to take Mr Balani for his bath. There is a frisson in the room. Mrs Balani's eyes light up and she exchanges a joke with Chirag. Mr Balani glowers. As Chirag walks across the room in front of him, Mr Balani slides down slowly in his chair and kicks out at him. The kick misses. Chirag and the women laugh. He will often lash out at Chirag, but that is just his way Pavita says.

Genograms

End of life care in the home is a different type of care giving. Palliative care professionals working in the community tend to see themselves as having a more intimate knowledge of their patients. A consequence of longer-term relationships with dying people and the conditional intimacies of entering into the sacred spaces of the home where people are less institutionalized.

These professionals are shown family photographs and the rising damp in the bedroom. They are introduced to friends, neighbours and the family cat. Many are competent cultural analysts, able to read the meanings and vocabulary of the arrangement of ornaments, photographs and furniture in a home. They often learn something of the hidden economy of herbal pharmacopoeia, hope and magic that connects homes in London and Birmingham to Beijing and Dhaka.

Nothing it seems can be taken-for-granted, so home carers have learned not to presume. They ask whether they should take off their shoes before entering some houses. Sensitive to variations in cultural decorum, they tread carefully.

Figure 11.4 Home furnishings.
Courtesy: Nadia Bettega

Tom, a palliative care social worker in North London describes meeting the family of a dying Rabbi in Golders Green.

> The main carer was his wife and I was just very conscious that as a man, I should not shake her hand. But as soon as I got in the door, she grabbed my hand and shook it and then we were really quite careful about how we addressed the Rabbi. She said, 'Oh, forget that, his name is so and so, call him that, that's fine.' Whereas in another household that wouldn't have been fine at all. So it's kind of gently feeling your way into that particular household, with that particular family.

The skills that are required in community palliative care are considerable. Carers are required to work between professional and institutional codes and regulation and the loitering surprises of every possible version of home imaginable: mansions, caravans, bed-sits, residential care homes, prisons. Domestic diversity can mean tea in china cups and the tasting of an array of specially prepared sweetmeats, or entering dilapidated buildings to tend to an anxious alcoholic.

In hospitals, the palliative care team – where there is one – will liaise with GPs. Hospital social workers will try to ensure that welfare benefits are being claimed and that any home help or occupational therapy has been arranged for when a patient is discharged home. Hospice home care teams are multidisciplinary and usually meet together every morning to discuss their patients. Team members will describe new patients to their colleagues and discuss developments and problems within their existing caseload. The level of detail is spectacular and the matter of their business makes home carers local historians with X-ray vision.

Genograms – maps of patient's kinship and personal relationships – are used to introduce new patients to the team. The symbols and codes are extensive. The most basic symbols signify gender (a square for a male, a circle for a female), with other signs denoting a spectrum of relationships: marriage, divorce, separation and co-habitation. Children are drawn in below their parents, ordered from the oldest to the youngest, left to right. Miscarriages, stillborn births and abortions are recognized. There are even symbols for family pets (a diamond).

A glance at a genogram can place the patient's generation and often their cultural background. The genograms of white, British, working-class families are wider and deeper than their middle-class counterparts. Cousins are given prominence in the networks of Caribbean patients and in common with South Asian patients there are an array of aunts and uncles. There is sometimes not enough space to map a full genogram for the connubial relationships of some Caribbean men. Amid such nuances, the commonalities are striking. Racism and resentment of migrants and minorities, especially South Asians, is most readily associated with the working-class, but the bare bones of a genogram reveals a depth of shared, caring relationships and structures between white working-class and South Asian families.

Working through an array of medical and demographic information, home care meetings are forensic, yet informal. Unrelenting technical jargon and a warts-and-all documenting of the small intimacies of what goes on behind closed doors. At a home care team meeting in a London hospice, I hear about Jim, aged 65, with cancer of the buttock and lung metastases. Jim's nurse, Lydia, tells her colleagues that Jim is becoming disorientated and anxious. He does not want his wife Tracy to leave him alone and becomes agitated even when she visits the toilet. He has demanded that Tracy pees in a bucket in their bedroom. The District Nurse is concerned about Jim's lack of appetite. Jim's son had phoned Lydia in distress, the hospital had told him that Jim has only a month to live. There are tuts of disapproval around the room. I hear a muttered 'outrageous'. The palliative care consultant suggests that the radical surgery on Jim's buttock was unnecessary. Reading the signs, she states matter-of-factly 'He's going to die at home'.

Then there is Jocy from Gibraltar, whose every need seems to be anticipated and met by her two daughters. Jocy has confided in her nurse that her daughters are unable to acknowledge that she is going to die, a situation made more difficult because Jocy has defied her prognosis repeatedly. 'I've been writing "death imminent" for ages and then she rallies' her nurse says, adding 'A lot of it is love that is keeping Jocy going'. When Carole announces 'Pat died yesterday' stillness descends upon the meeting. The sense of loss feels real and personalized. 'Very sad news' says a nurse beside me.

Bernadette introduces a new patient. Shirley, a Barbadian, is 54 with Motor Neurone Disease. She has two children. The youngest, 14-year-old Sebi, is being unusually helpful around the home. The team's social worker comments that it is a classic case of 'If I can be as good as I possibly can, Mummy won't die'.

Eileen McNaulty is 62, with cancer of the cervix. She lives by herself and is visited regularly by a granddaughter. There are concerns about Eileen's financial situation. She is a self-confessed shopoholic. The Citizens's Advice Bureau is helping Eileen to better manage her extensive debt. Eileen's immediate medical problem is her increased incontinence that is reducing her mobility. Eileen's nurse, Viv, comments that if anything, it is the incontinence that will keep Eileen to budget. She makes a note to visit her later on in the day.

The team meeting has taken one hour and five minutes. Thirteen patients have been discussed. Afterwards, team members return to their offices and check the central diary that contains information about the follow-up phone calls and visits that they need to make that day. They can be on the telephone for the next hour or so, talking to patients, family carers, GPs, occupational therapists and district nurses. Then they take to the road on home visits.

A view

Caring for dying people at home transforms locality and place. The view through a bus window or the car windscreen of a home palliative carer is more paranormal than panoramic. Neighbourhoods are corrugated with loss and peopled by ghosts. As they pass a block of flats, home-carers recall the smiling face of a child who would watch for their arrival. They relive the existential angst of kerbside conversations with family and friends. They know of the small, unseen tragedies that lie behind a home or shop that has come up for sale, the new conjugations between spouses in bereavement groups.

Home visits in cities traverse the infrastructures of biographies, households, cultures and continents. And often in a single street. The social discrepancies between deaths in London are vast. A report by Lord Darzi into health care in London in 2008, depicted socio-economic differences in life expectancy within the capital in stark terms. 'Just eight stops on the Jubilee line takes you from Westminster to Canning Town where life expectancy is seven years lower.'[16] A palliative care community nurse in West London,

> We've got lots of people living alone. Single mums with kids, and if they're asylum seekers they might be living away from their children. It's very, very varied here. And then of course you get the old traditional working class families. We still get a few of them, where they've got big families and there's lots of siblings and they all live nearby, but you don't get that very much anymore.

Home deaths for those living alone are the most difficult to achieve, unless there is a reliable network of friends and relatives who are willing to provide 24-hour support towards the end. But sometimes it is the very proximity of loved ones that is the problem.

On a visit to a Gujarati family in Wembley, there are nine members of the immediate household. Only four of them know the prognosis for the grandmother, Mrs Patel, who is semi-comatose and dying. The eldest son had taken the decision early on in his mother's illness not to tell her about her diagnosis. He feels that his mother would have *given up*, the truth hastening her death. As we leave the house, his wife, Meena, follows us out.

Meena tells us that Mrs Patel had asked several times about her diagnosis. As a non-English speaker she had been frightened by the partially explained tests she had had in hospital. The family always acted as her interpreters, filtering and blocking communication between Mrs Patel and health care professionals. Yet Mrs Patel seems to have known that something serious was unfolding in the energetic exchanges around her, that were transporting affects beyond anything that could ever be translated into language. For Meena it is apparent that her mother-in-law had insight into her condition. Shortly before her decline into unconsciousness, Mrs Patel had gathered the family together and distributed her jewellery among them.

The ethics of such family dynamics are gut churning for home carers and they draw heavily upon their skills in cultural diplomacy. They can get caught-up between a focus upon individual rights and autonomy and the need to remain open to more collective ways of being and decision-making. There are also the practical consequences of family conspiracies, regardless of culture, that need to be considered. When a dying person is unaware of their diagnosis, pain and symptoms can be more difficult to monitor and control. Patients can become unduly anxious and fearful. Family care can be more susceptible to breakdown, culminating in the blue-lighting of the dying person into an unfamiliar Accident and Emergency department where they can face a barrage of distressing and futile emergency procedures.

David, a Community Nurse Specialist, feels that there will be some improvement with time as more people talk about death and become aware of palliative care. His greatest challenge is working with generational accretions of culture within the same households.

> I remember a very large Muslim family. The younger generations were pushing for more active treatment and perhaps had more understanding about medications and understood decisions that were being made and wanted to take part in those decisions and wanted information. But at the other end of the family line were fiercely orthodox Muslims who said 'It's in god's hands. Nothing to do with us', and didn't really understand the nursing role either. So we were trying to manage all of this in one family, under one roof, and it was really difficult. At the end of the room I could see this patient but I just couldn't get to them. So, I called a family conference in the end to try and get some cards on the table, hear different people and let the family hear their different views, so they could actually understand one another and understand those motivations.

And did that work? I ask.

To an extent, but only for a little while and then they sort of went back into their corners.

Closeness to pain and suffering and to very different ways of dying can take its toll on home carers. In some cases, jangled nerves and insecurity can induce and reinforce crude stereotyping. At other times a stuttering in the taken-for-granted that makes itself felt as friction, foreignness, a murmur of other possibilities, extends routine and thought in a new directions. It brings a *style* to the lexicon of care. 'A style is managing to stammer in one's own language' the philosophers Gilles Deleuze and Claire Parnet have written, 'It is difficult because there has to be a need for such stammering . . . Being like a foreigner in one's own language. Constructing a line of flight.'[17]

Carmel speaks with such style in describing some of the difficulties she has encountered with Hindu and Sikh home deaths. But it is not the obstacles that have stayed with her.

> There can be a real exquisite sort of peacefulness about their approach to death, something very tender and really wonderful to be around. I think it's about handing things to god and about gaining some peace in terms of how you've lived your life and having some faith in that. It's something that I don't have much experience of, but it's inspiring to be a part of.

A cough

Rachel Gately is part of a district nursing team that operates out of what is not much more than a huddle of portakabins. District nurses provide most of the hands-on health care in home deaths, often seeing patients two or three times a day and fitting this palliative care into a generalist caseload that can include routines of wound-dressing, continence care and taking blood and urine samples. Rachel is accustomed to being a social and technical chameleon, adept at multi-tasking. She can eat, write-up notes and make phone-calls simultaneously. Rachel tells me that it is the unpredictability of her work that is especially stressful. Dying in localities has its own temporal rhythms, and death it seems can come in waves. Rachel's caseload can be palliative care free and then there can be up to six or eight dying people in the team's patch. At such times it is her other patients who can pay the price in more fleeting and trimmed-back visits.

Rachel's boss, Christine, has just returned to the office after trying to sort out the delivery of a hoist to a high-rise flat on a notoriously rough council estate in

South East London. The matriarch of a long-established, white, English family is dying. What should have been a routine delivery became fraught. Tempers flared and threats of violence ensued. The hoist would not fit into the one lift that was still working in the tower block. Health and Safety regulations prevented the delivery personnel from carrying the hoist up five flights of steep stairs. In the end the Health and Safety regulations were forgotten. The family enlisted the help of neighbours and together they carried the hoist up the stairs.

Rachel has spent most of the afternoon on the phone, tracking down a specialist, pressure-relieving mattress for a double bed. The mattress is for an elderly couple, originally from Jamaica. The husband has prostate cancer that has spread all over his body. He is not a talker, keeping his feelings and anxieties to himself. He comes from an era where stoicism and fortitude are the trademarks of manliness. As Edgar in King Lear put it 'Men must endure'. Rachel's assessment of the domestic situation is incisive.

> He knows he's dying and she knows he's dying, but they can't actually verbalize it together and he's keeping himself awake at night coughing, coughing and coughing. He keeps denying he's got pain, but you can see from his expressions that he's got physical as well as an awful lot of emotional pain.

Rachel had suggested medication to help her patient sleep. He had refused the sleeping tablets 'in case of a fire'. Reading between the lines, Rachel says,

> And his biggest fear is that if you give him something to help him sleep he won't wake up again and he'll die. So I think the cough is his way of trying to keep himself awake because he's afraid he'll die in his sleep. They have a very strong faith which I think is what's helping them through the whole time and the priest comes and he seems to be the one that's pulling them together and forging that bond. My staff nurse had seen him first and had ordered a highfaluting pressure mattress. So I went to see them and said 'My colleague has ordered this for you, where do you normally sleep?' And the wife said 'Well, we've slept in the same bed for forty-three years'. And I said 'Well how will you manage if we put your husband in a single bed?' 'Oh I'll sleep in a camp bed next to him.' I said 'Well at the moment things seem to be OK. If I get a double mattress would that be more preferable?' And that was what she wanted and that's what we've done.
>
> I think we will probably need to get a hospital bed and a super-duper mattress another two weeks down the line, but we've given them another three or four weeks of sleeping next to each other in bed, which I think is much more important for the moment while they build up their trust of us and cope with the loss of each other.

How to place a value on this mattress and the three to four extra weeks of sleeping together that Rachel brought to this couple? It will not be apparent in any accounting sheets or in audits, the medical case notes or even to Rachel's colleagues. There is a beauty to this poetic realism in care: unquantifiable, life and death changing and most often invisible. These rare places of sojourn for the combatants of reason and affect are as much a part of the richness of ordinary lives as they are the stuff of literary symbolism. In the Henry James novel *The Europeans*,[18] brother and sister, Felix and Eugenia, discuss the prospect of Felix's marriage. Eugenia muses that if Felix is as reasonable a husband as he has been a brother, his wife would have little to complain about.

> 'Felix looked at her a moment, smiling. "I hope," he said, "not to be thrown back on my reason."
>
> "It is very true," Eugenia rejoined "that one's reason is dismally flat. It's a bed with the mattress removed."'

What I learn from listening to Rachel and to other home care professionals is that care for stay-at-home patients can be deeply felt. It is without doubt a world of daily compromises, staff shortages and ongoing cost-cutting. And then in the midst of the everyday routines and frustrations there is also a world in which a mattress can extend love's time.

12

Pain

'I had a strange pain, started in the whole of my body you know, sometime in here' she explains touching her breast. 'Sometime in, in whole of my body, was circulating like blood.'

Pain needs a body. It relies upon flesh to receive and to register it, to allow it passage. Pain can come and go. It can linger immobile in a tangible 'here', it can engulf or move throughout the body so that it is everywhere *circulating like blood* in the words of Fatima, a Pakistani asylum seeker with terminal breast cancer that had metastasized to her bones.

With these properties, pain defies the ancient notion of a 'proper sensible' in which bodily organs remain faithful to autonomous senses 'each sense yielding access to only a single aspect of being'.[1] Despite efforts to metaphorize pain as numbers (0 is no pain, 10 is unbearable pain), faces (smiles, grimaces), rhythms (continuous, spasmodic, stabbing) or intensities (mild, intense), a distinguishing feature of pain lies in its abasement of categories and in the deficiencies of available descriptors and metaphors. 'I can't describe it' is a recurring refrain of the patients that I have talked with. 'How can you evoke pain in an image?' the artist Donald Rodney has asked. 'You can be sitting next to me and say you feel pain, but how do I know . . . whether you are feeling pain or not, or if your pain is anything like my pain?'[2] The philosopher Paul Harrison believes that 'experiences of suffering are quasicontradictory experiences in that they tend towards the limits of experience, towards the unexperienceable and irrecuperable.'[3]

At the borders of symbolization, pain entails, or demands, Elaine Scarry would argue, the shattering of language.

> Physical pain does not simply resist language but destroys it, bringing about an immediate reversion to a state anterior to language, to the sounds and cries a human being makes before language is learned.[4]

In Scarry's theorizing of pain as a destroyer of language, recognition is given to the role of pain translation and advocacy, to those such as physicians, where the success of the medical practitioner is dependent upon 'the acuity with which he or she can hear the fragmentary language of pain, coax it into clarity, and interpret it.'[5] This work of pain translation and advocacy also exists in the social sciences where the demands of researching pain, distress, trauma and suffering have been given sustained attention.

What characterizes these social science discussions is the belief that pain and suffering can be produced by the social: by inequality, exclusion, injustice, powerlessness and persecution. It is perhaps not surprising that such forms of suffering can manifest at the end of life for migrants, where lives are looked back on, and selves and bodies can become both more salient and more vulnerable as illness progresses and also at different stages of the care pathway that involve varying degrees and rhythms of exposure. In a Swedish study, nurses reported how caring for refugees and for survivors of the Nazi concentration camps sometimes entailed closer attention to the routines and technical procedures of care. 'We had a patient who had been in a concentration camp' one nurse said '. . . it was awful of course . . . talking about gas . . . she had great difficulty in breathing and it was extremely hard and there were so many memories involved in it all. . . .'[6] Cicely Saunders had also encountered similar experiences in her early work as a doctor in London in the 1960s. In an undated talk entitled 'The Problem Patient', Saunders presented a slide of Mrs P 'A patient with an extermination camp background who later developed severe depression with hallucinations, helped by E.C.T.'[7]

I have also found that at diagnosis common questions of 'Why?' and 'Why me?' can twist into 'Is it me?' Listen to this story from Mita, an Indian Hindu, Cancer Nurse Specialist, talking about an Indian Hindu patient with terminal cancer. The patient had been a teacher in India, a position that carries considerable prestige and status. In London he had applied repeatedly for teaching posts but had been unsuccessful. He ended up working in factories and then as a bus driver. Mita

> I think it had an impact on how he dealt with his condition, because unfortunately his diagnosis had been quite delayed. For a year he'd been going backwards and forwards to the GP, telling him all the classic symptoms of what he'd got. He said 'I know I'm educated and I know I'm completely in the wrong box. I think they haven't treated me properly because I am who I am, because saying I was only good enough for bus driving, not for teaching and for the same reason they

didn't think I was important enough to be diagnosed early enough to be treated in the right way.'

Mita found it difficult to know how to respond to and alleviate her patient's feelings of anguish and injustice and how the different injuries seemed to flow into each other. 'I mean what can you say?' she asked into the air 'What can I actually say to him that's actually going to make a difference to him?'

In the study *The Weight of the* World[8] first published in French in 1993, the sociologist Pierre Bourdieu used the term *social suffering* to name such experiences and to investigate the relationships between *la grande misère* – economic and spiritual impoverishment – and *la petite misère* or 'ordinary suffering'. *The Weight of the World* used ethnographic and interview methods, presenting its findings as a series of pen portraits in which there is a continuous overlapping between the social, the somatic and the 'spiritual' as Bourdieu calls it.

Louise B, an 80-year-old retired social worker, with degenerative arthritis, was interviewed by Gabrielle Balazs in a Parisian hospital emergency room as part of *The Weight of the World* project. Between 1965 and 1989 Balazs tells us 'the proportion of 60-year-olds or over in France has gone from 17 per cent to 19 per cent . . . more than three-quarters of people on their own aged 55 and over are women.'[9] Against this cultural background of the feminization of old age and the increasing isolation of older people in French society, Balazs found herself witnessing Louise's first steps into an irreversible process of institutionalized care. Of the interview Balazs says,

> The major problem revealed at the hospital is so painful that it cannot be completely articulated, or even thought: each time the interview brings her close to the truth of her solitude – she can no longer go home, her family cannot and does not want to take her in – she rapidly buries the lucidity that would kill her under a cascade of reassuring affirmations: 'I have friends,' 'I have caring people around me,' 'I'm lucky.'[10]

Because of the difficulties in expressing social suffering, sociological attentiveness to it has to be cultivated through 'active and methodological listening' Bourdieu argued.[11] In the study, interviewers often had a longstanding connection to, or at least some familiarity with, the research sites and the participants. It was a practice developed by the research team to reduce social asymmetries and the risks of a distanced denigration of those they were working with. Their goal Bourdieu tell us was 'to situate oneself in the place the interviewees occupy in the social space in order to understand them as necessarily *what they are*.[12] Bourdieu's purpose in trying to confect an extraordinary attunement in the interviews was to cut through the 'we've already seen and heard it all' worldly-wise cynicism of the researcher, and to move towards a practical understanding of how social structures and histories could be felt in each research participant's 'idiosyncrasy'.

The feminist cultural theorist, Angela McRobbie, has criticized Bourdieu's study for its sentimentality, lack of thick description and methodological rigour.[13] The careful documenting and exposition of the negotiation between subjectivity and objectivity and theoretical and practical knowledge that characterizes Bourdieu's empirical research, although present, are certainly more muted in this project. Instead, the pain translation and advocacy role of the researcher is emphasized and situated in her ability to give time, space and self to the research participant and 'like a mid-wife'[14] to bring deeply buried suffering and discontent into the world of expression and understanding. 'Against the old distinction made by Wilhem Dilthey' Bourdieu contends 'we must posit that *understanding and explaining are one*'.[15] In these and other qualifications, Bourdieu seems acutely aware of the controversial nature of his empirical approach to the study of suffering,

> . . . at the risk of shocking both the rigorous methodologist and the inspired hermeneutic scholar, I would say that the interview can be considered a sort of *spiritual exercise* that . . . aims at a *true conversion of the way we* look at other people in the ordinary circumstances of life. The welcoming disposition, which leads one to make the respondent's problems one's own, the capacity to take that person and understand them just as they are in their distinctive necessity, is a sort of *intellectual love*. . . .[16]

The words *spiritual* and *love* emphasized so provocatively – and that leap off the page to the scholastic eye – point to the limits of the scientific intent of social research. In its place Bourdieu institutes sociology as a 'craft', an unfolding and unpredictable bridging work between the interviewer and research participant, which,

> disposes one to improvise on the spot, in the urgency of the interview, strategies of self-presentation and adaptive responses, encouragement and opportune questions etc., so as to help respondents deliver up their truth, or, rather, to be delivered of it.[17]

Mindful of Angela McRobbie's critique of *Weight of the World*, there is something in Bourdieu's work – in the moment-by-moment improvisations, the communicating across differences in language and culture and the sense of witnessing the social birthing of painful experiences – that has relevance to my research experiences. So I have been especially interested in what Bourdieu and his colleagues were trying to get at with their flagrant, if ambivalent, detours outside of methodological orthodoxy and into the more-than-social.

In many respects a stubborn allegiance to, and focus upon the social constitution of pain and suffering is very much in evidence throughout *The Weight of the World*. This focus ensures that suffering remains firmly within sociological reach: social suffering can be comprehended, thematized and explained empirically. Yet there is also a more ambiguous recognition of how attentiveness to the *idiosyncrasy* of suffering can engender a move outside of disciplinary traditions, so that research relationships and practices overflow into such sublime matters as spirit and love that breach and offend scientific enterprise, categories and language.

Taking into account the long history of forensic attention to methodological practice that is the hallmark of Bourdieu's research, it seems to me that there is something more profound and artful going on than the 'sociological opportunism' that Angela McRobbie has read into the researchers' empirical rule-breaking.[18] Drawing from my work in palliative care, I want to suggest that Bourdieu's forays into the more-than-social intimate a contact with the vitality and anti-thematizing qualities of pain and the impossibility of limiting the affects and effects of pain and suffering to one sphere of life and being. Ibrahim and his plans for a post-mortem lifeline to his son (see Sweet Chariot), June Alexander and the mysteries of faith (see Moving On) are among those whom I have in mind, where I have had to think about and follow stories outside the domains of the social and linear time.

That pain and suffering can be produced by and experienced across a plurality of social and bodily sites is not of course only a problem for the social researcher. In observing, talking to and now teaching care practitioners, my thinking about pain has also been informed by their stories and dilemmas. I will elaborate upon what I have been learning by bringing into conversation sociological accounts of 'social suffering'[19] with what in palliative care is called 'total pain'. Total pain interpolates, and at times creolizes, physical, social, psychological and spiritual pain. It also gives recognition to pain that is accrued over a lifetime.

A distinctive value of the chorographic inventiveness of total pain is how it can allow for the assembling of diverse phenomena within its apprehending of pain. However, unlike a 'flat ontology',[20] it avoids a 'smear of equivalence'[21] between entities by not presupposing that phenomena have corresponding states and by allowing for that which is insecure and/or withdrawn; lacking a referent and/or inherent stable qualities. As I understand it, although the withdrawn can sometimes fracture the present, what is withdrawn is not fully accessible in the here and now, because there are planes of life and being that can bypass consciousness and symbolization. The philosopher Levinas has described such relations as being 'diachronic'.[22] Because life is marked by diachrony, Levinas has argued, we can never fully know either ourselves or others.

Total pain: 'All of me is wrong'

I remember one patient who said, when asked to describe her pain: 'Well, doctor, it began in my back but now it seems that all of me is wrong,' and she then described her other symptoms. She went on . . . 'I could have cried for the pills and injections but knew that I must not. My husband and son were wonderful but they were having to stay off work and lose their money.' She was suffering a 'total pain' . . . . It is, in a way, somewhat artificial thus to divide a whole experience but it may give an internal checklist on meeting a new patient.[23]

The challenges of alleviating the chronic pain that characterizes terminal disease preoccupied Cicely Saunders. She collected over a thousand patient case studies in the course of her work as a doctor, and used them, together with patient interviews, drawings, poems and paintings, to develop her ideas for hospice care and for pain alleviation. Saunders approached chronic pain as a 'situation' rather than an event, requiring practitioners to be 'attentive to the body, to the family and to [the] patient's inner life'.[24] Going against established medical conventions at the time, Saunders drew upon existing, but institutionally marginal practices, to advocate the regular giving of analgesics, including diamorphine, to keep chronic pain in remission, rather than administering analgesia in response to pain. And at the same time as giving attention to physical pain, Saunders returned time and again to the importance of listening to dying people and a concern with 'a whole experience suffered, endured, passed through'.[25]

Publications by Cicely Saunders without some reference to case study examples, and/or the stories of dying people or caregivers are rare. The archive of her work at King's College (London) is full of patient stories and hundreds of slides, poems and letters. Not all were collected for her clinical research. She was hopelessly curious about all forms of human experiencing and also the possibilities for inter-species learning about the alleviation of pain. She would follow up all manner of news reports and articles, once corresponding with a vet about his combined use of a morphine derivative and tranquilizer in the capture of square-lipped rhinoceros. In a file of transcribed conversations with patients, Saunders had collated a seemingly random collection of quotes that encompassed the sublime and the earthy; the sort of mundane yet magical fragments of life that are easily overlooked:

Mrs H: 'It seemed the pains went with me talking'

Mr S: 'Doctor, I think its time I went'

Mr F: 'Doctor, I won't see you again. Goodbye and thank you.'

Mr G: 'This injection is fine and will last me – till tomorrow morning (when he died)

Mrs I: 'I woke up and there were two of me'

Mrs C: Sister confiscates 'Lady Chatterley's Lover'

Mrs B: 'I'm bored underneath'.

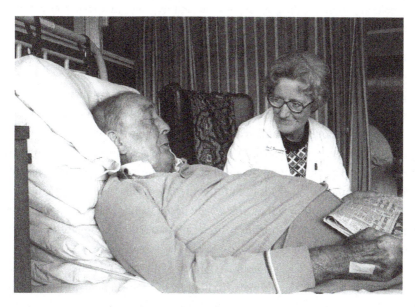

Figure 12.1 Cicely Saunders with patient.

Courtesy: St Christopher's Hospice

In an article first published in 1963 on 'The Treatment of Intractable Pain in Terminal Cancer' Saunders wrote,

> I once asked a patient who knew that he was dying what he wanted to see in the people who were looking after him. His answer, 'for someone to look as if they are trying to understand me' . . . It is indeed hard to understand another person but I always remember that he said 'trying'. He did not ask for success but only that someone should care to make the effort.[26]

Working with and from patient stories, Saunders believed that the constituency and temporality of pain had to be approached as a complex, moving heterogeneity that included the social, psychological and the spiritual. Her focus widened from the genre of disease, and from biochemistry and drugs, to the imperative of treating the many symptoms of a terminal condition. In a letter to her brother Christopher in 1966, Cicely described with low-key, if weary, clarity the challenges that her 'integrated approach' faced in the exigencies of everyday medicine.

> The main problem is, I think, that I am trying to talk about the art of medicine in a rather ill-fitting scientific dress but it is important to try and do this. I am very loth indeed to divide it up into two writings, one about the mental side of this type of pain and the other about the physical . . . I wanted to present it in a whole, in a form that the general physician and surgeon and student concerned with the care of these patients might possibly assimilate.

In the cosmology of Cicely's total pain, the plural phenomena of pain are allowed a mysterious ecology, tessellated and distinct, substantial and withdrawn, requiring multidisciplinary, but also experimental, care. 'If you listen to the tale of each one (symptom) and treat it separately, you will have so much less need for sedatives, tranquillizers and even analgesics'.[27] And while Saunders seemed to know that recognition of total pain would not always ensure effective pain relief, the effort of *trying* to respond to an-other's needs for care, even when one fails, remained significant to her for both the content and quality of care practices.

In similar ways to Bourdieu's *The Weight of the World*, Cicely Saunders' work with pain often strayed into matters of the immaterial and unquantifiable 'The spirit is more than the body which contains it'.[28]

Unlike Bourdieu, Cicely Saunders' work with death meant recognizing irredeemable loss and the ultimate limitations of the bridging work of care in responding to differing constituencies, temporalities and scales of pain. For every success story in Saunders' writing – a patient whose emotional distress is relieved by the right choice and dose of a tranquilizer – there was also sustained attention to those whose pain could not be understood or eased. Her notes about such instances are uncompromising, at times confessional: 'Miss H – I never got to grips with the situation and had discomfort . . . Lack of communication on my part' and for Mr H 'We were not very good with bowels – and he remained miserable? Sh'd have been more honest.'

In the case of emotional distress Cicely has written 'a good deal of suffering has to be lived through'. The role of the care practitioner in such circumstances is marked by a quintessential passivity 'We are not there to take away or explain, or even to understand but simply to "Watch with me" . . .'.[29] Here, a responsiveness to pain, and to that which might be unknown or withdrawn, is transposed into a non-acting standing-by of others. A receptiveness that the psychoanalyst and social work educator Margot Waddell has called 'serving'.[30]

In working between the quantitative empiricism of medical knowledge – observing, measuring, indexing, calculating, trialling – and what philosophers sometimes characterize as a fidelity to the unknown,[31] Cicely Saunders' notion of total pain reinstates care as a part of human adventuring requiring technical skills and expertise but also 'negative capability'. Negative capability is the term that the poet Keats[32] has used to denote the ability to tolerate incomplete understanding and mystery.

While not forgetting that the 'total' of total pain raises matters of medical imperialism and surveillance,[33] its domains and claims are not as totalizing as its name might suggest. Rather than signifying a closed system, total pain seems to point to the infinite, acknowledging that even with the recognition it can give to diverse registers and combinations of pain, it might never fully apprehend, control or alleviate someone's pain.

It is difficult to find concise examples from my research that demonstrate this side of total pain as an inventive, artful care practice. A story that comes very close, is the 'mattress story', told by the community-based nurse Rachel (see page 132). In the story Rachel worked hard to find a not easily available pressure-relieving mattress for a double bed for an anxious Caribbean man and his wife. The man was finding it difficult to sleep and had refused medication to help him. The mattress that Rachel managed to find was able to bring the couple three to four more weeks of sleeping together. Time that Rachel hoped might ease and contain their impending loss and fears and help to build more trusting relationships between the couple and care professionals.

From the perspective of total pain the qualities of the mattress can be thought of as an emotional and material substrate, continuing to connect and support the couple in Rachel's absence. As an affective subtending, the power of the mattress and its potential to relieve suffering is indivisible from its materiality; the extent to which its form and sensual qualities are themselves actants impressed by two variously suffering bodies, a cough, the physiology and metaphysics of sleep for a dying man and suspicion of professionals.

What captivated me about this story was how the offering of the mattress was both an inventive use of available resources *and* negative capability. Rachel could not verify the sources or different knots of pain that were involved in her patient's situation. She did not know for sure that the mattress would alleviate the man's pain and convey her recognition of the fear and anxieties that she felt this couple were living through. There were no clinical trials or evidence base that she could draw upon. Rather, Rachel's version of total pain was created and emerged from her relationship to the couple and out of some regard for materials and affects in their everyday lives. Such chorographic pain alleviation works off imagined interconnections between signs and the real. It seems cognizant of how emotions can materialize by 'sticking' to certain objects.[34] It also allows painful entities a non-presentness or mystery.

At first glance the basic tenets of total pain seem to operate much like a 'flat ontology',[35] one in which tumours as much as mattresses and coughs are recognized as contiguous, intra-acting components of pain. Indeed, emerging neuroscience investigations suggest that social and physical pain rely upon some of the same neurobiological substrates.[36] Yet, although total pain allows for such sharing it also leaves spaces for the effects of undisclosed and unfathomable entities that can defy the most bespoke titration of drugs or care-full listening. So in practice the 'total' of total pain can operate more as a provocation for care and as a tentative placeholder for a pluralized known and unknown.

Case stories

For me, the philosophy of total pain revitalizes social science discussions of the limits of understanding pain and suffering. It also raises questions of what might be at stake in the revisions and extensions to the empirical that I have suggested that total pain implies. These questions become less abstract when I apply them to my ongoing teaching with palliative care professionals. Consider what can happen in teaching when I use case stories generated from my research.

The case story of Maxine describes the end-of-life care of a 63-year-old hospice patient, a retired auxiliary nurse whose story I have documented in Chapter 4

'A Catch'. Maxine had talked to me in some detail, and over a period of months, about her life, recounting events of domestic and racist violence. In her stories Maxine was often more of a heroine than a victim, feisty and discerning. When admitted into the hospice for terminal care, she grew increasingly agitated. In the last days of her life, Maxine began to resist all hands-on care.

In multidisciplinary teaching sessions we discuss what might be involved in Maxine's situation. If it has not been raised, and drawing from the insights of feminist and psychoanalytic scholarship, I might suggest how histories of gendered and racialized violence are implicated in Maxine's anxieties about her body. In making sense of the care problematic, a doctor may layer my suggestions into what she has learned from 20 years of clinical practice and from evidence-based research: paranoia, agitation and hyper-sensitivity to touch and to noise can be caused by drugs and the biopathology of advanced disease. A social worker could draw upon pedagogies of anti-oppressive practice[37] and diversity training, relating the case story to his experiences of counselling survivors of war and women who have been raped, for whom physical care can be traumatic.

A crucial point is that the generation of these insights and possibilities is not about a semiotic expansion – a piling up of new symbolic categories onto existing knowledge in order to signify with greater accuracy, a previously unthought, but ultimately generalizable real. Neither is the aim to retrieve or to recover to the present a lost (explanatory) object of pain in Maxine's past. Rather, these interdisciplinary exchanges become highly focussed, contextualizing and specifying practices through which we can become variously sensitized to more possible registers of Maxine's pain, including those that elude us. In the process, it is attentiveness to the singularities of Maxine's situation that can produce shifts in what we think of as pain, so that the content of our experienced world expands.

This process is broadly akin to what Bruno Latour calls 'articulation', a bodily practice of 'learning to be affected by differences'.[38] It is a learning that does not rely upon an object/subject, nature/culture split or upon common, uncontested epistemologies. For Latour 'The more you articulate controversies, the wider the world becomes'.[39]

Being affected to learn

Latour's *learning to be affected* is defined as a bodily practice and is relevant to the embodied thinking and practising of ethics in empirical research: how might the attentiveness of research be articulated? There is a supplement that I would like to add. In my teaching and learning with care professionals it is apparent that we are already affected by our encounters with pain, suffering and vulnerability. At the same time there are aspects of entities and others that cannot be fully recuperated into a taught interdisciplinary or sensual affectedness. No matter how many different perspectives, experiences and levels of analysis are brought to the interpretation of Maxine's case-storied life, no matter how questions of disciplinary knowledge production are kept in sight, there are always aspects of her experience that are untranslatable. So while our worlds have expanded through our encounters with Maxine and with each other, we cannot claim to ever fully understand the sources, routes, levels, temporality and meanings of Maxine's pain.

And so within learning, to be affected, there is also the unintelligible and the undecidable. It is this unintelligibility – an empirical counterpart of the withdrawn in philosophies of total pain – that can become an inspiration for the bridging work of sociological attentiveness and the improvisations of methodology. In other words, there are circuits or relays of interdependence between learning to be affected and being affected to learn which gain traction and impetus from the things we cannot resolve, recover or connect, but which nevertheless have a status as a response.[40]

'Incomprehensibility' Derrida writes '. . . is not the beginning of irrationalism but the wound or inspiration which opens speech and then makes possible every logos or every rationalism'.[41] There are two notions of fidelity at work here: remaining faithful to the idiom and the milieu of what is unknowable, while also searching for and using every possible means by which to know it differently. I have in mind the commonplace but often under-described 'wounding' inspirations of empirical research: Bourdieu's struggles with the 'infidelities' of transcribing interviews – his admission that it took him over a decade (with repeated listening to an interview recording) to better appreciate the depth of the precarious existence of two farmers whom he had known personally for a long time. And there is my own turn to poetry and creative writing to evoke and commemorate non-linearities and enigma.[42] As Graham and Thrift have recognized, despite its origins in failure and fault, in improvisation there is always the hope of a provisional responsiveness and learning.

> Improvisation allows the work of maintenance and repair to go on when things
> may seem bleak and it takes in a whole series of responses, from simple repetition
> (such as trying it again) through to attempts to improve communication so as to

be clear exactly what the problem is, through disagreement over causes, through to complex theorizing, responses which are often the result of long and complex apprenticeships and other means of teaching. . . .[43]

Of course we need to be careful about valorizing or embracing the unintelligible too readily. The unknown as beyond question risks becoming complicit with the mystifications that are part of the apparatus of social and political abjection.[44] We can also neglect the more mundane ways in which empirical inquiry can itself be 'dumb', stifled by a 'dramatically poor repertoire of sympathies and antipathies'.[45]

Thinking about the status of what is inaccessible, mysterious or unlocatable is also to think about differential histories and scales of existence and how these histories and scales are rendered and approached – and always *in media res* – from different disciplinary perspectives. But, it is also to return to basics: to recognize that critical methodologies, as much as care, are driven by a desire (and for some, a responsibility) to oppose unnecessary suffering 'it is precisely the radical destructibility of life that makes it a matter of care'.[46] And so, the unintelligible for me is not so much a bounded territory or domain, an empirical no-go zone. Rather, it simultaneously signifies and problematizes the underlying drive of the attentiveness of social research as an imperative to uncover and to do something about unnecessary suffering.

Learning from the improvisations of dying migrants and care practitioners, I want to suggest that the unintelligible involves something more than being the opposite or absence of intelligibility. Carrying the capacity to put into motion, touch, interrupt and halt it is the very condition of future 'live'[47] empirical activity; a site of problem-making and accounting for. An opening to the creation of different methodological practices, knowledge and ways of thinking about the usefulness of what we do and also about what is 'sociologically unspeakable'.[48]

I am still very much learning about the demands of doing research in pain-full settings. At this stage of my thinking there are two matters that I feel are important. First, attentiveness to a range of different materials out of which attempts at intersubjective bridging and communication can be produced, and which can exceed the social, the material and the temporally linear. And second the cultivating of an empirical sensibility that is hospitable to the withdrawn.

The Foreigner Question – An Epilogue

In 1996, the philosopher Jacques Derrida took part in a series of seminars in Paris that culminated in the book *Of hospitality*,[1] presented as a dialogue with the psychoanalyst and philosopher Anne Dufourmantelle. The conversational form of the seminars/essays is important. It makes present the dialogic terms of hospitality – which presupposes a host and a guest – and where hospitality harbours more menacing conditions, such as having your generosity abused – and of deconstruction where meaning hinges upon exclusions and opposites.

In the opening essay 'Foreigner Question: Coming from Abroad/from the Foreigner' (*Question d'etranger: venue de l'etranger*), Derrida, our teacher, hooks us in – as all good teachers do – with a puzzle. 'Isn't the question of the foreigner [*l'etranger*] a foreigner's question?' he asks 'Coming from the foreigner, from abroad [*l'etranger*]?'[2] And then the questions keep coming, through circularities and small changes in emphasis and angle that disclose and release other meanings.

> The question of the foreigner is a question of the foreigner, addressed to the foreigner. As though the foreigner were first of all the one who puts the first question or the one to whom you address the first question. As though the foreigner were being-in-question, the very question of being-in-question, the question-being or being-in-question of the question.[3]

This type of writing can make you feel giddy. There are bouts of confusion and enlightenment. This is another point expressed in form of the deconstructionist effort to think differently by making language and meaning insecure and difficult. I have learned to stick with these texts, moving with the play of meanings as they coalesce and disperse, just letting the writing fizz and wash over me at times.

So with Derrida, the foreigner is a figure who questions our own existence and belonging. I go back over the text, back over the text. *I didn't get that – what did he just say?* Anne Dufourmantelle who sits to the left of me in the split text format of this seminar/writing is some comfort. She is both a helpful guide (don't worry he's obsessed) and a pedagogue, authoritative and erudite. The obsessing Dufourmantelle tells us is Derrida being Derrida 'drawing the contours of an impossible, illicit geography of proximity'[4] where what is foreign is right here. In other words, otherness or alterity is not so much a spatial problem, a problem of the cultural and experiential distance between me and you. It is a problem of time. A problem of genealogy, inheritance, anticipation and of not ever knowing what the future holds. This is also the other-within, the alterity within each of us that I wrote of in the Introduction.

So this is the foreigner – a 'being-in-question' – as an unknowable, ultimately uncategorizable Other that disturbs our being at home with ourselves and in the world. 'To the pacified reason of Kant' Dufourmantelle explains 'Derrida opposes the primary haunting of a subject prevented by alterity from closing itself off in its peacefulness.'[5]

Derrida's tracing of the figure of the foreigner is formidable, moving through readings of Kant, Plato, Sophocles, Levinas, Joyce and Kafka, histories of colonization and decolonization such as French colonial rule in Algeria, and anthropological texts. It is significant that the seminars open with Derrida's citing of a Tupinamba weeping ceremony of welcoming and hospitality performed by women and taken from Jean de Léry's *History of a Voyage to the Land of Brazil, Otherwise Called America*. As Julia Emberley[6] has pointed out, Derrida's use of the Tupinamba ceremony for the purpose of radicalizing and advancing a European cosmopolitan hospitality is problematic when the effects of colonization on indigenous peoples in North and South America have been disavowed, especially for women.

Emberley is interested in excavating 'an indigenous ethics of hospitality, homelessness, and homecoming'[7] that builds upon Derrida's opening up of hospitality to aboriginality, territorial dispossession and sexual difference. Emberley takes up Derrida's invitation to consider the domestic playing out of hospitality and the question of the unwanted violating guest through a discussion of Doris Pilkington's novel *Rabbit Proof Fence*.[8]

Rabbit Proof Fence is the story of the forcible taking away of 'half-caste' children from their aboriginal mothers to British colonial boarding schools in 1930s Australia. Emberley's is a multi-sited telling, showing how 'The history of the movement of bodies is not a simple one, it is complicated and troubled by histories of violence, uprootings, various kinds of fascisms and racisms.'[9] Crucial to this recognizing of the historical inflections of transnational hospitality are shifting notions of territory as ground, soil and earth for figures as diverse as the aborigine, the nomad and the violating European refugee turned settler.

Rabbit Proof Fence stories the dramatic escape of three Nyungar children – Molly, Daisy and Gracie – from their colonial boarding school. Using the rabbit proof fence as their guide, the girls walk 1,200 miles from the Moore River Native Settlement to their mother's camp. Their homecoming is commemorated with a weeping welcoming/mourning ceremony where tears, blood and soil merge. 'The wailing began softly at first then grew louder as more people joined the group.'[10] The ceremony is performed at the meeting point of material, affective and symbolic borders. For Emberley, the ceremony makes audible and feelable an emergent ethics of hospitality and story telling, where homelessness and the desire for a homecoming flow into each other. She writes,

> This narrative of flight, I want to suggest, is also a story of homecoming, returning to their mother's camp, and to their mothers. Thus, the motivation to flee was not only due to the oppressive conditions of the Moore River Native Settlement but also to their desire to return to their mother's camp. Strangely enough, the way back is guided by a barbed-wire fence, which on the one hand is the rabbit-proof fence, a boundary created for colonial containment, and ironically, as Pilkington writes 'a symbol of love, home and security' (109). It was their umbilical connection to their home, their kin, and their land.[11]

Such moments of hospitality as a homecoming on ambivalent ground resonate with the dispossession from the warmth and aqueous security of the womb for Emberley. In watering the soil, the weeping/mourning ceremonies 'reproduce the original fluidity of home and dispossession'.[12]

I would like to contribute another final story to this palimpsest of hospitalities. It is a story in which birth and death are intimates and where homecoming is dispersed across debilitated paternity, migration trajectories and life itself.

Sweet chariot

I interviewed Ibrahim, a refugee from Ghana, in his hospice bed ten days before he died. When I think of Ibrahim he comes to me as breath.

When we met, Ibrahim's pain was not under control. The audio record of our interview and the written transcript is indented by pauses, hesitations and laboured breathing. The breathing came both from Ibrahim and from the mechanical sighs of the syringe driver that was pumping liquid opioids into his blood stream. Scattered throughout the interview are ellipses, the transcription denotation for pauses. I have yet to find a code that comes close to symbolizing the tempo and varying presence of breath.

In our interview Ibrahim talked of his fears for his partner and 16-month-old baby in London and for his two older children in Ghana. How would they survive financially without him? He worried aloud about the cultural identity of his baby son, a concern that echoes with what the United Nations has called the 'intangible cultural heritage' of language, oral history, rituals and craft skills.[13]

At the time, hospice doctors were overhauling Ibrahim's drugs to better control his pain and symptoms. Hospice social workers had secured a small grant to ease the family's financial burdens. Ibrahim had come up with his own solution to the problem he saw facing his baby. He wanted to be buried in Ghana.

> I want my son to [. . .] one day not just melt away into this society, but think of a place where he comes from and one day, or once in a while go back there, and when he goes there and then there's this grave stone standing there and say 'Oh that's your Dad lying down there' just gives him some kind of attachment to a place which I will cherish [. . .] yeah. But if he stays here, just melts away into society and that's the end [. . .].

The repatriation of the dead is a practice that follows in the footsteps of Ghanaian diasporic rituals. It is not so unusual. Yet, the problem of how to ensure that a baby known in the present connects in the future with a place he has no experience of – and where his father was himself endangered and excluded in the past – is a novel predicament, full of uncertainty, paradoxes and strange temporalities. It is one where Ibrahim's desire to cultivate a sense of a transnational belonging for his son is made by casting an experimental lifeline fabricated from the only materials that he has left: his imagination and his body.

And because this reiteration of a Ghanaian diasporic death ritual comes from a dying refugee it complicates, if not subverts, the sentimentalizing of the nation as a vital territory and ground of belonging. 'Ghana is a difficult country and in this situation if you send me back you are going to make some people's lives worse for them . . . If you have to die, just die here [. . .] I don't want to compound anybody's misery.' Ibrahim's imagined post-mortem future hosting of his son in Ghana is not that of the paternal despot in Derrida's writing, who lays down the laws of hospitality.[14] This is a father without a home, and on temporal ground that is fast moving out from under him.

In his essay on 'Sly Civility' Homi Bhabha notes the unsettled root of the word territory '. . . "territory" derives from both *terra* (earth) and *terrere* (to frighten), whence territorium, "a place from which people are frightened off"'.[15] That Ibrahim could imagine a return to Ghana only in death, and then through a risky investment in a cultural trust fund, moves between subservience to and flouting of the *terrere* of the nation-state and its borders.

Refugee flesh, Ghanaian soil, patrilineality and an ambivalent territorial identification all circulate in Ibrahim's imagined return to Ghana under the cover of death's darkness. It is a fantasy shorn of the immediate constraints of economic resources and uneven claims to citizenship. It is a burial plan and a site of future welcoming and hospitality that is fleshy, earthy and imaginative. Speech acts are always uncertain. They can do things – like name ships or turn a relationship into a marriage – but only if the conditions are right to help them get 'uptake'. Ibrahim's morbid umbilicus of a speech act extending between father and son is the wispy breathless desire of a marginal citizen. It is especially tenuous. It can only be hoped for, and dreamed of, rather than assumed or relied upon.

From graves to monuments, archives, rituals, stories and dreams the dead live on – continuing to commune with the living, sometimes nurturing them and the natality of an unknown future.[16] 'Like human dwelling, the afterlife needs places to take place in' Robert Pogue Harrison concludes. 'If humans dwell, the dead, as it were indwell – and very often in the same space.'[17] Ibrahim's place of hospitality and a homecoming to come, for a child that has yet to feel the soil of this home between his toes, is one which rests upon and exceeds Ghanaian territory and tradition. It is a place in the sense of Plato's chora. A realm of future encountering, a web of coordinates and organic metaphors. 'Not at all a determined place, which would be a topos' Peter Van Wyck reminds us of chorographic place-making 'but a manner of *spacing* in which things may come to take place'.[18]

Ibrahim could not be buried in Ghana because his partner did not have the money for the repatriation of his body and the burial costs. But I do not know how the story of this fragile, spirited hospitality will end. I imagine that Ibrahim's son has some inkling. I hope so.

> Love insists upon making a . . . leap over death . . . because the beloved constitutes the most particular and differentiated image of which the human imagination is capable. Every hair of your head.[19]

Geese[20]

It happens every time.
We wonder about the geese
on our drive to work –
        passing the ferry
or slowing amongst the fields
of water and reeds –

and they come
        out of nowhere
resuming the game they will make
of distance.

It's reassuring then
        to think
that anything could be
so punctual and loud
their voices splashing in the sky
above us
        and the bodies surging on
towards the light.

In school
        we were taught to admire
the homing instinct
        animate and sharp
        behind the eyes
ignoring this vast delight
        this useless motion.

I'd think of them gorged on savannah
        or native corn
an African heat laid down
        in the well-oiled feathers
or mingling with salt and berries
        in the blood.

I'd think of tundra
　　birchwoods under snow
hectares of lake and ozone
　　and the odd
glimmer of random light
amongst the trees

but I couldn't imagine the maps
by which they travelled:
　　miles of surface
etched into the brain's
　　wet geometry.

I couldn't imagine
　　the pull and sway of home
unless it was play they intended:
　　that no good reason
of purposed joy.

Round here
　　they mostly arrive
in sixes and sevens
dropping to rest for a time
　　at the edge of the firth
then moving on

　　but once
in the first grey of morning
　　travelling north
I saw them in their hundreds:
　　one broad
wave of black and white
　　the motion
verging on standstill.

I parked the car
　　and stepped out
to the rush of it:

a rhythm I had waited years
to feel in the meat of my spine
    and the bones of my face

and a long time after they passed
I could feel it still:
not what my teachers had seen
    that mechanical
flicker of instinct
nothing magnetic
    no skill
and no sense of direction

but homing
    in the purer urgency
of elsewhere
    which is nothing like the mind's
intended space
    but how the flesh belongs.

John Burnside

Appendix: Research and Methods

The stories in this book have come out of encounters and relationships – interviews, ethnographic observation and anecdodes – drawn mainly from a hospice ethnography and a narrative-based project called 'Stories That Matter' run by the voluntary organization *Priae* (The Policy Research Institute in Ageing and Ethnicity). I have also drawn upon my teaching experiences in palliative care and from my membership of various working groups in palliative care organizations.

Th hospice ethnography was a three-year doctoral research study that began in 1995.[1] I had started off trying to research and compare two sites: a hospice and a local teaching hospital. I spent one-day a week for six months accompanying two Macmillan nurses at the hospital. I also carried out five group interviews with doctors and nurses there. I had wanted to interview patients, but towards the end of my fieldwork I had conducted only four interviews and there were few people from ethnically minoritized groups on the nurses' case load at the time. With the advice of the nurses I decided to focus upon the hospice ethnography.

The ethnography entailed hundreds of hours of being in the hospice and accompanying nurses on visits in the community. I spent three months observing two different home-care teams. I also volunteered in the hospice day centre for six months, working one day a week, helping with a pottery class, making and serving drinks and food, talking to patients and cleaning-up. Whatever it was that I was doing, I made notes everyday of my observations, experiences and feelings. I also organized what I called 'emotions in fieldwork' supervision sessions with Colin Murry Parkes, a psychiatrist and global expert in grief and loss, who had worked with Cicely Saunders in the early days of the hospice movement. We met every six weeks or so during my fieldwork, and the sessions became a space for me to explore my feelings, dilemmas and thoughts. Each session was tape-recorded and transcribed, becoming integrated as a part of the study's 'data'.

The discussions with Colin were important in recognizing and responding to the emotional demands that I was facing in working with dying and loss. They also provided a novel approach to reflexivity in research, as a practice which aims to interrogate how tacit assumptions and one's own social positioning can affect the research process. A shortcoming of reflexivity, is that lone researchers, or indeed research teams, have vested interests and unconscious biases that can lead to blind-spots and collusive tendencies. It is a predicament of modern knowledge production that the philosopher Michel Foucault saw metaphorized in Diego Velázquez's painting *Las Meninas* (painted in 1656), that plays with ideas about perspective and the relationship between inside/outside.[2] For Foucault, one of the questions posed by *Las Meninas* is whether it is possible to be both inside (subjectively involved) and outside (distant and objective) a social scene, or in Foucauldian terms, a power-knowledge nexus.

A difficulty with critical reflection in research or for care practitioners is its superficial interpretation. Describing and thinking about what you have done, or how you felt at the time, so often becomes an easy stand-in for critical reflective practice. It fails to engage with what we cannot see, or worse still how we negate other experiences by incorporating them into our own experience and viewpoints. 'Any purely reflexive discourse runs the risk of leading the experience of the outside back to the dimension of interiority' Foucault argues, continuing

> reflection tends irresistibly to repatriate it to the side of consciousness . . . it risks setting down readymade meanings that stitch the old fabric of interiority back together in the form of an imagined outside.[3]

Opening up the research process to those who are independent from the research and who also bring with them very different worldviews is something that I found valauble in helping to question and contest my interpretations. Towards the end of the hospice research, I also experimented with setting up a 'talking wall' type installation in the hospice, where I summarized and displayed key findings, together with blank sheets of paper where responses to the research could be recorded.

The hospice study involved: 33 interviews with 23 patients; migrants mainly from South Asia, Africa and the Caribbean; and 14 group interviews with 38 members of staff. Five of these discussion groups were held with three white women social workers over a 12-month period, giving me a deeper insight into the quotidian unfolding of hospice life. All of the hospice interviews were in English, tape-recorded and fully transcribed by me.

When I began the research I knew nothing about narrative methods and was nudged towards them by the patients that I was interviewing. After listening to the first of my five pilot, semi-structured interviews, I realized that my interview schedule was being skilfully by-passed. I was being given wide-ranging biographical narratives. Following some haphazard discoveries of literature and training in the Biographical Narrative Interpretive Method,[4] I moved towards a more open, non-directive approach and this is what I used in the *Stories that Matter* project. The basic idea in biographical narrative interviewing is to start with an open question, some variation of 'Tell me about the story of your life' or as I phrased it more narrowly 'Tell me something about yourself and your experiences of illness and care'. After this first question, the interviewer listens, noting down in chronological order the topics as they are narrated, asking for more narrative about each topic and in the order in which they were raised, but only after the initial freely-associated narrative has been completed.[5]

The single most important lesson that I have learned as an interviewer is that in order to elicit narrative and stories you need to ask narrative-inducing questions. These are open 'Do you remember what happened?' type questions, rather than questions that ask directly for opinion, rationalization or feelings. This is because opinions and rationalized accounts of behaviour or emotions can be constrained by what is felt to be socially acceptable or desirable. Some people can find questions about what they think or feel threatening. Opinions are also often pre-formulated and rehearsed, providing insight into autobiographical theory but remaining somewhat distant from experience.

I now see the role of the interviewer, in similar ways to Pierre Bourdieu,[6] as a midwife to narrative, with questions and attentiveness helping and coaxing a fragile narrative into the world.

My hospice study was followed by three other related projects:

1. 'Stories That Matter' – a narrative project for the Policy Research Institute on Ageing and Ethnicity, with 'minority ethnic' elders and carers, and health and social care professionals in cities in England (2003–7).[7]
2. 'The Listening Study' – on patient priorities for cancer research in the United Kingdom using focus group and nominal group techniques for Macmillan Cancer Support (2004–6).[8]
3. 'Involving people of diverse ethnicities in cancer research' – a project using semi-structured and narrative interviews with patients and research nurses in England for Macmillan Cancer Support (2008–10).[9]

All of these three projects have contributed to the writing of this book, especially the narrative interviews in the *Stories That Matter* project. The project involved

33 interviews with elders and carers from racialized minorities and 11 group interviews with 56 health and social care professionals in London, Berkshire, Bradford, Hertfordshire, Nottingham and Leicester. The older people and carers who were interviewed came from a range of ethnic and cultural backgrounds (broadly speaking South Asian, African, Caribbean, Portuguese and Chinese). Fifteen interviews were conducted in English and 17 in the preferred language of the older person/carer. Twelve of the interviews conducted in a language other than English were conducted through an interpreter (Cantonese, Portuguese, Gujarati, Hinkoo). The remaining five interviews were done in Hindi, Punjabi and Urdu by the project worker, Neera Deepak. All of the interviews were audio-recorded (expect for one spontaneous and elder-initiated telephone interview with his daughter) and transcribed verbatim by an external transcriber.

There is certainly a difference between what people tell you in interviews and what you can take in when you see them interacting with others or in their home environments *au naturel*, with a grandchild clamped onto a waist, an aroma of spices in the air or neighbours popping in and out for a chat and a spliff. And there is always more going on in interviews than what is being said. Contrary valences and nuances can be conveyed in the tonality of a voice, gestures and switches to dialect. And because most of the interviews took place in homes – and in the case of professionals, in the institutions in which they worked – I was able to see localities, kitchens, bathrooms, institutional cultures and architecture. So as an ethnographer I am not entirely convinced or happy about the often derogatory differentiations that are made between ethnography and interviews (where ethnography is always superior), or the claims that ethnography is 'naturalistic' and interviews are not. It very much depends on what sort of ethnography and what sort of interviews you are doing.

Stories, writing, care

The writer and environmental activist Arundhati Roy describes the relationship between stories and human life as a zone of contact where the forces of volition and choice can flow in unconventional directions 'a kind of reverse colonization' as Avery Gordon might describe it.[10] Although 'Writers imagine that they cull stories from the world' Roy asserts,

> I'm beginning to believe that vanity makes them think so. That it's actually the other way around. Stories cull writers from the world. Stories reveal themselves

to us. The public narrative, the private narrative – they colonize us. They commission us. They insist on being told.[11]

Roy's poetic observation is not the hyperbole of the artist. Can we not also think of the objects, events, sights, sounds, tastes and smells that we encounter in research (and in life) in this way? Research 'materials' as much as stories can animate and inhabit us. At times they seem to choose us and carry us away with them, revealing their demands and messages at a pace that has little respect for place or mechanical clock time, for whether you are waiting at a bus stop or trying to meet a book deadline.

For Arthur Frank, stories are our companion species. 'Stories work with people, for people, and always stories work *on* people' Frank writes in his book *Letting Stories Breathe*.[12] Yet the way in which stories (read also research materials) work on us, their power over us, is not as one-sided as Arundhati Roy would seem to suggest. The power of stories in the jargon of the social sciences is said to be 'relational'. The meanings and impacts that a story has on those who participate in it and receive it are a part of continually moving properties, energies and connections. Mariam Motamedi Fraser makes this point so clearly with regard to stories as research methods, materials and as relationships, 'for what are methods, after all, but different modes of relating?' she asks.[13] What is so valuable in these discussions of the relationality of stories and research methods is the restoring of vitality to research and to writing.

Trying to understand, write and assemble the stories that I have gathered here has been slow. Very, very slow. I have produced academic articles along the way. I have also written poems and short stories. And all the while I have found myself returning time and again to the same materials, re-reading transcripts and fieldnotes, listening to the recordings of interviews, picking up sensory clues that I had missed before, understanding the research materials in new ways as my life and thinking changed. There is also something specific in all of this about working with people at the end of their lives and who are often in pain.

I interviewed Ibrahim, a 46-year-old Ghanaian refugee with kidney cancer in his hospice bed, ten days before he died (see Sweet Chariot). Ibrahim's pain filled-up the room, pushing itself under the skin of the interview. There were the frequent recuperative pauses that he took when speaking. The restless shifting of his body as he tried to find a comfortable position, the rhythmic whirring of a syringe driver delivering his morphine. All of these sounds burrowed into the audio-record of our conversation that I would return to, layering more detail into the transcript of the interview that is heavily punctured by ellipses – [. . .] – the transcription code used for pauses. Was that a spasm of pain in the rise and fall of his intonation? Why does that sentence trail off? What was that half-formed word?

During the interview I became increasingly unsure of how to tell the difference between ordinary bodily movements and pain-relieving adjustments. Even the smallest, most innocuous of movements unnerved me.

Do you want to lie down at all?

No it's all right, I am just lifting my leg away.

And then shortly before I took the decision to end the interview there were two more variations on the following type of exchange,

You seem to be in a bit of discomfort now though is it –?

No.

No? You're OK?

If I am, I will let you know.

But would he let me know? At what point would that be? And what sort of pain were we talking about? How to carry on talking and listening when pain is evident but someone wants to carry on with an interview and to tell you their story? How to write a story that is true to the amiguities of sensuality and spirit and to what cannot be known? 'Undecidability . . . names the condition of impossibility that underwrites decisive action', the geographer Clive Barnett has explained of Jacques Derrida's use of the term '. . . in the sense that what is impossible is founding action on a saturation of knowledge'.[14] Working with the undecidable is what ethics in research and in writing has come to mean for me.

Ethics is not only about what we do (and what we fail to do). It is also about the timing of what we do. It is about responding to and negotiating two distinct but related times: the compelling urgency of acting in the now together with a patient respect and openness to a future that can never be adequately known or planned for, but must still be cared for and oriented to.

This long-drawn-out time of thinking, digesting, being acted upon and hesitant writing, concerns situations and qualities that I think are a trans-methodological excess – a surplus value reaching beyond what any method was designed and intended for. By 'situation' I mean something that happens during research (and in everyday life) that has a punctal[15] quality, a piercing donated by convention that alters the ebb and flow of the routinized processes of research – the question-putting, the listening, the transcribing, the writing-up. A situation is a disturbance that reminds you of, or reaffirms, the indeterminacy of life and meaning. It is space of chora: enigmatic, provocative, generative, spirited.

Despite rigorous, sometimes arduous methodological training, we cannot control or prepare for how such situations will unfurl or makes themselves felt. They can be immediate, such as in those real-time electric intensities in an interview or interaction. They can also accrue and emerge much later as ghostly disturbances, where despite concerted effort and collaborations, a story or event continues to elude and trouble interpretation and analysis. It just keeps coming back, wanting more. It says 'I'm not finished with you yet'.

I have taken to calling this strange unsettlement and *longue durée* of understanding and writing 'vital time'; my colleague Nirmal Puwar in one of her profound, off-the-cuff comments has called it a 'In your own time'. It is a temporality that breaches linear clock time and far exceeds the research cycle that is timetabled and funded accordingly. It incites thinking about how creativity inheres in life and in research materials themselves.[16]

The voluptuous curly Sinhalese alphabet is an example of what I am talking about, about how materials can cultivate and draw out thinking and writing. Michael Ondaatje

> I still believe the most beautiful alphabet was created by the Sinhalese. The insect of ink curves into a shape that is almost sickle, spoon, eyelid. The letters are washed blunt glass which betray no jaggedness. Sanskrit was governed by verticles, but its sharp grid features were not possible in Ceylon. Here the Ola leaves which people wrote on were too brittle. A straight line would cut apart the leaf and so a curling alphabet was derived from its Indian cousin.[17]

I started off writing this with stories and methods in mind and I have found myself thinking about good care in this way, as being pulled and inspired by the bodies, objects and spaces that it encounters. I hope that this movement between what is good care and what is good research and writing flows throughout the book.

Notes

Preface

1 Pierre Bourdieu, *The Weight of the World: Social Suffering in Contemporary Society*, 1st edn (Cambridge: Polity, 1999), 4.

2 Joy Melville, *St Christopher's Hosipce* (London: Together Publishing Company, 1990), 54.

3 Maureen Mackintosh, Parvati Raghuram and Leroi Henry, 'A Perverse Subsidy: African Trained Nurses and Doctors in the NHS', *Soundings* no. 34 (2006): 103–13.

4 Alan Maynard and Arthur Walker, Doctor Manpower 1975–2000: Alternative Forecasts and Their Resource Implications. In *The Royal Commission on the National Health Service, Research Paper Number 4* (London: Her Majesty's Stationary Office, 1974).

5 Edward Sissman, *Night Music: Poems* (New York: Houghton Mifflin Harcourt, 1999), 57.

6 Veena Das, *Life and Words: Violence and the Descent into the Ordinary* (Berkeley and London: University of California Press, 2007), 2.

7 Arundhati Roy, 'Come September', *Tamilnation.org*, 18 September 2002, http://tamilnation.co/intframe/roy/arundhati1.htm

Chapter 1: Death and the Migrant – An Introduction

1 Jacques Derrida, *Aporias: Dying – Awaiting (One Another at) the 'Limits of Truth'*, trans. Thomas Dutoit (Stanford, CA: Stanford University Press, 1993).

2 Christopher Bollas, 'Introducing Edward Said', in *Freud: And the Non-European* (New York and London: Verso Books, 2003), 8.

3 Mustafa Dikeç, Nigel Clark and Clive Barnett, 'Extending Hospitality: Giving Space, Taking Time', *Paragraph* 32, no. 1 (March 2009): 11.

4 Claus Leggewie, 'Transnational Citizenship: Ideals and European Realities', *Eurozine*, 3 April 2013, www.eurozine.com/articles/2013-02-19-leggewie-en.html

5 James Clifford, *Routes: Travel and Translation in the Later Twentieth Century.* (Cambridge: Harvard University Press, 1997).

6 Novalis quoted in Friedrich Heiler, *Prayer: A Study in the History and Psychology of Religion* (London: Oxford University Press, 1932), viii.

7   Charles Hirschkind, *The Ethical Soundscape: Cassette Sermons and Islamic Counterpublics* (New York: Columbia University Press, 2006).

8   Emma White, 2011 Census: Key Statistics for England and Wales, March 2011, *Office for National Statistics*, 11 December 2012, www.ons.gov.uk/ons/rel/census/2011-census/key-statistics-for-local-authorities-in-england-and-wales/stb-2011-census-key-statistics-for-england-and-wales.html#tab - -Provision-of-unpaid-care

9   Pierre Bourdieu, *The Logic of Practice* (Cambridge: Polity, 1990).

10 Gilles Deleuze, 'Ethology: Spinoza and Us', in *Incorporations*, ed. Jonathan Crary and Sanford Kwinter, trans. Robert Hurley (New York: Zone, 1992), 624–33, 626.

11 Nirmal Puwar, 'Aaj Kaal (Yesterday, Today, Tomorrow)', *Darkmatter, in the Ruins of Imperial Culture*, 3 April 2012, www.darkmatter101.org/site/2012/04/03/aaj-kaal-yesterday-today-tomorrow-video/

12 Yasmin Gunaratnam, *Call for Care* (London: Health Education Authority, 1991).

13 Nirmal Puwar, 'Mediations on Making Aaj Kaal', *Feminist Review* 100, no. 1 (March 2012): 136, doi:10.1057/fr.2011.70

14 Ibid., 137.

15 Bridget Anderson, *Us and Them: The Dangerous Politics of Immigration Control* (Oxford: Oxford University Press, 2013).

16 See Eithne Luibhéid, *Queer/Migration* (Durham and London: Duke University Press, 2008).

17 Rutvica Andrijasevic, 'Sex on the Move: Gender, Subjectivity and Differential Inclusion', *Subjectivity* 29, no. 1 (December 2009): 389–406, 403.

18 See 'Women Try to Take Body on Plane', *BBC*, 6 April 2010, sec. England, http://news.bbc.co.uk/1/hi/england/8604663.stm

19 John Berger and Jean Mohr, *A Seventh Man*, 2nd edn (London and New York: Verso, 2010), 11.

20 United Nations Department of Economic and Social Affairs Population Division, *Trends in International Migration Stock: Migrants by Age and Sex* (United Nations database, POP/DB/MIG/Stock/Rev.2010, 2011).

21 Berger and Mohr, *A Seventh Man*, 68.

22 Carlos Vargas-Silva, *Global International Migrant Stock: The UK in International Comparison. Migration Observatory Briefing* (Oxford: COMPAS, University of Oxford, UK, March 2011), http://migrationobservatory.ox.ac.uk/briefings/global-international-migrant-stock-uk-international-comparison

23 Cinzia Rienzo, *Migrants in the UK Labour Market: And Overview. Migration Observatory Briefing* (Oxford: COMPAS, the Migration Observatory at the University of Oxford, 2012), http://migrationobservatory.ox.ac.uk/briefings/migrants-uk-labour-market-overview

24 Jacques Derrida and Anne Dufourmantelle, *Of Hospitality* (Stanford, CA: Stanford University Press, 2000).

25 Alphonso Lingis, *The Community of Those Who Have Nothing in Common* (Bloomington: Indiana University Press, 1994), 12.

26 The Lancet, 'Migrant Health: What Are Doctors' Leaders Doing?' *The Lancet* 371 (19 January 2008): 178.

27 Will Ross, 'Sent Home, Abandoned and Saved in Ghana', *BBC*, 17 January 2008, sec. From Our Own Correspondent, http://news.bbc.co.uk/1/hi/programmes/from_our_own_correspondent/7193366.stm

28 Edward Mills, Steve Kanters, Amy Hagopian, Nick Bansback, Jean Nachega, Mark Alberton, Christopher G Au-Yeung, Andy Mtambo, Ivy L Bourgeault, Samuel Luboga, Robert Hogg and Nathan Ford, 'The Financial Cost of Doctors Emigrating from sub-Saharan Africa: Human Capital Analysis', *BMJ* 343 (November 24, 2011): d7031–d7031, doi:10.1136/bmj.d7031.

29 Médecins du monde, *Access to Health Care for Vulnerable Groups in the European Union in 2012: An Overview of the Condition of Persons Excluded from Healthcare Systems in the EU* (Médecins du monde, 2012), 16, www.medecinsdumonde.org/…/european_advocacy_paper_pd

30 'Maternal Mortality Across the World', *BBC*, 26 October 2009, sec. Africa, http://news.bbc.co.uk/1/hi/world/africa/8320781.stm

31 Franklin Oikelome, *The Recruitment and Retention of Black and Minority Ethnic Staff in the National Health Service* (London: Race Equality Foundation, 2007).

32 Jasbir K. Puar, 'Prognosis Time: Towards a Geopolitics of Affect, Debility and Capacity', *Women & Performance: a Journal of Feminist Theory* 19, no. 2 (July 2009): 166, doi:10.1080/07407700903034147.

33 Thomas Lynch, Stephen Connor and David Clark, 'Mapping Levels of Palliative Care Development: A Global Update', *Journal of Pain and Symptom Management* (24 September 2012), doi:10.1016/j.jpainsymman.2012.05.011, 14.

34 John Berger, 'Foreword', in *The Algebra of Infinite Justice*, Arundhati Roy, 5th edn (London: Flamingo, 2002), xiii–xxi.

35 Sarah Lochlann Jain, 'Living in Prognosis: Toward an Elegiac Politics', *Representations* 98, no. 1 (May 2007): 77–92, doi:10.1525/rep.2007.98.1.77.

36 Ibid., 85.

37 Julie Livingston, *Improvising Medicine: An African Oncology Ward in an Emerging Cancer Epidemic*, 1st edn (Durham and London: Duke University Press, 2012).

38 Ibid., 7.

39 *WHO. Ensuring Balance in National Policies on Controlled Substances* (Geneva: World Health Organization, 2011).

40 European Association of Palliative Care, Regulatory Barriers to Access and Availability of Opioids for the Management of Cancer Pain, 29 September 2012,

www.eapcnet.eu/Themes/Policy/Opioidaccessibilitysurvey/Untreatedcancerpain. aspx See also Human Rights Watch and Diederik Lohman, '*Please, Do Not Make Us Suffer Any More-*': *Access to Pain Treatment As a Human Right* (New York: Human Rights Watch, 2009).

41 Pain and Policy Group, Opiod consumption data, 2010, www.painpolicy.wisc.edu/global

42 Help the Hospices, *Hospice and Palliative Care Directory 2011–2012* (London: Help the Hospices, 2011).

43 World Health Organization, *WHO Definition of Palliative Care* (Geneva: World Health Organization, 2010).

44 Jacques Ranciere, *The Politics of Aesthetics*, trans. Gabriel Rockhill (New York and London: Continuum International Publishing Group, 2006).

45 Julia Kristeva, *Revolution in Poetic Language* (New York: Columbia University Press, 1984), 26.

46 Peter Van Wyck, *The Highway of the Atom* (Montreal, Kingston, London and Ithaca: McGill-Queen's University Press, 2010), 136.

47 Gregory L. Ulmer, *Heuretics: The Logic of Invention* (Baltimore and London: JHU Press, 1994), 67.

48 Martin Heidegger, *Being and Time*, trans. John Macquarrie and Edward Robinson, new edn (Oxford: Wiley-Blackwell, 1978). See also Graham Harman, *The Quadruple Object* (Winchester UK: Zero books).

49 David Clark, 'Wither the Hospices?' in *The Future of Palliative Care*, ed. David Clark (Buckingham: Open University Press, 1993).

50 Dawn Hill and Dawn Penso, *Opening Doors: Improving Access to Hospice and Specialist Palliative Care Services by Members of the Black and Ethnic Minority Communities* (London: National Council for Hospice and Specialist Palliative Care Services, 1995).

51 Mirca Madianou and Daniel Miller, 'Polymedia: Towards a New Theory of Digital Media in Interpersonal Communication', *International Journal of Cultural Studies* 16, no. 2 (1 March 2013): 169–87.

52 Eleonore Kofman and Parvati Raghuram, *The Implications of Migration for Gender and Care Regimes in the South* (Geneva: UNRISD, 2009), www.unrisd.org/80256B3 C005BCCF9/%28httpPublications%29/9C17B4815B7656B0C125761C002E9283?O penDocument

53 Nari Rhee and Carol Zabin, 'Aggregating Dispersed Workers: Union Organizing in the "care" Industries', *Geoforum* 40, no. 6 (November 2009): 969–79, doi:10.1016/j. geoforum.2009.08.006.

54 Carol Wolkowitz, *Bodies at Work* (London: Sage, 2006).

55 Libby Sallnow, Suresh Kumar and Allan Kellehear (eds), *International Perspectives on Public Health and Palliative Care*, 1st edn (London: Routledge, 2011).

56 Libby Sallnow, Suresh Kumar and Mathews Numpeli, 'Home-based Palliative Care in Kerala, India: The Neighbourhood Network in Palliative Care', *Progress in Palliative Care* 18, no. 1 (2010): 14–17.

57 Suresh Kumar and Mathews Numpeli, 'Neighborhood Network in Palliative Care', *Indian Journal of Palliative Care* 11, no. 1 (2005): 6.

58 Charles Leadbeater and Jake Garber, *Dying for Change* (London: Demos, 2010), www.demos.co.uk/publications/dyingforchange/

59 Zygmunt Bauman, *Liquid Modernity* (Cambridge: Polity, 2000), 184.

60 Tony Walter, Rashid Hourizi, Wendy Moncur and Stacy Pitsillides, 'Does the Internet Change How We Die and Mourn? Overview and Analysis', *Omega (Westport)* 64, no. 4 (1 January 2011): 275–302.

61 Stacey Pitsillides, Janis Jefferies and Martin Conreen, 'Museum of the Self and Digital Death: An Emerging Curatorial Dilemma for Digital Heritage', in *Heritage and Social Media: Understanding Heritage in a Participatory Culture*, ed. Elisa Giaccardi (New York: Routledge, 2012), 56–68.

62 Margrit Shildrick and Janet Price, 'Deleuzian Connections and Queer Corporealities: Shrinking Global Disability', *Rhizomes* 11/12 (Spring 2006), www.rhizomes.net/issue11/shildrickprice/index.html

Chapter 2: Eros

1 Melville, *St Christopher's Hospice*, 54.

2 Stephen Verderber and Ben J. Refuerzo, *Hospice Architecture* (Oxford and New York: Taylor and Francis, 2006).

3 Mary Bains, Why Practice in a Hospice? Personal Communication, 23 May 2012.

4 Cicely Saunders, A Personal Therapeutic Journey, *BMJ* 313, no. 7072 (21 December 1996): 1599–1601, doi:10.1136/bmj.313.7072.1599.

5 Cicely Saunders, The Evolution of the Hospices, in *The History of the Management of Pain: From Early Principles to Present Practice. The Proceedings of a Conference Organised by the Section of the History of Medicine of the Royal Society of Medicine, London*, ed. Ronald Mann (Carnforth: Parthenon Publishing Group, 1988), 20.

6 Melville, *St Christopher's Hospice*, 55.

7 Ibid., 54.

8 Mica Nava, *Visceral Cosmopolitanism: Gender, Culture and the Normalisation of Difference*, 1st edn (Oxford and New York: Berg Publishers, 2007).

9 Gordon Brown, *Courage: Eight Portraits*, 1st edn (London: Bloomsbury Publishing, 2007), 180.

10 Karen Armstrong, *The Case for God: What Religion Really Means* (London: Bodley Head, 2009).

11 Rachel Lichtenstein and Iain Sinclair, *Rodinsky's Room*, new edn (London: Granta Books, 2000), 68.

12 Rajeswari Sunder Rajan, *Real and Imagined Women: Gender, Culture, and Postcolonialism* (London and New York: Routledge, 1993), 6.

13 Mariam Motamedi Fraser, Once Upon a Problem, *The Sociological Review* 60 (2012): 92, doi:10.1111/j.1467–954X.2012.02118.x.

14 Ibid., 88.

15 Jacques Derrida, *Archive Fever: A Freudian Impression* (Chicago and London: University of Chicago Press, 1998).

16 Irit Rogoff, The Exergue – All is Fair in Love and War, Dictionary of War, June 2006–February 2007. http://dictionaryofwar.org/node/415.

17 Derrida, *Archive Fever*.

18 Michel Foucault, *The Archaeology of Knowledge* (Abingdon, Oxon: Routledge, 2002), 27.

19 Amanda Bingley, Carol Thomas, Janice Brown, Joanne Reeve and Sheila Payne Developing Narrative Research in Supportive and Palliative Care: The Focus on Illness Narratives, *Palliative Medicine* 22, no. 5 (2008): 653–8.

20 Light for Cicely, *Light for Cicely*, 2010, www.light-for-cicely.net/

21 Jeni Walwin, *Jeniwalwin*, 2013, www.walwin.co.uk/pastprojects7.html

22 Paul Weindling, *John W. Thompson: Psychiatrist in the Shadow of the Holocaust* (New York: University Rochester Press, 2010), 97.

23 Viktor E. Frankl, *Man's Search For Meaning: The Classic Tribute to Hope from the Holocaust*, trans. Ilse Lasch, new edn (London: Rider, 2004), 60.

24 Robert G. Twycross, *Time to Die* (London: Christian Medical Fellowship, 1984), 19.

25 Brown, *Courage*, 179.

26 Ibid., 182.

27 Lichtenstein and Sinclair, '*Rodinsky's Room*', 68.

28 David Clark, Neil Small, Michael Wright, Michelle Winslow and Nic Hughes, *A Bit of Heaven for the Few?: An Oral History of the Modern Hospice Movement in the United Kingdom* (Observatory Publications, 2005), 19.

29 Alessandro Portelli, *The Death of Luigi Trastulli, and Other Stories: Form and Meaning in Oral History* (New York: SUNY Press, 1991), 2.

30 Shirley Du Boulay, *Cicely Saunders*, new edn (London: Hodder & Stoughton Religious, 1987), 57.

31 Carolyn Steedman, *Dust* (Manchester and New York: Manchester University Press, 2001).

32 Cicely Saunders, David Tasma, *Hospice Information Bulletin* (2004): 6.

33 Hannah Arendt, 'Introduction – Walter Benjamin 1892–1940', in *Illuminations*, trans. Harry Zorn, new edn (London: Pimlico, 1999), 7–55.

34 Saunders, David Tasma.

35 Roland Barthes, *Camera Lucida: Reflections on Photography*, trans Richard Howard new edn (London: Vintage Classics, 2000).

36 Nela Milic, *Balkanising Taxonomy*, 2008, www.goldsmiths.ac.uk/balkanising-taxonomy/

37 Nirmal Puwar, 'Im/possible Inhabitations', in *The Situated Politics of Belonging*, ed. Nira Yuval-Davis, Kalpana Kannabiran and Ulrike Vieten (London: Sage, 2006), 82.

38 Saunders, David Tasma, 6.

39 Boulay, *Cicely Saunders*, 56.

40 Bonnie Honig, *Democracy and the Foreigner* (Princeton, NJ: Princeton University Press, 2001).

41 Arthur Frank, *The Wounded Storyteller: Body, Illness, and Ethics* (Chicago: University of Chicago Press, 1997), 98.

42 Alphonso Lingis, *Trust* (Minneapolis, MN: University of Minnesota Press, 2004), 64.

43 Robert Pogue Harrison, *The Dominion of the Dead* (Chicago and London: University of Chicago Press, 2003).

44 Ibid., x.

Chapter 3: Thanatos

1 Edith Wyschogrod, *Saints and Postmodernism: Revisioning Moral Philosophy* (Chicago and London: University of Chicago Press, 1990).

Chapter 4: A Catch

1 Thomas J Csordas, Intersubjectivity and Intercorporeality, *Subjectivity* 22, no. 1 (May 2008): 114, doi:10.1057/sub.2008.5.

2 Trinh T. Minh-ha, *Reassemblage*, 1982, www.ced.berkeley.edu/faculty/bourdier/trinh/TTMHFilmRE.htm

3 Doreen Massey, *For Space* (London, Thousand Oaks, CA and New Delhi: Sage Publications, 2005), 140.

4 Marilyn Frye, *Politics of Reality: Essays in Feminist Theory* (Trumansburg, NY: Crossing Press, 1983), 2, cited in Ahmed, 2010, 66.

5 Sara Ahmed, *The Promise of Happiness* (Durham and London: Duke University Press, 2010).

6 Gary Sibbald, Diane Krasner and James Lutz, 'Tip the SCALE Toward Quality End-of-life Skin Care', *Nursing Management (Springhouse)* 42, no. 3 (March 2011): 24–32, doi:10.1097/01.NUMA.0000394052.84595.dc.

7   Frantz Fanon, *Black Skin, White Masks*, 2nd edn (London: Pluto, 1986), 60.

8   Ahmed, *The Promise of Happiness*, 84.

9   Suzanne Hall, *City, Street and Citizen: The Measure of the Ordinary* (London and New York: Routledge, 2012), 5.

10 See Alex Rhys-Taylor's ethnography of East End Markets for an innovative approach to the sensuality of multicultural life. *Coming to Our Senses: A Multi-sensory Ethnography of Class and Multiculture in East London*. Doctoral thesis, Goldsmiths, University of London, http://eprints.gold.ac.uk/3226/

11 Kramer Ann, *Many Rivers to Cross: Caribbean People in the NHS 1948–69* (London: The Stationery Office, 2006), 1. The book and Website Many Rivers to Cross include oral history accounts from Caribbean people who have worked for the NHS, including those who worked as auxiliary nurses.

12 George Mavrommatis, 'A Racial Archaeology of Space: A Journey Through the Political Imaginings of Brixton and Brick Lane, London,' *Journal of Ethnic and Migration Studies* 36, no. 4 (April 2010): 561–79.

13 Macmillan Cancer Support, Common Questions About Macmillan Nurses Document, January 2013, www.macmillan.org.uk/HowWeCanHelp/Nurses/YourQuestions.aspx

14 Ague, 2012, http://en.wiktionary.org/wiki/ague1. Ague is a Middle English word for fever. Thanks to Suzanne Scafe for helping me to identify the possible origins and the meanings of this word.

15 Elisabeth Grosz, *Chaos, Territory, Art: Deleuze and the Framing of the Earth* (New York: Columbia University Press, 2008).

Chapter 5: Never Mind

1   Michel Serres, *The Troubadour of Knowledge*, trans. Sheila Faria Glaser and William Paulson (Ann Arbor: University of Michigan Press, 1997), 15.

2   Ibid., 3.

3   See the photo stories Bedside Archaeology on the Website *After Cicely* http://aftercicely.com/photo-stories-bedside-archaeology

4   Allan Kellehear, Edwin Pugh and Lynda Atter, 'Home Away from Home? A Case Study of Bedside Objects in a Hospice,' *International Journal of Palliative Nursing* 15, no. 3 (1 March 2009): 148.

5   Kathryn Linn Geurts, *Culture and the Senses: Bodily Ways of Knowing in an African Community* (Berkeley, CA: University of California Press, 2003).

6   Didier Anzieu, *The Skin Ego* (New Haven: Yale University Press, 1989).

7   Julia Lawton, *The Dying Process: Patients' Experiences of Palliative Care* (London: Routledge, 2000).

8   Bruno Latour, 'How to Talk About the Body? The Normative Dimension
    of Science Studies', *Body & Society* 10, no. 2–3 (1 June 2004): 7,
    doi:10.1177/1357034X04042943.

9   Jamaica Kincaid, *A Small Place* (New York: Farrar, Straus and Giroux, 2000), 34.

10 Ibid., 30.

11 Paul Virilio, *Open Sky*, trans. Julie Rose (London: Verso, 1997).

12 Julia Lawton, 'Contemporary Hospice Care: The Sequestration of the Unbounded
    Body and "Dirty Dying"', *Sociology of Health & Illness* 20, no. 2 (1998): 134,
    doi:10.1111/1467-9566.00094.

13 Hideto Sonoda, Shunji Kohnoe, Tetsuro Yamazato, Yuji Satoh, Gouki Morizono,
    Kentaro Shikata, Makoto Morita, Akihiro Watanabe, Masaru Morita, Yoshihiro
    Kakeji, Fumio Inoue and Yoshihiko Maehara, 'Colorectal Cancer Screening with
    Odour Material by Canine Scent Detection', *Gut* 60, no. 6 (June 2011): 814–19,
    doi:10.1136/gut.2010.218305.

14 see Alison Fairlie, *Baudelaire: Les Fleurs Du Mal* (London: Edward Arnold, 1960).

15 Anna Andreevna Akhmatova, *Twenty Poems*, trans. Jane Keyon (Minneapolis, MN:
    Eighties Press and Ally Press, 1985), 45.

Chapter 6: Dissimulation

1   Health Protection Agency, 'HIV in the United Kingdom: 2011 report', 2011, www.
    hpa.org.uk/Publications/InfectiousDiseases/HIVAndSTIs/1111HIVintheUK2011re
    port/

2   Margaret May, Mark Gompels, Valerie Delpech, Kholoud Porter, Frank Post,
    Margaret Johnson, David Dunn, Adrian Palfreeman, Richard Gilson, Brian
    Gazzard, Teresa Hill, John Walsh, Martin Fisher, Chloe Orkin, Jonathan Ainsworth,
    Loveleen Bansi, Andrew Phillips, Clifford Leen, Mark Nelson, Jane Anderson and
    Caroline Sabin 'Impact of Late Diagnosis and Treatment on Life Expectancy in
    People with HIV-1: UK Collaborative HIV Cohort (UK CHIC) Study', *BMJ* 343, no.
    oct11 2 (11 October 2011): d6016–d6016, doi:10.1136/bmj.d6016.

3   Chimaraoke O Izugbara and Eliud Wekesa, 'Beliefs and Practices about
    Antiretroviral Medication: A Study of Poor Urban Kenyans Living with HIV/AIDS,
    Beliefs and Practices about Antiretroviral Medication: A Study of Poor Urban
    Kenyans Living with HIV/AIDS', *Sociology of Health & Illness, Sociology of Health &
    Illness* 33, no. 6, (4 March 2011): 869–83, 869.

4   World Health Organization | HIV/AIDS, *WHO*, www.who.int/hiv/en/ (accessed
    December 11, 2012).

5   World Health Organization, *WHO | Global Health Sector Strategy on HIV/AIDS
    2011–2015* (Switzerland: World Health Organization, 2011), www.who.int/hiv/pub/
    hiv_strategy/en/index.html

6 Mark Freeman, *Hindsight: The Promise and Peril of Looking Backward*, 1st edn (New York: Oxford University Press, 2009).

7 Dilip Ratha and Ani Silwal, *Remittance Flows in 2011: An Update, Migration and Development Brief 18* (The World Bank, Remittances Unit, 23 April 2012), http://web.worldbank.org/WBSITE/EXTERNAL/TOPICS/0,,contentMDK:21924020~pagePK:5105988~piPK:360975~theSitePK:214971,00.html

8 Barbara Browning, *Infectious Rhythm: Metaphors of Contagion and the Spread of African Culture* (New York and London: Routledge, 1998), 10.

9 *With Antiretroviral Drugs (ARVs), Does HIV Still Matter?* 2008, www.youtube.com/watch?v=oOa08oDhnC4&feature=youtube_gdata_player

10 Marsha Rosengarten, *HIV Interventions: Biomedicine and the Traffic Between Information and Flesh (In Vivo: The Cultural Mediations of Biomedical Science)* (Seattle and London: University of Washington Press, 2009).

11 Norman K. Denzin, *Interpretive Ethnography: Ethnographic Practices for the 21st Century* (Thousand Oaks, CA and London: Sage, 1997), 278.

12 Andreas Lommel, *Prehistoric and Primitive Man* (London: McGraw-Hill, 1966).

13 Mau Mau Massacre Cover-up Detailed in Newly-opened Secret Files, *The Guardian*, 30 November 2012, www.guardian.co.uk/world/2012/nov/30/maumau-massacre-secret-files

14 Donald. W. Winnicott, *Playing and Reality*, 2nd edn (London: Routledge, 2005).

15 Ann Michaels, The Winter Vault (London, Berlin, New York: Bloomsbury, 2010), 183.

Chapter 7: Moving On

1 Paul Connerton, *How Societies Remember* (Cambridge: Cambridge University Press,1989).

2 Helen F. Wilson, 'Passing Propinquities in the Multicultural City: The Everyday Encounters of Bus Passengering', *Environment and Planning A* 43, no. 3 (2011): 634–49.

3 Edward W. Said, *Reflections on Exile: And Other Essays* (Cambridge, MA: Harvard University Press, 2000).

4 The Food Programme, Fasting Old and New, 1 April Radio 4, www.bbc.co.uk/programmes/b01rl1dl

5 Cancer Research UK, 'Myeloma' Document, 30 November 2012, www.cancerresearchuk.org/cancer-help/type/myeloma/

Chapter 8: Music

1 Therese Schroeder-Sheker, 'Music for the Dying: a Personal Account of the New Field of Music-thanatology – History, Theories, and Clinical Narratives', *Journal*

of Holistic Nursing: Official Journal of the American Holistic Nurses' Association 12, no. 1 (March 1994): 90.

2   Ibid., 87.

3   Ibid., 87–8.

4   Gilles Deleuze, *Francis Bacon: The Logic of Sensation*, trans. Daniel. W. Smith (Minneapolis, MN: University of Minnesota Press, 2003), 47.

5   Ching Kung, 'A Possible Unifying Principle for Mechanosensation', *Nature* 436, no. 7051 (4 August 2005): 647, doi:10.1038/nature03896.

6   Margaret Alexiou, *The Ritual Lament in Greek Tradition*, 2nd edn (Cambridge: Cambridge University Press, 2002), 15.

7   Gail Holst-Warhaft, 'Death and the Maiden: Sex, Death, and Women's Laments', in *Women, Pain and Death: Rituals and Everyday Life on the Margins of Europe and Beyond*, ed. Evy Johanne Häland (Newcastle-upon-Tyne: Cambridge Scholars, 2008), 23.

8   The social significance and manipulation of mourning is not consigned to the past. The Essex-based company Rent-a-Mourner, where professional and 'polite' mourners cost about 45 pounds for two hours, states that 'We are typically invited to help increase visitors to funerals where there may be a low turnout expected. This can usually be a popularity issue or being new to an area, or indeed, the country.' 'Rent a Mourner', 2011, www.rentamourner.co.uk/index.html

9   Kathryn Conrad, 'Keening the Nation: The Bean Chaointe, the Sean Bhean Bhocht, and Women's Lament in Irish Nationalist Literature', in *Irish Literature: Feminist Perspectives*, ed. Patricia Coughlan and Tina O'Toole (Dublin: Carysfort Press, 2008), 40–1.

10   Shirley Firth, *Dying, Death and Bereavement in a British Hindu Community* (Bondgenotelaan: Peeters Publishers, 1997).

11   Nirmal Puwar, *Space Invaders: Race, Gender and Bodies Out of Place*, 1st edn (Oxford: Berg Publishers, 2004).

12   Quoted in Melville, *St Christopher's Hosipce*, 55.

13   World Health Organization, *Environmental Health Inequalities in Europe. Assessment Report*, www.euro.who.int/en/what-we-publish/abstracts/environmental-health-inequalities-in-europe.-assessment-report

14   Robert Pogue Harrison, *The Dominion of the Dead* (Chicago and London: University of Chicago Press, 2003).

15   Peter Bailey, 'Breaking the Sound Barrier: A Historian Listens to Noise', *Body and Society* 2, no. 2 (1 June 1996): 49–66.

16   John Kay, Alex Peake and Lynsey Haywood, 'Mosque Call Outrages Oxford', *The Sun*, www.thesun.co.uk/sol/homepage/news/622919/News-Mosque-call-outrages-Oxford-Residents-angered.html

17   'Mosque's Plan to Broadcast Call to Prayer from Loudspeaker "Will Create Muslim Ghetto"', *Mail Online*, www.dailymail.co.uk/news/article-504373/Mosques-plan-broadcast-prayer-loudspeaker-create-Muslim-ghetto.html

18 Kay et al., 'Mosque Call Outrages Oxford'.

19 Nick Cumming-Bruce and Steven Erlanger, 'Swiss Ban Building of Minarets on Mosques', *The New York Times*, 30 November 2009, sec. International/Europe, www.nytimes.com/2009/11/30/world/europe/30swiss.html

20 Étienne Balibar and Immanuel Maurice Wallerstein, *Race, Nation, Class: Ambiguous Identities* (London: Verso, 1991), 21.

21 Rosalyn Diprose, *Corporeal Generosity: On Giving with Nietzsche, Merleau-Ponty, and Levinas*, SUNY Series in Gender Theory (Albany: SUNY Press, 2002), 8.

22 Norbert Elias, *The Civilizing Process: The History of Manners and State Formation and Civilisation*, trans. Edmund Jephcott (Oxford: Blackwell, 1994).

23 Jacques Derrida, *The Gift of Death*, Religion and Postmodernism (Chicago: University of Chicago Press, 1996).

24 Ibid.

25 Melville, *St Christopher's Hosipce*, 54.

26 Schroeder-Sheker, 'Music for the Dying', 84.

27 Corinne May, 'Corrinne May – Angel in Disguise Lyrics', *LetsSingIt*, http://artists.letssingit.com/corrinne-may-lyrics-angel-in-disguise-3s5nf6w#axzz2GunEXMuc

28 Diprose, *Corporeal Generosity*, 12.

Chapter 9: The Prince and the Pee

1 Yasmin Gunaratnam, 'The Bed', in *Relating Experience: Stories from Health and Social Care: An Anthology About Communication and Relationships*, ed. Caroline Malone et al. (London: Routledge, 2004), 120–1.

2 Bertrand Russell, *History of Western Philosophy* (London: Routledge, 2012), 250.

3 Cato Maior De Senectute, *Loeb Classical Library*, 1923, http://penelope.uchicago.edu/Thayer/E/Roman/Texts/Cicero/Cato_Maior_de_Senectute/text*.html

4 Yoav Ben-Shlomo, Simon Evans, Fowzia Ibrahim, Biral Patel, Ken Anson, Frank Chinegwundoh, Cathy Corbishley, Danny Dorling, Bethan Thomas, David Gillatt, Roger Kirby, Gordon Muir, Vinod Nargund, Rick Popert, Chris Metcalf and Raj Persad on behalf of the PROCESS study group, The Risk of Prostate Cancer Amongst Black Men in the United Kingdom: The PROCESS Cohort Study', *European Urology* 53, no. 1 (January 2008): 99–105.

5 BME Cancer Communities, *Hear me Now: The Uncomfortable Reality of Prostate Cancer in Black African-Caribbean Men*, February 2013, www.bmecancer.com/index.php/cancers/prostate-cancer/82-embed-template

6 Brett StLouis, 'Readings Within a Diasporic Boundary: Transatlantic Black Performance and the Poetic Imperative in Sport', in *Un/Settled Multiculturalisms: Diasporas, Entanglement, Transruptions*, ed. Barnor Hesse (Zed Books, 2000), 51–72.

7   Anatole Broyard, 'About Men: Intoxicated by my Illness', 12 November 1989, www.
    nytimes.com/1989/11/12/magazine/about-men-intoxicated-by-my-illness.html

8   Sue Wilkinson and Celia Kitzinger, 'Thinking Differently About Thinking Positive:
    A Discursive Approach to Cancer Patients' Talk', *Social Science & Medicine (1982)*
    50, no. 6 (March 2000): 797–811.

9   Margaret Wetherell and Nigel Edley, 'Negotiating Hegemonic Masculinity:
    Imaginary Positions and Psycho-Discursive Practices', *Feminism & Psychology* 9,
    no. 3 (1 August 1999): 335–56.

10 Steven Dunstan, *General Lifestyle Survey Overview A Report on the 2010 General
    Lifestyle Survey* (London: Office for National Statistics, 2012), www.ons.gov.uk

11 Daniel Miller, *The Comfort of Things* (Cambridge and Malden, MA: Polity, 2008), 7.

12 Ibid., 8.

13 Daniel Miller and Fiona Parrott, 'Loss and Material Culture in South London', in
    Death Rites and Rights, ed. Belinda Brooks-Gordon, Fatemeh Ebtehaj, Jonathan
    Herring, Martin Johnson and Martin Richards (Oxford: Hart Publishing, 2007),
    147–61.

14 Gunaratnam, 'The Bed'.

Chapter 10: Failing, Falling

1   Margaret Clarke, Ilora Finlay and Ian Campbell, 'Cultural Boundaries in Care',
    Palliative Medicine 5, no. 1 (1 January 1991): 63.

2   Ibid., 64.

3   Ibid.

4   Shirley Firth, *Dying, Death and Bereavement in a British Hindu Community*
    (Bondgenotelaan: Peeters Publishers, 1997).

5   Dev Jootun, 'Nursing with Dignity. Part 7: Hinduism', www.nursingtimes.net/
    nursing-with-dignity-part-7-hinduism/206286.article

6   Natalie Evans, Arantza Menaca, Johnathan Koffman, Richard Harding, Irene
    Higginson, Robert Pool, Marjolein Gysels, PRISMA. 'Cultural Competence in
    End-of-Life Care: Terms, Definitions, and Conceptual Models from the British
    Literature', *Journal of Palliative Medicine* 15, no. 7 (July 2012): 812–20.

7   Roger Burrows and Nicholas Gane, 'Geodemographics, Software and Class',
    Sociology 40, no. 5 (1 October 2006): 793–812.

8   Apple, 'CultureGPS', n.d., www.culturegps.com/About.html

9   Yasmin Gunaratnam, 'Cultural Vulnerability: A Narrative Approach to Intercultural
    Care', *Qualitative Social Work* 12, no. 2 (March 2013): 104–18.

10 Graham Ixer, 'There's No Such Thing As Reflection', *British Journal of Social Work*
    29, no. 4 (1 August 1999): 513–27.

11 Anthony Giddens, *Modernity and Self-Identity: Self and Society in the Late Modern Age* (Cambridge: Polity, 1991).

12 Ibid., 182.

13 Clarke et al., 'Cultural Boundaries in Care', 65.

14 AnneMarie Mol, *The Logic of Care: Health and the Problem of Patient Choice* (Oxford and New York: Routledge, 2008).

15 Ibid., 96.

16 Ibid., 101.

17 Clarke et al., 'Cultural Boundaries in Care', 65.

18 Margot Waddell, 'Living in Two Worlds: Psychodynamic Theory and Social Work Practice', *Free Associations* 15 (1989): 11–35.

19 Sayantani Dasgupta, 'Narrative Humility', *The Lancet* 371, no. 9617 (March 2008): 980, doi:10.1016/S0140–6736(08)60440–7.

20 Ibid., 981.

21 Margot Waddell, 'Living in Two Worlds: Psychodynamic Theory and Social Work', *Free Associations* 15 (1989): 13; original emphasis.

22 Julie Livingston, *Improvising Medicine: An African Oncology Ward in an Emerging Cancer Epidemic*, 1st edn (Durham and London: Duke University Press Books, 2012).

23 Monica Greco, 'On the Art of Life: A Vitalist Reading of Medical Humanities', *The Sociological Review* 56 (2008): 26; original emphasis.

24 Gunaratnam, 'Cultural Vulnerability'.

25 Sara Ahmed, 'Embodying Diversity: Problems and Paradoxes for Black Feminists', *Race Ethnicity and Education* 12, no. 1 (2009): 48.

26 Lena Dominelli, *Anti-Oppressive Social Work Theory and Practice* (New York: Palgrave Macmillan, 2002).

27 Yasmin Gunaratnam and Gail Lewis, 'Racialising Emotional Labour and Emotionalising Racialised Labour: Anger, Fear and Shame in Social Welfare', *Journal of Social Work Practice: Psychotherapeutic Approaches in Health, Welfare and the Community* 15, no. 2 (2001): 131.

28 Marie De Hennezel, *Intimate Death: How the Dying Teach Us to Live*, trans. Carol Brown Janeway, new edn (London: Time Warner Paperbacks, 1998), 6.

29 Kaichiro Tamba, 'Care Mind in Thirty-one Syllables', *Progress in Palliative Care* 14, no. 5 (2006): 252–4.

30 Christina Mason (ed.), *Journeys into Palliative Care: Roots and Reflections* (London: Jessica Kingsley, 2002), 26–7.

31 Alison Worth, Tasneem Irshad, Raj Bhopal, Duncan Brown, Julia Lawton, Elizabeth Grant,1 Scott Murray, Marilyn Kendall, James Adam, Rafik Gardee and Aziz Sheikh, 'Vulnerability and Access to Care for South Asian Sikh and Muslim Patients with Life Limiting Illness in Scotland: Prospective Longitudinal Qualitative Study', *BMJ* 338, no. feb03 1 (3 February 2009): b183–b183, doi:10.1136/bmj.b183.

32 Étienne Balibar and Immanuel Maurice Wallerstein, *Race, Nation, Class: Ambiguous Identities* (London: Verso, 1991).

33 Mustafa Dikeç, Nigel Clark and Clive Barnett, 'Extending Hospitality: Giving Space, Taking Time', *Paragraph* 32, no. 1 (March 2009): 1–14; 12 original emphasis.

34 Audre Lorde, 'The Uses of Anger', in *Sister Outsider* (California: The Crossing Press, 1984), 124.

35 Ibid., 129.

36 Jeanette Winterson, *The World And Other Places*, new edn (London: Vintage, 1999), 14.

Chapter 11: Home

1 Joanne Lynn and David M. Adamson, 'Living Well at the End of Life', Product Page, 2003, www.rand.org/pubs/white_papers/WP137.html

2 Barbara Gomes and Irene J. Higginson, 'Where People Die (1974–2030): Past Trends, Future Projections and Implications for Care', *Palliative Medicine* 22, no. 1 (1 January 2008): 33–41.

3 Charles Leadbeater and Jake Garber, *Dying for Change* (London: Demos, 2010), 68, www.demos.co.uk/publications/dyingforchange/

4 Department of Health, 'End of Life Care Strategy Article', 2011, www.dh.gov.uk/ health/category/policy-areas/social-care/end-of-life/

5 Nisar Ahmed, Janine Bestall, Sam Ahmedzai, Sheila Payne, Bill Noble and David Clark, 'Systematic Review of the Problems and Issues of Accessing Specialist Palliative Care by Patients, Carers and Health and Social Care Professionals', *Palliative Medicine* 18, no. 6 (September 2004): 525–42.

6 Julia Twigg, Carol Wolkowitz, Rachel Lara Cohen and Sarah Nettleton, *Body Work in Health and Social Care: Critical Themes, New Agendas* (Oxford: John Wiley & Sons, 2011).

7 Maliha Safri and Julie Graham, 'The Global Household: Toward a Feminist Postcapitalist International Political Economy', *Signs* 36, no. 1 (2010): 99–126, 100.

8 Jean-Louis Chrétien, *The Call and the Response*, trans. Anne Davenport (New York: Fordham University Press, 2004), 83.

9 Carol Wolkowitz, *Bodies at Work* (London: Sage, 2006), 147.

10 Kim England and Isabel Dyck, 'Managing the Body Work of Home Care', *Sociology of Health & Illness* 33, no. 2 (2011): 206–19.

11 Richard Sennett, *The Craftsman* (London: Penguin UK, 2009).

12 See Christian Heath, 'Embarrassment and Interactional Organization', in *Erving Goffman: Exploring the Interaction Order*, ed. Paul Drew and Anthony Wooton (Cambridge: Polity, 1988), 136–60.

13 Nari Rhee and Carol Zabin, 'Aggregating Dispersed Workers: Union Organizing in the "care" Industries', *Geoforum* 40, no. 6 (November 2009): 969–79.

14 Women Watch, United Nations Inter-Agency Network on Women and Gender Equality, 'Gender Equality & Trade Policy', 2010, www.un.org/womenwatch/ feature/trade/Labour-Mobility-and-Gender-Equality-Migration-and-Trade-in-Services.html

15 See also Cigdem Esin and Corinne Squire, 'Visual Autobiographies in East London: Narratives of Still Images, Interpersonal Exchanges, and Intrapersonal Dialogues', *Forum Qualitative Sozialforschung/Forum: Qualitative Social Research* 14, no. 2 (12 March 2013), www.qualitative research.net/index.php/fqs/article/view/1971

16 Ara Darzi, *A Framework for Action* (London: Health Care for London, 2008), 18; www.nhshistory.net/darzilondon.pdf

17 Gilles Deleuze and Claire Parnet, *Dialogues II* (New York and Chichester, West Sussex: Columbia University Press, 2007), 4.

18 Henry James, *The Europeans* (London: Penguin Classics, 2007).

Chapter 12: Pain

1 Jean-Louis Chrétien, *The Call and the Response*, trans. Anne Davenport (New York: Fordham Univ Press, 2004), 33.

2 Interview with Ruth Kelly, London, 11 March 1994, www.iniva.org/autoicon/DR/ interv2.htm

3 '"How Shall I Say It . . .?" Relating the Nonrelational', *Environment and Planning A* 39, no. 3 (2007): 590–608, 595.

4 Elaine Scarry, *The Body in Pain: The Making and Unmaking of the World* (New York and Oxford: Oxford University Press, 1987), 4.

5 Ibid., 6.

6 Solvig Ekblad, Anneli Marttila and Maria Emilsson, 'Cultural Challenges in End-of-life Care: Reflections from Focus Groups', Interviews with Hospice Staff in Stockholm', *Journal of Advanced Nursing* 31, no. 3 (2000): 628.

7 'The problem patient' talk was in K/PP149 Box 14 of 37 in the Cicely Saunders Archive, King's College, London.

8 Pierre Bourdieu, Alain Accardo, Gabrielle Balazs, Stephane Beaud, Francois Bonvin, Emmanuel Bourdieu, Philippe Bourgois, Sylvain Broccolichi, Patrick Champagne, Rosine Christin, Jean-Pierre Faguer, Sandrine Garcia, Remi Lenoir, Francoise Oeuvrard, Michel Pialoux, Louis Pinto, Denis Podalydes, Abdelmalek Sayad, Charles Soulie and Loic Wacquant, *The Weight of the World: Social Suffering in Contemporary Society*, trans. Priscilla Parkhurst Ferguson, 1st edn (Cambridge: Polity, 1999).

9 Ibid., 599.

10 Ibid., 600.

11 Ibid., 609.

12 Ibid., 613.

13 Angela McRobbie, 'A Mixed Bag of Misfortunes? Bourdieu's Weight of the World', *Theory, Culture & Society* 19, no. 3 (2002): 129–38.

14 Bourdieu, *The Weight of the World*, 621.

15 Ibid., 613; author's emphasis.

16 Ibid., 614; original emphasis.

17 Ibid., 621.

18 McRobbie, 'A Mixed Bag of Misfortunes?', 14.

19 Bourdieu, *The Weight of the World*.

20 Manuel DeLanda, *Intensive Science and Virtual Philosophy* (London and New York: Continuum International Publishing Group, 2002).

21 Hayden Lorimer, 'Cultural Geography: The Busyness of Being "more-than-representational"', *Progress in Human Geography* 29, no. 1 (2005): 83–94.

22 Emmanuel Levinas, *Time and the Other*, trans. Richard Cohen (Pittsburgh, PA: Duquesne University Press, 1994).

23 Cicely Saunders, 'The Evolution of the Hospices', in *The History of the Management of Pain: From Early Principles to Present Practice. The Proceedings of a Conference Organised by the Section of the History of Medicine of the Royal Society of Medicine, London*, ed. Ronald Mann (Carnforth: Parthenon Publishing Group, 1988), 171–2.

24 Cicely Saunders, 'Nature and Management of Terminal Pain', in *Matters of Life and Death* (London: Dartman, Longman and Todd, 1970), 217.

25 Cicely Saunders and David Clark, *Cicely Saunders: Selected Writings 1958–2004* (Oxford University Press, 2006), 217.

26 Ibid., 64.

27 Cicely Saunders, *Uncertainty and Fear. Proceedings of a Conference on Long-term Illness and Its Implications, October 19, 1962* (London: Queen's Institute of District Nursing, 1962), 8.

28 Cicely Saunders, 'A Patient', *Nursing Times*, 31 March 1961, 396.

29 Saunders and Clark, *Cicely Saunders*, 219.

30 Margot Waddell, 'Living in Two Worlds: Psychodynamic Theory and Social Work Practice', *Free Associations* 15 (1989): 11–35.

31 Alain Badiou, *Ethics: An Essay on the Understanding of Evil* (London and New York: Verso, 2002).

32 John Keats, 'Letter to George and Tom Keats, 21 December, 1817', in *The Letters of J. Keats: 1814–1821*, ed. H. E. Rollins (Cambridge: Cambridge University Press, 1958), 193.

33   David Clark, "'Total Pain", Disciplinary Power and the Body in the Work of Cicely Saunders, 1958–1967', *Social Science and Medicine* 49, no. 6 (1999): 727–36.

34   Sara Ahmed, *The Cultural Politics of Emotion* (Edinburgh University Press, 2004).

35   DeLanda, *Intensive Science and Virtual Philosophy*.

36   Naomi I. Eisenberger, 'The Pain of Social Disconnection: Examining the Shared Neural Underpinnings of Physical and Social Pain', *Nature Reviews. Neuroscience* 13, no. 6 (June 2012).

37   Lena Dominelli, *Anti-Oppressive Social Work Theory and Practice* (New York: Palgrave Macmillan, 2002).

38   Bruno Latour, 'How to Talk About the Body? The Normative Dimension of Science Studies', *Body & Society* 10, no. 2–3 (1 June 2004): 205–29.

39   Ibid., 211.

40   Harrison, 'How Shall I Say It . . .?'.

41   Jacques Derrida, *Writing and Difference*, 2nd edn (London: Routledge, 1978), 98.

42   Yasmin Gunaratnam, 'Where Is the Love? Art, Aesthetics and Research', *Journal of Social Work Practice* 21, no. 3 (2007): 271–87.

43   Stephen Graham and Nigel Thrift, 'Out of Order', *Theory, Culture & Society* 24, no. 3 (1 May 2007): 1–25, 4.

44   Gayatri Chakravorty Spivak, 'Can the Subaltern Speak?' in *Marxism and the Interpretation of Culture*, ed. Cary Nelson and Lawrence Grossberg (London: Macmillan, 1988).

45   Latour, 'How to Talk About the Body?' 219.

46   Martin Hagglund, 'Radical Atheist Materialism: A Critique of Meillassoux', in *The Speculative Turn: Continental Materialism and Realism*, ed. Levi Bryant, Nick Smicek and Graham Harman (Melbourne, Australia: re.press, 2011), 124.

47   For a discussion of 'Live Sociology' see Les Back, *The Art of Listening* (Oxford and New York: Berg, 2007) and Les Back and Nirmal Puwar's edited collection, *Live Methods* (Oxford: Sociological Review/Wiley-Blackwell, 2013).

48   Avery Gordon, *Ghostly Matters: Haunting and the Sociological Imagination*, 2nd edn (Minneapolis, MN: University of Minnesota Press, 2008), 178.

Chapter 13: The Foreigner Question – An Epilogue

1   Jacques Derrida and Anne Dufourmantelle, *Of Hospitality* (Stanford, CA: Stanford University Press, 2000).

2   Ibid., 3.

3   Ibid.

4   Ibid., 2.

5   Ibid., 4.

6 Julia Emberley, 'Epistemic Encounters: Indigenous Cosmopolitan Hospitality, Marxist Anthropology, Deconstruction, and Doris Pilkington's Rabbit-Proof Fence', *ESC: English Studies in Canada* 34, no. 4 (2008): 147–70.

7 Doris Pilkington, *Rabbit-proof Fence* (New York: Miramax Books, 2002), 149.

8 Pilkington, *Rabbit-proof Fence.*

9 Ibid., 164.

10 Ibid., 123.

11 Ibid., 165.

12 Ibid., 166.

13 UNESCO, *UNESCO Convention For Safeguarding the Intangible Cultural Heritage* (UNESCO, 2003), www.unesco.org/culture/ich/index.php?lg=en&pg=00022

14 Derrida and Dufourmantelle, *Of Hospitality.*

15 Homi K. Bhabha, *The Location of Culture* (London and New York: Routledge, 1994), 142; original emphasis.

16 Robert Pogue Harrison, *The Dominion of the Dead* (Chicago and London: University of Chicago Press, 2003), x.

17 Ibid.; original emphasis.

18 Peter Van Wyck, *The Highway of the Atom* (Montreal, Kingston, London and Ithaca: McGill-Queen's University Press, 2010), 136; original emphasis.

19 John Berger, *And Our Faces, My Heart, Brief as Photos* (London: Bloomsbury, 1984).

20 John Burnside, 'Geese' in *The Asylum Dance* (London: Jonathan Cape, 2000), 9–11.

Chapter 14: Appendix: Research and Methods

1 Yasmin Gunaratnam, 'Researching and Representing Ethnicity: A Qualitative Study of Hospice Staff and Service Users' (Unpublished PhD thesis, London School of Economics, 1999).

2 Michel Foucault, *The Order of Things: Archaeology of the Human Sciences*, 2nd edn (London and New York: Routledge, 2001).

3 Michel Foucault and Maurice Blanchot. *The Thought from Outside*, trans. Brian Massumi and Jeffrey Mehlman, reprint (New York: Zone Books, 1987), 21.

4 Tom Wengraf, *Qualitative Research Interviewing: Biographic Narrative and Semi-Structured Methods* (London: Sage, 2001).

5 For more about my approach to biographical narrative interviewing see Yasmin Gunaratnam, 'Narrative Interviews and Research', in *Narrative and Stories in Health Care: Illness, Dying and Bereavement*, ed. Yasmin Gunaratnam and David Oliviere (Oxford: Oxford University Press, 2009), 47–62.

6 Pierre Bourdieu, *The Weight of the World: Social Suffering in Contemporary Society*, 1st edn (Cambridge: Polity, 1999).

7 Yasmin Gunaratnam, From Competence to Vulnerability: Care, Ethics, and Elders from Racialized Minorities, *Mortality: Promoting the Interdisciplinary Study of Death and Dying* 13, no. 1 (2008): 24–41.

8 Jessica Corner, David Wright, Jane Hopkinson, Yasmin Gunaratnam, John McDonald and Claire Foster, 'The Research Priorities of Patients Attending UK Cancer Treatment Centres: Findings from a Modified Nominal Group Study', *British Journal of Cancer* 96, no. 6 (26 March 2007): 875–81.

9 Ikumi Okamoto, Phil Cotterell, David Wright, Yasmin Gunaratnam and Claire Foster, 'Minority Ethnic Patients' Involvement in Cancer Research: An Exploration of Experiences, Attitudes and Barriers', Monograph, 2010, http://eprints.soton. ac.uk/184007/

10 Avery Gordon, *Ghostly Matters: Haunting and the Sociological Imagination*, 2nd edn (Minneapolis, MN: University of Minnesota Press, 2008), 98.

11 Arundhati Roy, 'Come September', *Tamilnation.org*, 18 September 2002, http:// tamilnation.co/intframe/roy/arundhati1.htm

12 Arthur W. Frank, *Letting Stories Breathe: A Socio-Narratology* (Chicago and London: University of Chicago Press, 2010), 3; original emphasis.

13 Fraser, 'Once Upon a Problem', 102, doi:10.1111/j.1467–954X.2012.02118.x.

14 Clive Barnett, 'Deconstructing Radical Democracy: Articulation, Representation, and Being-with-others', *Political Geography* 23, no. 5 (June 2004): 520.

15 Roland Barthes, *Camera Lucida: Reflections on Photography*, trans. Richard Howard, new edn (London: Vintage Classics, 2000).

16 Motamedi Fraser, 'Once Upon a Problem'.

17 Michael Ondaatje, *Running in the Family* (London: Picador, 1983), 83.

Bibliography

Ahmed, Sara. *The Cultural Politics of Emotion*. Edinburgh University Press, 2004.

—. *Queer Phenomenology: Orientations, Objects, Others*. Durham and London: Duke University Press, 2005.

—. 'Embodying Diversity: Problems and Paradoxes for Black Feminists'. *Race Ethnicity and Education*, 12 (2009), 48–52.

Akhmatova, Anna Andreevna. *Twenty Poems*, trans. Jane Keyon. Minneapolis, MN: Eighties Press [and] Ally Press, 1985.

Alexiou, Margaret. *The Ritual Lament in Greek Tradition*, 2nd edn. Cambridge: Cambridge University Press, 2002.

Anderson, Bridget. *Us and Them: The Dangerous Politics of Immigration Control*. Oxford: Oxford University Press, 2013.

Arendt, Hannah. 'Introduction – Walter Benjamin 1892–1940'. In *Illuminations*, trans. Harry Zorn, new edn. London: Pimlico, 1999 7–55.

Armstrong, Karen. *The Case for God: What Religion Really Means*. London: Bodley Head, 2009.

Back, Les. *The Art of Listening*. Oxford and New York: Berg, 2007.

Balibar, Étienne and Wallerstein, Immanuel. *Race, Nation, Class: Ambiguous Identities*. London: Verso, 1999.

Barnett, Clive. 'Deconstructing Radical Democracy: Articulation, Representation, and Being-with-others'. *Political Geography*, 23 (2004), 503–28.

Bar-On, Daniel. *The Indescribable and the Undiscussable*. Budapest: Central European University Press, 1999.

Barthes, Roland. *Camera Lucida: Reflections on Photography*, trans. Richard Howard, new edn. London: Vintage Classics, 2000.

Bastian, Michelle. 'The Contradictory Simultaneity of Being with Others: Exploring Concepts of Time and Community in the Work of Gloria Anzaldúa'. *Feminist Review*, 97 (2011), 151–67.

Becker, Howard. 'Visual Evidence: A Seventh Man, the Specified Generalization, and the Work of the Reader'. *Visual Studies*, 17 (2002), 3–11.

Berger, John. 'Foreword'. In *The Algebra of Infinite Justice*, Arundhati Roy, 5th edn. London: Flamingo, 2002, xiii–xxi.

Berger, John and Mohr, Jean. *A Seventh Man*, 2nd edn. London and New York: Verso, 2010.

Berlant, Lauren. 'Slow Death: Sovereignty, Obesity, Lateral Agency'. *Critical Inquiry*, 33 (2007), 754–80.

Bhabha, Homi. *The Location of Culture*, 2nd edn. London and New York: Routledge, 2004.

Bingley, Amanda, Thomas, Carol, Brown, Janice, et al. 'Developing Narrative Research in Supportive and Palliative Care: The Focus on Illness Narratives'. *Palliative Medicine*, 22 (2008), 653–8.

Bollas, Christopher. 'Introducing Edward Said'. In *Freud: And the Non-European*. Edward W. Said. New York and London: Verso Books, 2003, 1–9.

Bourdieu, Pierre. *The Logic of Practice*. Cambridge: Polity, 1990.

Bourdieu, Pierre, Accardo, Alain, Balazs, Gabrielle, et al. *The Weight of the World: Social Suffering in Contemporary Society*, 1st edn. Cambridge: Polity, 1999.

Brown, Gordon. *Courage: Eight Portraits*, 1st edn. London: Bloomsbury, 2007.

Browning, Barbara. *Infectious Rhythm: Metaphors of Contagion and the Spread of African Culture*. New York and London: Routledge, 1998.

Burrows, Roger and Gane, Nicholas. 'Geodemographics, Software and Class'. *Sociology*, 40 (2006), 793–812.

Butler, Judith. *Precarious Life: The Power of Mourning and Violence*. London and New York: Verso, 2004.

Calarco, Matthew. 'On the Borders of Language and Death – Derrida and the Question of the Animal'. *Angelaki Journal of the Theoretical Humanities*, 7 (2002), 17–25.

Chrétien, Jean-Louis. *The Call and the Response*, trans. Anne Davenport. New York: Fordham University Press, 2004.

Clark, David. *Wither the Hospices? In The Future of Palliative Care*, ed. David Clark. Buckingham: Open University Press, 1993, 167–77.

—. '"Total pain", Disciplinary Power and the Body in the Work of Cicely Saunders, 1958–1967'. *Social Science and Medicine*, 49 (1999), 727–36.

—. 'Total Pain: The Work of Cicely Saunders and the Hospice Movement'. *American Pain Society Bulletin*, 10 (2000). Available at: www.ampainsoc.org/library/bulletin/jul00/hist1.htm (accessed 20 April 2008).

Clark, David, Small, Neil, Wright, Michael, et al. *A Bit of Heaven for the Few?: An Oral History of the Modern Hospice Movement in the United Kingdom*. Lancaster: Observatory Publications, 2005.

Clarke, Margaret, Finlay, Illora and Campbell, Ian. 'Cultural Boundaries in Care'. *Palliative Medicine*, 5 (1991), 63–5.

Clifford, James. *Routes: Travel and Translation in the Later Twentieth Century*. Cambridge: Harvard University Press, 1997.

Connerton, Paul. *How Societies Remember*. Cambridge: Cambridge University Press, 1989.

Conrad, Kathryn. 'Keening the Nation: The Bean Chaointe, the Sean Bhean Bhocht, and Women's Lament in Irish Nationalist Narrative'. In *Irish Women's Writing: Feminist Perspectives*, ed. Patricia Coughlan, R. O'Dwyer and Tina O'Toole. Dublin: Carysfort Press, 2002, 39–57.

Cvetkovich, Michèle Aina. *An Archive of Feelings: Trauma, Sexuality, and Lesbian Public Cultures*. Durham and London: Duke University Press, 2003.

Das, Veena. *Life and Words: Violence and the Descent into the Ordinary*. Berkeley and London: University of California Press, 2007.

DasGupta, Sayantani. 'Narrative Humility', *The Lancet*, 371 (9617) (March 2008), 980–1.

De Hennezel, Marie. *Intimate Death: How the Dying Teach Us to Live*, trans. Carol Brown Janeway. London: Time Warner Paperbacks, 1998.

DeLanda, Manuel. *Intensive Science and Virtual Philosophy*. London and New York: Continuum International Publishing Group, 2002.

Deleuze, Gilles. 'Ethology: Spinoza and Us'. In *Incorporations*, ed. Jonathan Crary and Sanford Kwinter, trans. Robert Hurley. New York: Zone, 1992, 624–33.

—. *Francis Bacon: The Logic of Sensation*, trans. Daniel. W. Smith. Minneapolis, MN: University of Minnesota Press, 2003.

Denzin, Norman K. *Interpretive Ethnography: Ethnographic Practices for the 21st Century*. Thousand Oaks, CA and London: Sage, 1997.

Derrida, Jacques. *Writing and Difference*. London: Routledge, 1978.

—. 'Aporias: Dying – Awaiting (One Another at) the "Limits of Truth"', trans. Thomas Dutoit. Stanford, CA: Stanford University Press, 1993.

Derrida, Jacques and Dufourmantelle, Anne. *Of Hospitality*. Stanford, CA: Stanford University Press, 2000.

Dikeç, Mustafa, Clark, Nigel and Barnett, Clive. 'Extending Hospitality: Giving Space, Taking Time'. *Paragraph*, 32 (2009), 1–14.

Diprose, Rosalyn. *Corporeal Generosity – On Giving Nietzche, Merleau-ponty and Levinas*. New York: SUNY Press, 2002.

Dominelli, Lena. *Anti-Oppressive Social Work Theory and Practice*. New York: Palgrave Macmillan, 2002.

Du Boulay, Shirley. *Cicely Saunders*, new edn, London: Hodder & Stoughton Religious, 1987.

Eisenberger, Naomi I. 'The Pain of Social Disconnection: Examining the Shared Neural Underpinnings of Physical and Social Pain, Nature Reviews'. *Neuroscience*, 13, (June 2012), 421–34.

Ekblad, Solvig, Marttila, Anneli and Emilsson, Maria. 'Cultural Challenges in End-of-life Care: Reflections from Focus Groups' Interviews with Hospice Staff in Stockholm'. *Journal of Advanced Nursing*, 31 (2000), 623–30.

Elias, Norbert. *The Civilizing Process: The History of Manners and State Formation and Civilisation*, trans. Edmund Jephcott. Oxford: Blackwell, 1994.

Emberley, Julia. 'Epistemic Encounters: Indigenous Cosmopolitan Hospitality, Marxist Anthropology, Deconstruction, and Doris Pilkington's Rabbit-Proof Fence'. *ESC: English Studies in Canada*, 34 (2008), 147–70.

Evans, Natalie, Menaca, Arantza, Koffman, Johnathan, et al. 'Cultural Competence in End-of-Life Care: Terms, Definitions, and Conceptual Models from the British Literature'. *Journal of Palliative Medicine*, 15 (2012), 812–20.

Fairlie, Alison. *Baudelaire: Les Fleurs Du Mal*. London: Edward Arnold, 1960.

Firth, Shirley. *Dying, Death and Bereavement in a British Hindu Community*.
    Bondgenotelaan: Peeters Publishers, 1997.

Foucault, Michel and Maurice Blanchot. *The Thought from Outside*, trans. Brian
    Massumi and Jeffrey Mehlman, Reprint. New York: Zone Books, 1987.

—. *The Order of Things: Archaeology of the Human Sciences*, 2nd edn. London and New
    York: Routledge, 2001.

Frank, Arthur W. *The Wounded Storyteller : Body, Illness, and Ethics*. Chicago:
    University of Chicago Press, 1997.

—. *Letting Stories Breathe: A Socio-Narratology*. Chicago and London: University of
    Chicago Press, 2010.

Frankl, Viktor E. *Man's Search For Meaning: The Classic Tribute to Hope from the
    Holocaust*, trans. Ilse Lasch, new edn. London: Rider, 2004.

Geurts, Kathryn Linn. *Culture and the Senses: Bodily Ways of Knowing in an African
    Community*. Berkeley, CA: University of California Press, 2003.

Giddens, Anthony. *Modernity and Self-Identity: Self and Society in the Late Modern Age*.
    Cambridge: Polity, 1991.

Gordon, Avery. *Ghostly Matters: Haunting and the Sociological Imagination*, 2nd edn.
    Minneapolis, MN: University of Minnesota Press, 2008.

Grosz, Elizabeth. 'Notes towards a Corporeal Feminism'. *Australian Feminist Studies*, 2
    (1987), 1–16.

—.*Chaos, Territory, Art: Deleuze and the Framing of the Earth*. New York: Columbia
    University Press, 2008.

Gunaratnam, Yasmin. 'Implications of the Stephen Lawrence Inquiry for Palliative Care'.
    International Journal of Palliative Nursing, 6 (3) (March 2000), 147–9.

—. '"We mustn't Judge People … but": Staff Dilemmas in Dealing with Racial
    Harassment amongst Hospice Service Users'. *Sociology of Health & Illness*, 23 (2001),
    65–84.

—. '"Bucking and Kicking": Race, Gender and Embodied Resistance in Health Care'. In
    Biographical Methods and Professional Practice: An International Perspective, ed. Prue
    Chamberlayne, Joanna Bornat and Ursula Apitzsch. Bristol: Policy Press, 2004, 207–19.

—. 'Where Is the Love? Art, Aesthetics and Research'. *Journal of Social Work Practice*, 21
    (2007), 271–87.

—. 'From Competence to Vulnerability: Care, Ethics, and Elders from Racialized Minorities'.
    Mortality: Promoting the Interdisciplinary Study of Death and Dying, 13 (2008), 24–41.

—. 'Narrative Interviews and Research', in *Narrative and Stories in Health Care: Illness,
    Dying and Bereavement*, ed. Yasmin Gunaratnam and David Oliviere (Oxford:
    Oxford University Press, 2009), 47–62.

—. 'Learning to be Affected: Social Suffering and Total Pain at Life's Borders'. *The
    Sociological Review*, 60 (Issue Supplement. S1) (2012), 108–23.

—. 'Cultural Vulnerability: A Narrative Approach to Intercultural Care'. *Qualitative
    Social Work*, 12 (2) (March 2013), 104–18.

Hagglund, Martin. 'Radical Atheist Materialism: A Critique of Meillassoux'. In *The Speculative Turn: Continental Materialism and Realism*, ed. Levi Bryant, Nick Smicek and Graham Harman. Melbourne, Australia: re.press, 2011, 113–29.

Hall, Suzanne. *City, Street and Citizen: The Measure of the Ordinary*. London and New York: Routledge, 2012.

Harrison, Paul. '"How shall I say it …?" Relating the nonrelational'. *Environment and Planning A*, 39 (2007), 590–608.

Harvey, David. *Spaces of Hope*. Berkeley, CA: University of California Press, 2000.

Health Protection Agency. 'HIV in the United Kingdom: 2011 report', 2011, www.hpa. org.uk/Publications/InfectiousDiseases/HIVAndSTIs/1111HIVintheUK2011report/ (accessed 12 December 2012).

Heidegger, Martin. *Being and Time*, trans. John Macquarrie and Edward Robinson, new edn. Oxford: Wiley-Blackwell, 1978.

Heiler, Friedrich. *Prayer: A Study in the History and Psychology of Religion*. London: Oxford University Press, 1932.

Hill, Dawn and Penso, Dawn. *Opening Doors: Improving Access to Hospice and Specialist Palliative Care Services by Members of the Black and Ethnic Minority Communities*. London: National Council for Hospice and Specialist Palliative Care Services, 1995.

Hirschkind, Charles. *The Ethical Soundscape: Cassette Sermons and Islamic Counterpublics*. New York: Columbia University Press, 2006.

Holst-Warhaft, Gail. 'Death and the Maiden: Sex, Death, and Women's Laments'. In *Women, Pain and Death: Rituals and Everyday Life on the Margins of Europe and Beyond*, ed. Evy Johanne Häland. Newcastle upon Tyne: Cambridge Scholars Publishing, 2008, 15–33.

Honig, Bonnie. *Democracy and the Foreigner*. Princeton, NJ: Princeton University Press, 2001.

Horton, Richard. 'GBD 2010: Understanding Disease, Injury, and Risk'. *The Lancet*, 380, no. 9859 (December 2012), 2053–4.

Human Rights Watch and Lohman, Diederik. *'Please, Do Not Make Us Suffer Any More': Access to Pain Treatment As a Human Right*. New York: Human Rights Watch, 2009.

International Council on Security and Development (ICOS). Icosgroup.net, 25 October 2007, www.icosgroup.net/2007/media/media-press-releases/european_parliament/ (accessed 11 July 2011).

Ixer, Graham. 'There's No Such Thing As Reflection'. *British Journal of Social Work*, 29 (1999), 513–27.

Izugbara, Chimaraoke O and Wekesa, Eliud. 'Beliefs and Practices about Antiretroviral Medication: A Study of Poor Urban Kenyans Living with HIV/AIDS, Beliefs and Practices about Antiretroviral Medication: A Study of Poor Urban Kenyans Living with HIV/AIDS'. *Sociology of Health & Illness, Sociology of Health & Illness* 33, (2011), 869–83.

Jain, Sarah Lochlann. 'Living in Prognosis: Toward an Elegiac Politics'. *Representations*, 98 (2007), pp. 77–92.

Keats, John. 'Letter to George and Tom Keats, 21 December, 1817'. In *The Letters of J. Keats: 1814–1821*, ed. Hyder Edward Rollins. Cambridge: Cambridge University Press, 1958, 193.

Kellehear, Allan, Pugh, Edwin and Atter, Lynda. 'Home Away from Home? A Case Study of Bedside Objects in a Hospice'. *International Journal of Palliative Nursing*, 15 (2009), 148–52.

Kincaid, Jamaica. *A Small Place*. New York: Farrar, Straus and Giroux, 2000.

Kramer, Ann. *Many Rivers to Cross: Caribbean People in the NHS 1948–69*. London: Stationery Office, 2006.

Kristeva, Julia. *Revolution in Poetic Language*. New York: Columbia University Press, 1984.

Kung, Ching. 'A Possible Unifying Principle for Mechanosensation'. *Nature*, 436 (4 August 2005), 647–54.

Latour, Bruno. 'How to Talk About the Body? The Normative Dimension of Science Studies'. *Body & Society*, 10 (2004), 205–29.

Lawton, Julia. *The Dying Process: Patients' Experiences of Palliative Care*. London: Routledge, 2000.

Leadbeater, Charles and Garber, Jake. *Dying for Change*. London: Demos, 2010, www. demos.co.uk/publications/dyingforchange/

Leggewie, Claus. 'Transnational Citizenship: Ideals and European Realities'. *Eurozine*, April 3 (2013), www.eurozine.com/articles/2013-02-19-leggewie-en.html (accessed 4 March 2013).

Levinas, Emmanuel. *Time and the Other*. Pittsburgh, PA: Duquesne University Press, 1994.

Lichtenstein, Rachel and Sinclair, Iain. *Rodinsky's Room*, new edn. London: Granta Books, 2000.

Lingis, Alphonso. *The Community of Those Who Have Nothing in Common*. Bloomington: Indiana University Press, 1994.

—. *Trust*. Minneapolis, MN: University of Minnesota Press, 2004.

Livingston, Julie. *Improvising Medicine: An African Oncology Ward in an Emerging Cancer Epidemic*, 1st edn. Durham and London: Duke University Press, 2012.

Lommel, Andreas. *Prehistoric and Primitive Man*. London: McGraw-Hill, 1966.

Lorimer, Hayden. 'Cultural Geography: The Busyness of Being "More-than-representational"'. *Progress in Human Geography*, 29 (2005), 83–94.

Lynch, Thomas, Connor, Stephen and Clark, David. 'Mapping Levels of Palliative Care Development: A Global Update'. *Journal of Pain and Symptom Management* (24 September 2012) doi: 10.1016/j.jpainsymman.2012.05.011; 45(6) (June 2012), 1094–106.

Mackintosh, Maureen, Raghuram, Parvati and Henry, Leroi. 'A Perverse Subsidy: African Trained Nurses and Doctors in the NHS'. *Soundings*, 34 (2006), 103–13.

Madianou, Mirca and Miller, Daniel. 'Polymedia: Towards a New Theory of Digital Media in Interpersonal Communication'. *International Journal of Cultural Studies*, 16 (2) (2013), 169–87.

Mason, Christina (ed.). *Journeys into Palliative Care: Roots and Reflections*. London: Jessica Kingsley Publishers, 2002.

Mavrommatis, George. 'A Racial Archaeology of Space: A Journey Through the Political Imaginings of Brixton and Brick Lane, London'. *Journal of Ethnic and Migration Studies*, 36 (2010), 561–79.

McRobbie, Angela. 'A Mixed Bag of Misfortunes? Bourdieu's Weight of the World'. *Theory, Culture & Society*, 19 (2002), 129–38.

Médecins du monde. 'Access to Health Care for Vulnerable Groups in the European Union in 2012: An Overview of the Condition of Persons Excluded from Healthcare Systems in the EU'. *Médecins du monde*, www.medecinsdumonde.org/.../european_ advocacy_paper_pdf (accessed 8 August 2012).

Mezzandra, Sandro and Neilson, Brett. 'Border as Method, or, the Multiplication of Labor'. *European Institute for Progressive Cultural Policies*. 2008. http://eipcp.net/ transversal/0608/mezzadraneilson/en (accessed 28 April 2010).

Michaels, Ann. The Winter Vault. London, Berlin, New York: Bloomsbury, 2010.

Milic, Nela. *Balkanising Taxonomy*. 2008. www.goldsmiths.ac.uk/balkanising-taxonomy/ (accessed 10 July 2011).

Miller, Daniel. *The Comfort of Things*. Cambridge and Malden, MA: Polity, 2008.

Miller, Daniel and Parrott, Fiona. 'Loss and Material Culture in South London'. In *Death Rites and Rights*, ed. Belinda Brooks-Gordon, Fatemeh Ebtehaj, Jonathan Herring et al. Oxford: Hart Publishing, 2007, 147–61.

Mol, Ann-Marie. 'Proving or Improving: On Health Care Research as a Form of Self-Reflection'. *Qualitative Health Research*, 16 (2006), 405–14.

—. *The Logic of Care: Health and the Problem of Patient Choice*. Oxford and New York: Routledge, 2008.

Motamedi Fraser, Mariam. 'Once Upon a Problem'. *Sociological Review*, 60 (Issue Supplement. S1) (2012), 84–107.

Oikelome, Franklin. *The Recruitment and Retention of Black and Minority Ethnic Staff in the National Health Service*. London: Race Equality Foundation, 2007.

Okamoto, Ikumi, Cotterell, Phil, Wright, David, et al. 'Minority Ethnic Patients' Involvement in Cancer Research: An Exploration of Experiences, Attitudes and Barriers'. 2010. Monograph http://eprints.soton.ac.uk/184007/ (accessed 8 January 2013).

Ondaatje, Michael. *Running in the Family*. London: Picador, 1983.

Portelli, Alessandro. *The Death of Luigi Trastulli, and Other Stories: Form and Meaning in Oral History*. New York: SUNY Press, 1991.

Puar, Jasbir. 'Mapping US Homonormativities'. *Gender, Place and Culture*, 13 (2006), 67–88.

—. 'Prognosis Time: Towards a Geopolitics of Affect, Debility and Capacity'. *Women & Performance: A Journal of Feminist Theory*, 19 (2009), 161–72.

Puwar, Nirmal. *Space Invaders: Race, Gender and Bodies Out of Place*. Oxford: Berg Publishers, 2004.

—. 'Im/possible Inhabitations'. In *The Situated Politics of Belonging*, ed. Nira Yuval-Davis, Kalpana Kannabiran and Ulrike Vieten. London: Sage, 2006, 75–83.

—. 'Aaj Kaal (Yesterday, Today, Tomorrow), Darkmatter, in the Ruins of Imperial Culture', 3 April 2012, www.darkmatter101.org/site/2012/04/03/aaj-kaal-yesterday-today-tomorrow-video/ (accessed 21 July 2012).

—. 'Mediations on Making Aaj Kaal'. *Feminist Review* 100 (2012), 124–41.

Rancière, Jacques. *The Politics of Aesthetics*, trans. Gabriel Rockhill. New York and London: Continuum International Publishing Group, 2006.

Ratha, Dilip and Silwal, Anil. Remittance Flows in 2011: An Update, Migration and Development Brief 18. The World Bank, Remittances Unit, 23 April 2012. http://web.worldbank.org/WBSITE/EXTERNAL/TOPICS/0,,contentMDK:21924020~page PK:5105988~piPK:360975~theSitePK:214971,00.html (accessed 18 December 2012).

Rhee, Nari and Zabin, Carol. 'Aggregating Dispersed Workers: Union Organizing in the "care" Industries'. *Geoforum*, 40 (2009), 969–79.

Rienzo, Cinzia. 'Migrants in the UK Labour Market: And Overview. Migration Observatory Briefing'. Oxford: COMPAS, the Migration Observatory at the University of Oxford, 2012. http://migrationobservatory.ox.ac.uk/briefings/migrants-uk-labour-market-overview (accessed 13 January 2013).

Rosengarten, Marsha. *HIV Interventions: Biomedicine and the Traffic Between Information and Flesh*. Seattle and London: University of Washington Press, 2009.

Ross, Will. 'Sent Home, Abandoned and Saved in Ghana'. *BBC*, 17 January 2008. From Our Own Correspondent, http://news.bbc.co.uk/1/hi/programmes/from_our_own_correspondent/7193366.stm (accessed 25 January 2008).

Roy, Arundhati. 'Come September'. Tamilnation.org, 18 September 2002. http://tamilnation.co/intframe/roy/arundhati1.htm (accessed 4 August 2012).

Safri, Maliha and Graham, Julie. 'The Global Household: Toward a Feminist Postcapitalist International Political Economy'. *Signs*, 36 (2010), 99–126.

Sallnow, Libby, Kumar, Suresh and Numpeli, Mathews. 'Home-based Palliative Care in Kerala, India: The Neighbourhood Network in Palliative Care'. *Progress in Palliative Care* 18 (1) (2010), 14–17.

Sallnow, Elizabeth, Kumar, Suresh and Kellehear, Allan (eds). *International Perspectives on Public Health and Palliative Care*. London: Routledge, 2011.

Saunders, Cicely. 'A Patient'. *Nursing Times* (1961), 394–7.

—. 'Care of patients suffering from terminal illness at St. Joeseph's Hospice, Hackney, London'. *Nursing Mirror*, 14 (1964), vii–x.

—. 'Nature and Management of Terminal Pain'. In *Matters of Life and Death*, ed. Edward Shotter. London: Dartman, Longman and Todd, 1970, 15–26.

—. 'The Evolution of the Hospices'. In *The History of the Management of Pain: From Early Principles to Present Practice. The Proceedings of a Conference Organised by the Section of the History of Medicine of the Royal Society of Medicine, London*, ed. Ronald Mann. Carnforth: Parthenon Publishing Group, 1988, 167–78.

—. 'Spiritual Pain'. In *Cicely Saunders: Selected Writings 1958–2004*. Oxford: Oxford University Press, 2006, 217–21.

Scarry, Elaine. *The Body in Pain: The Making and Unmaking of the World*. New York and Oxford: Oxford University Press, 1987.

Scheff, Thomas J. 'Shame and the Social Bond: A Sociological Theory'. *Sociological Theory*, 18 (2000), 84–99.

Schroeder-Sheker, Therese. 'Music for the Dying: A Personal Account of the New Field of Music-thanatology—History, Theories and Clinical Narratives'. *Journal of Holistic Nursing*, 12 (1994), 83–99.

Serres, Michel. *The Troubadour of Knowledge*, trans. Sheila Faria Glaser and William Paulson. Ann Arbor: University of Michigan Press, 1997.

Shildrick, Margrit and Price, Janet. 'Deleuzian Connections and Queer Corporealities: Shrinking Global Disability'. *Rhizomes*, 11/12 (Spring 2006), www.rhizomes.net/issue11/shildrickprice/index.html (accessed 28 April 2010).

Sissman, Edward. *Night Music: Poems*. New York: Houghton Mifflin Harcourt, 1999.

Smith, Tony. 'Problems of Hospices'. *BMJ* 288 (6425) (21 April 1984), 1178–9.

Spivak, Gayathri. 1988. 'Can the Subaltern Speak?' In *Marxism and the Interpretation of Culture*, ed. Cary Nelson and Lawrence Grossberg. London: Macmillan, 1988, 271–313.

Steedman, Carolyn. *Dust*. Manchester and New York: Manchester University Press, 2001.

St Louis, Brett. 'Readings Within a Diasporic Boundary: Transatlantic Black Performance and the Poetic Imperative in Sport'. In *Un/Settled Multiculturalisms: Diasporas, Entanglement, Transruptions*, ed. Barnor Hesse. London: Zed Books, 2000, 51–72.

Strong-Wilson, Teresa. *Bringing Memory Forward: Storied Remembrance in Social Justice Education With Teachers*. New York: Peter Lang, 2008.

Sunder Rajan, Rajeswari. *Real and Imagined Women: Gender, Culture, and Postcolonialism*. London and New York: Routledge, 1993.

Tamba, Kaichiro. 'Care Mind in Thirty-One Syllables'. *Progress in Palliative Care*, 14 (2006), 252–4.

The International Council on Security and Development. 'ICOS'. Icosgroup.net, 25 October 2007. www.icosgroup.net/2007/media/media-press-releases/european_parliament/ (accessed 24 May 2012).

The Lancet. 'Migrant Health: What Are Doctors' Leaders Doing?' 371 (19 January 2008), 178.

Twycross, Robert G. *Time to Die*. London: Christian Medical Fellowship, 1984.

Ulmer, Gregory L. *Heuretics: The Logic of Invention*. Baltimore and London: JHU Press, 1994.

Van Wyck, Peter. *The Highway of the Atom*. Montreal and Kingston, London. Ithaca: McGill-Queen's University Press, 2010.

Vargas-Silva, Carlos. 'Global International Migrant Stock: The UK in International Comparison'. Migration Observatory Briefing. Oxford: COMPAS, University of

Oxford, 2011. http://migrationobservatory.ox.ac.uk/briefings/global-international-migrant-stock-uk-international-comparison (accessed 12 December 2012).

Verderber, Stephen and Refuerzo, Ben J. *Hospice Architecture*. Oxford and New York: Taylor and Francis, 2006.

Virilio, Paul. *Open Sky*, trans. Julie Rose. London: Verso, 1997.

Waddell, Margot. 'Living in Two Worlds: Psychodynamic Theory and Social Work Practice'. *Free Associations*, 15 (1989), 11–35.

Walter, Eugene. *Placeways: A Theory of the Human Environment*. Chapel Hill: University of North Carolina Press Books, 1988.

Walter, Tony. *The Revival of Death*. London: Routledge, 1994.

Walter, Tony, Hourizi, Rashid, Moncur, Wendy and Pitsillides, Stacy. 'Does the Internet Change how We Die and Mourn? Overview and Analysis'. *Omega: Journal of Death & Dying*, 64 (2011), 275–302.

Wengraf, Tom. *Qualitative Research Interviewing: Biographic Narrative and Semi-Structured Methods*. London: Sage, 2001.

Wilkinson, Sue and Kitzinger, Celia. 'Thinking Differently About Thinking Positive: A Discursive Approach to Cancer Patients' Talk'. *Social Science & Medicine*, 50 (2000), 797–811.

Winnicott, Donald W. *Playing and Reality*, 2nd edn. London: Routledge, 2005.

Wolkowitz, Carol. *Bodies at Work*. London: Sage, 2006.

Worth, Alison, Irshad, Tasneem, Bhopal, Raj, et al. 'Vulnerability and Access to Care for South Asian Sikh and Muslim Patients with Life Limiting Illness in Scotland: Prospective Longitudinal Qualitative Study'. *BMJ* 338 (2009), b183.

Wyschogrod, Edith. *Saints and Postmodernism: Revisioning Moral Philosophy*. Chicago and London: University of Chicago Press, 1990.

Index

absolute responsibility 89
abstract systems 105
Adamson, David M. 177n. 1
Ahmed, Nisar 177n. 5
Ahmed, Sara 48, 109, 169n. 5, 170n. 8,
    176n. 53, 180n. 34
air diffuser, in hospice ward 85
Akhmatova, Anna Andreevna 66, 171n. 15
Alexiou, Margaret 173n. 6
Anderson, Bridget 8, 164n. 15
Andrijasevic, Rutvica 164n. 17
anger 72, 108, 109, 112–13
Ann, Kramer 170n. 11
anti-oppressive practice 109, 143
antiretroviral drugs (ARVs) 67, 72
anxiety 48, 50, 54, 65, 73, 112, 128, 143
Anzieu, Didier 59, 170n. 6
Aquinas, Thomas 82
Arendt, Hannah 35, 168n. 33
Armstrong, Karen 26, 167n. 10
Atter, Lynda 170n. 4
auxiliary nursing 51–2

Back, Les 180n. 47
Badiou Alain 179n. 31
Bailey, Peter 173n. 15
Bains, Mary 167n. 3
Balazs, Gabrielle 135
Balibar, Étienne 87, 174n. 20, 177n. 32
Balkanising Taxonomy (exhibition) 36–8
Bamber, Helen 29
Barnett, Clive 111, 160, 163n. 3, 177n. 33,
    182n. 14
Barthes, Roland 36, 169n. 35, 182n. 15
Baudelaire, Charles
    Recueillement 65
Bauman, Zygmunt 21, 167n. 59
Benjamin, Walter 35
Ben-Shlomo, Yoav 174n. 4
Berger, John 11, 164nn. 19, 21, 165n. 34,
    181n. 19
Bettega, Nadia 5

Bhabha, Homi 181n. 15
    'Sly Civility' 151
Bingley, Amanda 168n. 19
biomedicine 15
Black Africans 67
BME Cancer Communities
    Hear me Now 92
body work *see* incapacitation
Bohusz-Szyszko, Marian 25
Bollas, Christopher 3, 163n. 2
Bourdieu, Pierre 6, 135–7, 163n. 1, 164n.
    9, 178n. 8, 179nn. 9–12, 14–17, 19,
    182n. 6
    The Weight of the World 135, 137
Brady, Denise 99
Brah, Avtar 7
Brown, Gordon 167n 9, 168nn. 25–6
Browning, Barbara 72, 172n. 8
Broyard, Anatole 93, 175n. 7
Burnside, John 154, 181n. 20
Burrows, Roger 175n. 7

Campbell, Ian 99, 101, 105–7, 175nn. 1–3
cancer, accounts of smell of 64
cancer patients, battle of 44–5
    see also individual entries
case studies
    Alexander, June 77
        faith of 78–80
    Mr. Balani 120–3
    Edwin
        home of 94–7
        prostate cancer of 91–4
    Eve 85–8
    Mr. Gupta 116–20
    James 67–76
        death of 75
        and love for Kenya 75
        shock of 68–73
    Lawrence, Violet 57–8
        breast cancer of 58–9
        imposed captivation of 63–4

Janice's apprehension of 60–1
Janice's perseverance towards 61–2
lack of presence of 60
last days of 65–6
Lewis, Maxine 44, 142–3
  and attempt to escape hospital 45
  last days of 46–7
  paranoia of 47–8
  patience of 52–5
  stories of 50–2
  suspicion, about hospice nurses and
    volunteers 46
Nusrat 71
Chapman, Allan 87, 88
Ching Kung 82, 173n. 5
choice, logic of 107
Chrétien, Jean-Louis 117, 177n. 8,
  178n. 1
The Cicely Saunders Institute of Palliative
  Care (King's College campus,
  London) 28
Cicero 94
  De Senectute 92, 174n. 3
Citizens's Advice Bureau 126
Clark, David 165n 33, 166n. 49, 179nn. 25–6,
  29, 180n. 33
Clark, Nigel 111, 163n. 3, 177n. 33
Clarke, Margaret 99, 101, 105–9, 175nn. 1–3,
  176n. 13
Clifford, James 163n. 5
Cluny monastery 90
Cohen, Rachel Lara 177n. 6
community, significance of 12
community palliative care 102
Connerton, Paul 172n. 1
Connor, Stephen 165n. 33
Conrad, Kathryn 83, 173n. 9
Conreen, Martin 167n. 61
Corner Jessica 182n. 8
corporeal anticipation 118
corporeal generosity 88
Csordas, Thomas 44, 169n. 1
cultural authenticity 8
cultural competence 103, 105–7
  reversal of 108
cultural insensitivity 110
Culture GPS tool 104
Cumming-Bruce, Nick 174n. 19

Daily Mail 87
Darzi, Ara 127, 178n. 16
Das, Veena 164n. 6
DasGupta, Sayantani 108, 177nn. 19–20
deambulatorium angelorum 90
DeLanda, Manuel 179n 20, 180n. 35
de Léry, Jean
  *History of a Voyage to the Land of Brazil,
    Otherwise Called America* 148
Deleuze, Gilles 6–7, 82, 129, 164n. 10,
  173n. 4, 178n. 17
Denzin, Norman 73, 172n. 11
Derrida, Jacques 12, 27, 79, 144, 147–8,
  150, 160, 163n. 1, 165n. 24, 168nn.
  15, 17, 174nn. 23–4, 180nn. 1–5,
  41, 181n. 14
  Of hospitality 147
diachrony 138
Dias, Arthur V. 43
diasporic dying 8–12
differentialist racism 87–8
Dikeç, Mustafa 111, 163n. 3, 177n. 33
Diprose, Rosalyn 88, 90, 174nn. 21, 28
dissimulation
  case study of James 67–76
Dominelli, Lena 176n 26, 180n. 37
Du Boulay, Shirley 33, 168n. 30,
  169n. 39
Dufourmantelle, Anne 147, 148, 165n. 24,
  180n. 1, 181n. 14
Dunstan, Steven 175n. 10
Dyck, Isabel 177n. 10

Edley, Nigel 175n. 9
Eisenberger, Naomi I. 180n. 36
Ekblad, Solvig 178n. 6
Elias, Norbert 174n. 22
Emberley, Julia 148, 181n. 6
emotional distress 14, 140–1
end of life care *see* home and care; pain
England, Kim 177n. 10
Erlanger, Steven 174n. 19
Esin, Cigdem 178n. 15
Evans, Natalie 175n. 6
exergue 27–8

Fairlie, Alison 171n. 14
faith, significance of 78–80

Fanon, Frantz 170n. 7
  Black Skin, White 48
fear 9, 10, 13, 34, 43, 49, 50, 64, 65, 67, 70,
    74, 88, 107, 110, 112, 128, 130, 141,
    142, 150
  immobilization of 104
Finlay, Illora 99, 101, 107–11, 175nn. 1–3
Firth, Shirley 173n 10, 175n. 4
foreign founder, significance of 38–9
Foucault, Michel 156, 168n. 18, 181nn. 2–3
Frank, Arthur 169n 41, 182n. 12
  Letting Stories Breathe 159
Frankl, Viktor E. 29, 168n. 23
Freeman, Mark 172n. 6
Frye, Marilyn 169n. 4
fungating wounds 59

Gaitskell, Hugh 25
Gane, Nicholas 175n. 7
Garber, Jake 167n 58, 177n. 3
Geurts, Kathryn Linn 170n. 4
Giddens, Anthony 105, 176nn. 11–12
global care chain 120
Gomes, Barbara 177n. 2
Gordon, Avery 158, 180n. 48, 182n. 10
Graham, Julie 115, 177n. 7
Graham, Stephen 180n. 43
Greco, Monica 109, 176n. 23
Grosz, Elisabeth 170n. 15
guilt 110–13
Gunaratnam, Yasmin 164n 12, 174n. 1,
    175nn. 9, 14, 176nn. 24, 27, 180n. 42,
    181nn. 1, 5, 182n. 7
  Eros 12

Hagglund, Martin 180n. 46
Hall, Suzanne 170n. 9
Harman, Graham 166n. 48
Harrison, Paul 133, 180n. 40
Harrison, Robert Pogue 151, 169nn. 43–4,
    173n. 14, 181nn. 16–17
  The Dominion of the Dead 40
Haywood, Lynsey 173n. 16
Heath, Christian 177n. 12
Heidegger, Martin 166n. 48
Heiler, Friedrich 163n. 6
Hennezel, Marie De 176n. 28
Henry, Leroi 163n. 3

Higginson, Irene J. 177n. 3
Highly Active Antiretroviral Therapy
    (HAART) 72
Hill, Dawn 168n. 48
Hirschkind, Charles 164n. 7
HIV 67–9, 72–3, 75–6, 85
  disease impostors 73
  test 67, 69
Holocaust 29, 34, 39
Holst-Warhaft, Gail 83, 173n. 7
home and care 115–16, 127–31
  and case studies of incapacitation 116–23
  and genograms 124–7
Honig, Bonnie 169n. 40
  Democracy and the Foreigner 38
hospice-tality and geo-social 12–16
Hourizi, Rashid 167n. 60
Howe, Darcus 93
humic foundation 40

Imbuga, Francis 73
improvisation, significance of 144–5
inadequacy 39, 112, 113
incapacitation
  case study of Mr. Balani 120–3
  case study of Mr. Gupta 116–20
incomprehensibility 144
inert existing 59
infirmity 65
information capitalism 104
intercultural care 99–101, 104–6
Irish Sisters of Charity 25
Ixer, Graham 175n. 10
Izugbara, Chimaraoke O 171n. 3

Jain, Sarah Lochlan 14, 165nn. 35–6
James, Henry 178n. 18
  The Europeans 131
Jefferies, Janis 167n. 61
Jootun, Dev 175n. 5

Kay, John 173n 16, 174n. 18
Keats, John 179n. 32
Kellehear, Allan 166n 55, 170n. 4
Kelly, Ruth 178n. 2
Kincaid, Jamaica 171nn. 9–10
  A Small Place 63
Kitzinger, Celia 175n. 8

Kofman, Eleonore 166n. 52
Kovats, Tania
  Birch 28
Krasner, Diane 169n. 6
Kristeva, Julia 18, 166n. 45
Kübler, Elisabeth 29
Kumar, Suresh 166n 55, 167nn. 56–7
Kumar, Vipin 7

lamentation 83
The Lancet 13, 165n. 26
Latour, Bruno 60, 143, 171n. 8, 180nn. 38–9, 45
Lawton, Julia 59, 64, 170nn. 7, 12
Leadbeater, Charles 167n 58, 177n. 3
'learning to be affected by differences' 143–4
Leggewie, Claus 4, 163n. 4
Levinas, Emmanuel 108, 111, 138, 179n. 22
Lewis, Gail 176n. 27
Lichtenstein, Rachel 168nn. 11, 27
  Rodinsky's Room 26
Lingis, Alphonso 12, 39, 165n. 25, 169n. 42
Livingston, Julie 15, 16, 109, 165nn. 37–8, 176n. 22
Lommel, Andreas 172n. 12
lonely deaths, implications of 64
Lorde, Audre 177nn. 34–5
  The Uses of Anger 113
Lorimer, Hayden 179n. 21
Luibhéid, Eithne 164n. 16
Lutz, James 169n. 6
Lynch, Thomas 165n. 33
Lynn, Joanne 177n. 1

McCarthy, Caroline
  Light for Cicely 28
Mackintosh, Maureen 163n. 3
McRobbie, Angela 136, 137, 179nn. 13, 18
Madianou, Mirca 166n. 51
Mann, Cass 72
Mason, Christina 176n. 30
Massey, Doreen 46, 169n. 3
Mavrommatis, George 170n. 12
May, Corinne 174n. 27
May, Margaret 171n. 2
Maynard, Alan 163n. 4
Melville, Joy 163n 2, 167nn. 1, 6–7, 173n. 12, 174n. 25

Michaels, Ann
  The Winter Vault 76
Michniewicz, Antoni 25, 30
Milic, Nela 36, 169n. 36
Miller, Daniel 166n 51, 175nn. 11–13
Miller, David 95
Mills, Edward 165n. 28
Minh-ha, Trinh T. 44, 169n. 2
Mohr, Jean 164nn. 19, 21
Mol, AnneMarie 107, 176nn. 14–16
Moncur, Wendy 167n. 60
moral responsibility, giving away of 105
moral rhetoric 63
mortal chorographies 16–19
Motamedi Fraser, Mariam 27, 168nn. 13–14, 182nn. 13, 16
mourning 83, 173n. 8
music 81
  as spiritualization of body 82
Mutahi, Wahome 73

narrative humility 108
National Health Service (NHS) 9, 13, 14, 68
Nava, Mica 25, 167n. 8
negative capability 108, 141, 142
Neighbourhood Network in Palliative Care 21
Nettleton, Sarah 177n. 6
Ngomo, Dorothy 14
noise 81–6
  Eve's story on 85–6
  and hospice-tality 87–90
non-compliant patients 62
Numpeli, Mathews 167nn. 56–7
Nursing With Dignity 102

Oikelome, Franklin 165n. 31
Okamoto, Ikumi 182n. 9
Ondaatje, Michael 161, 182n. 17
otherness 42, 44, 108, 111, 148
Our Lady's Hospice (Harold Cross, Dublin) 25
over-spilling bodies 64

pain 133
  approach to, at the end of life 24–5
  case stories of 142–3
  and notion of learning to be affected by differences 143–5
  physical 133

total 16, 29, 36, 137–42
translation and advocacy 134, 136
palliative care 14, 16, 17, 20, 30, 53, 74,
    109–11, 125, 137
  community 102
  cross-cultural 99–101
  problems in accessing 115
  racism operating in 111
Palliative Medicine (journal) 99
Panesar, Jasbir 7
paranoia 47–50
Parkes, Colin Murray 155
Parnet, Claire 129, 178n. 17
Parrott, Fiona 175n. 13
passivity 108, 141
'A Patient who Made Me' 19
Peake, Alex 173n. 16
Penso, Dawn 166n. 50
perseverance 61–2, 78
Pilkington, Doris 181nn. 7–12
  Rabbit Proof Fence 148–9
Pipkin, Lillian 24
Pitsillides, Stacy 167nn. 60–1
Plato 18
Plutarch 82–3
polymedia 20
Portelli, Alessandro 31–2, 168n. 29
Powell, Enoch 25
Priae (The Policy Research Institute in
    Ageing and Ethnicity) 155
Price, Janet 22, 167n. 62
Puar, Jasbir K. 165n. 32
public mourning and women 83
Pugh, Edwin 170n. 4
Puwar, Nirmal 7, 161, 164nn. 11, 13–14,
    169n. 37, 173n. 11, 180n. 47

racism 48, 51, 62–3, 96, 109–14
  differentialist 87–8
  as unhappy signifier 109
Raghuram, Parvati 163n 3, 166n. 52
Rancière, Jacques 17–18, 166n. 44
Ratha, Dilip 172n. 7
reflexivity 156
Refuerzo, Ben J. 167n. 2
relationality 159
Rent-a-Mourner 173n. 8
Rhee, Nari 166n 53, 178n. 13
Rhys-Taylor, Alex 170n. 10

Rienzo, Cinzia 164n. 23
Rogoff, Irit 168n. 16
Rosengarten, Marsha 72–3, 172n. 10
Ross, Will 13, 165n. 27
Roy, Arundhati 158–9, 163n.7, 182n. 11
Royal Brompton Hospital 25
Ruganda, John 73
Russell, Bertrand 174n. 2
Ryder, Sue 29

Safri, Mahila 115, 177n. 7
Said, Edward W. 172n. 3
St. Christopher's Hospice (Sydenham,
    London) 23–5, 30, 84, 99
St Joseph's Hospice (Hackney, London) 25
StLouis, Brett 174n. 6
St Luke 24–5
St Thomas' hospital 78, 79
Sallnow, Libby 166n 55, 167n. 56
Saunders, Cicely 24–6, 29, 29, 34, 134,
    138–9, 155, 167nn. 4–5, 168nn. 32,
    34, 169n. 38, 179nn. 23–9
  and David Tasma's window 30–1
  diary of 33
  and hospice philosophy 33
  in absentia ventriloquism of 32
  relationship with David Tasma 30
  'The Treatment of Intractable Pain in
    Terminal Cancer' 140
Scarry, Elaine 133, 178nn. 4–5
Schroeder-Sheker, Therese 81, 90, 172n. 1,
    173nn. 2–3, 175n. 26
secrecy, significance of 73–4
Sennett, Richard 177n. 11
Serres, Michel 57, 170nn. 1–2
servicing 108
seselelame 64, 66
  meaning of 59
shame 64, 74, 110, 112, 119
Shildrick, Margrit 22, 167n. 62
Sibbald, Gary 169n. 6
Silwal, Ani 172n. 7
Sinclair, Iain 168nn. 11, 27
  Rodinsky's Room 26
Sissman, Edward 163n. 5
skin ego 59
social game, of photographic ritual 36
social suffering 135
social workers, of hospice 49

Sonoda, Hideto 171n. 13
Spivak, Gayatri Chakravorty 180n. 44
Squire, Corinne 178n. 15
Steedman, Carolyn 34, 168n. 31
stigma 71
Stories That Matter project 101, 155, 157
Sumani, Ama 13
The Sun 87
Sunder Rajan, Rajeswari 27, 168n. 12

Tamba, Kaichiro 176n. 29
Tasma, David 25, 26, 28, 29, 30, 33, 36,
   168n. 34, 169n. 38
   and Cicely Saunders, window of *31*
   death of 37–8
   early life of 34
   enigma of 39
   grave of *32*
   personal life of 34–5
   photograph of *35*
   relationship with Cicely Saunders 30
Tasma-Saunders window 31
terminal restlessness 48
thanatos 41
Thiongo, Ngugi wa 73–4
Thompson, John W. 29
Thrift, Nigel 180n. 43
throwntogetherness 46, 48
total pain 16, 18, 36, 137–42
   as inventive artful care practice 141–2
transmigrants 4 *see also individual entries*
Twigg, Julia 177n. 6
Twycross, Robert G. 168n. 24

Ulmer, Gregory 18, 167n. 47
unintelligibility 144, 145

Van Wyck, Peter 151, 166n. 46,
   181n. 18
Vargas-Silva, Carlos 164n. 22
Velázquez, Diego
   Las Meninas 156
Verderber, Stephen 167n. 2
Virilio, Paul 63, 171n. 11
visceral cosmopolitanism 25

Waddell, Margot 108, 141, 176nn. 18, 21,
   179n. 30
Walker, Arthur 163n. 4
Wallerstein, Immanuel 87, 174n. 20
Walter, Tony 167n. 60
Walwin, Jenni 28–9, 168n. 21
Weindling, Paul 29, 168n. 22
Wekesa, Eliud 171n. 3
Wengraf, Tom 181n. 4
Wetherell, Margaret 175n. 9
What's killing Darcus Howe? (TV
   documentary) 93
White, Emma 164n. 8
Wilkinson, Sue 175n. 8
Wilson, Helen F. 172n. 2
Winnicott, Donald 74, 172n. 14
Winterson, Jeanette 113, 177n. 36
withdrawnness 18
Wolkowitz, Carol 166n 54, 177nn. 6, 9
Woolf, Virginia 25
World Health Organization (WHO) 16
   on noise 84–5
Worth, Alison 176n. 31
Wyschogrod, Edith 42, 169n. 1

Zabin, Carol 166n 53, 178n. 13
Zoladex 93